Novel
Theories and Practices

Novel

Theories and Practices

Edited by

Partha Kumar Mukhopadhyay

ATLANTIC

PUBLISHERS & DISTRIBUTORS (P) LTD

Published by
ATLANTIC
PUBLISHERS & DISTRIBUTORS (P) LTD
7/22, Ansari Road, Darya Ganj,
New Delhi-110002
Phones : +91-11-40775252, 23273880, 23275880, 23280451
Fax : +91-11-23285873
Web : www.atlanticbooks.com
E-mail : orders@atlanticbooks.com

Branch Office
5, Nallathambi Street, Wallajah Road,
Chennai-600002
Phones : +91-44-64611085, 32413319
E-mail : chennai@atlanticbooks.com

ISBN 978-81-269-1664-1

Printed in India at Glorious Printers, A-13, D.S.I.D.C., Jhilmil Industrial Area, Delhi-110095

Dedicated to

Late Snehalata Debi, my grandmother, who helped me form value judgements on novels, in my tender years

Contents

Preface

"The Novel is a Death; it transforms life into destiny, a memory into a useful act, duration into an oriented and meaningful time. But this transformation can be accomplished only in full view of society", so writes Ronald Barthes about a literary genre which has become the main literary medium in today's world. The growth of novel in its different phases and over ages witnessed also the spate of various theories on novel which explain the art of fiction with apt discussion of character, plot, time, narrative manner, language, politics, poetics of social realism and vision of life. Fiction and theories of fiction are thus allied to each other.

The Protestant and bourgeois background of the rise of novel as elaborated in Ian Watt's book, *The Rise of the Novel: Studies in Defoe, Richardson and Fielding* (1957) comes under criticism in *The True Story of the Novel* (1996) written by Margaret Anne Doody. Doody argues that the novel is a very old form which was in practice in the Greek and Roman ages and even during the Middle ages and the Renaissance. Doody's argument that the novels of the ancient and non-Christian oriental world should occupy a central place in any discussion of the origin of novel almost defies Watt's theory of the Protestant and bourgeois origin of the novel and its massive output in the eighteenth century England. Thus, the flexibility of the novel form as perceived by Doody offers a sharp contrast to the autonomy of this genre as claimed by Watt and others. Northrop Frye's *Anatomy of Criticism* (1957) also indirectly throws light upon the origin of novel when he equates myth with literature marked by archetypal patterns and traces in the diversity of the novel form enough flexibility to accommodate comedy, romance and tragedy as well as irony and confession.

The traditional exponents of the art of fiction viewed the novel genre from different perspectives, though D.H. Lawrence and Henry James ascribe importance to the artistic unity of the novel. James thinks that the English novel is deficient in the expression of artistic coherence and consciousness. "A novel is a living thing, all one and continuous, like any other organism, and in proportion as it lives will it be found, I think, that in each of the parts, there is something of each of other parts", James observes. Gustave Flaubert presents an art in his novels where part and whole, form and subject matter, are inseparable. James also takes care in pointing out, "The story and the novel, the idea and the form, are the needle and thread, and I never heard of a guild of tailors who recommended the use of the thread without the needle, or the needle without the thread." F.R. Leavis traces in the works of great novelists like Austen, James and Conrad human values and awareness which are under threat in today's decaying consumers' civilization. D.H. Lawrence, on the other hand, considers the novel as a proper medium of responding to the world and with its 'tremulation' value, the novel, he thinks, bears the essence of great creations of all ages. E.M. Forster, however, opines, "The novel tells a story", though he takes due note of the roles of people, plot, fantasy, prophecy and pattern in novels. Forster argues, "History develops, art stands still. The novelist of the future will have to pass all the new facts through the old, if variable, mechanism of the creative mind" (*Aspects of the Novel,* 1927).

Critics of the "moralistic" school are mainly concerned with the reformative role of the novel. Madame de Staël's theory of fiction upholds the mission of novels in reforming men, manners and even social ills. "Mme de Staël's perception of the relationship between domestic morality and the novel interestingly foreshadows the theories of the twentieth century critic Ian Watt" (J.A. Bull, *The Framework of Fiction,* 1988).

Among the Marxist critics, Mikhail Bakhtin's significant contribution to the study of novels can be traced in his viewing the language medium of novels as a dynamic process signifying class struggle and consciousness. In his theoretical formulation, verbal context implies various world views and beliefs. Thus, Bakhtin's theory of novel launches an attack on the theory of organic unity of novel framed by the traditional theoreticians of this genre. George Lukács, on the other hand, feels that social reality and class conflict incorporating dialectical advancement should form the content of novels. Fredric Jameson, however, attempts to coordinate the 'inner' form and external reality within the creative process of novel which embraces personal and social values, past and future.

Novels and theories of novels have assumed different colours and contours with the advance of post-modernism, post-colonialism and feminism. They have left indelible marks on the growth of fiction in the modern periods. Modernism, in John Barth's view, is an attack on the nineteenth century bourgeois social order and its values, whereas post-modernist fiction "simply carries to its logical and questionable extremes, the antirationalist, antirealist, antibourgeois program of modernism". Finally, we may refer to Ursula K. Heise, mentioning those theoreticians who view narrative time in novels as a way of escaping from human time "crucially shaped by mortality".

Besides a brief survey of some major theories of fiction, some articles in the present book dwell on some specific theories of fiction. The correlation between theory and its practical application in works of art can only illustrate a literary work in all dimensions. This anthology of critical papers on some celebrated theoreticians' views on the web and texture of fiction also focuses on their myriad shades of applications in different texts. This book thus incorporates into a single design, discussions of the creative processes of fiction as well as fictions of enduring values and popularity.

In her elaborate exploration of the feminist literary theories and their embodiments in fictional writings, Santwana Halder shows how the feminist theories contribute a lot in evaluating novels and how the feminist theorists are drawing inspiration from fictional writings in support of their theories and movements. In discussing the interaction between post-modernism and feminist theories, she surveys the writings of Simon de Beauvoir, Mary Ellman and Kate Millet to finally discuss Doris Lessing's *The Golden Notebook* (1962) which embraces the concept of chaos in a world confronted by a new pattern of cataclysms, but simultaneously shows the humanist in Lessing aspiring for a unity in the world system. Post-colonialism and feminism are associated in her discussion of Kiran Desai's *The Inheritance of Loss* and Amitav Ghosh's *Sea of Poppies* demonstrating that the upper class people's claim to social supremacy is not much different from the colonial and patriarchal mindset now criticised by the feminist and cultural studies group. Santwana Halder also discusses gynocriticism and ecofeminism to demonstrate how Amitav Ghosh's *The Hungry Tide* (2004) illustrates a movement born out of the union of feminist and ecological theories, as the social mindset which oppresses women, is similar to the one that abuses nature and natural environment. Thus, Halder's paper establishes the bond of intimacy between fictions and current feminist theories.

Anita Myles takes up another aspect of feminism when she discusses the black feminist movement in the American context. Like other feminist movements, this movement is aggressive towards the social construction of gender and other cultural postulations that nourish it and finds proper voice in the writings of Alice Walker, Paul Marshall and Toni Morrison, who earnestly write about the triumphs and tragedies of African American women to establish that sexism and racism are of all ages. Myles in her illuminating article substantiates that the study of Black Feminism may enrich even fictional theories and studies of fiction.

Feminism appears again in Shabina Nishat Omar's article which elaborates on the marginalised consciousness of the feminine self in today's repressive and racial society to demonstrate that Tehmina Durrani's *My Feudal Lord* reveals a personal feminine experience adequately exposing the hollowness of the patriarchal discourse. This novel, Shabina argues, shows how a powerless lady revolts against the barren traditional ways to emerge as an empowered woman and how Durrani interrogates the basic relationship between gender, spatial-cultural location and identity.

The traditional theories of novel engage V.M. Madge's attention in his perceptive article, "The novel tells you a story, dear!" It illustrates Henry James' theoretical formulation on novel as expounded in his "The Art of Fiction," along with D.H. Lawrence's and E.M. Forster's views on fiction. Whereas Lawrence thinks that novel with its flexibility is capable of representing the whole of humanity, James is preoccupied with the English novelists' "cavalier approach to their art". E.M. Forster's analysis of novel with its demarcation between story and plot, and flat and round characters offers better pronouncements on the theory of novel than what is offered by James. Madge further argues that James appears most vulnerable as a theorist of fiction in his neglect of the story element because "the conceptual contours of story are not as fuzzy as James tries to make them". Even Solzhenitsyn emulates novelists like Tolstoy and Dostoevsky as they are impressive storytellers and interpreters of life with social responsibility.

Piyali Das, in her paper "Theorizing fiction..." offers a comparative study of the traditional theoreticians' views on fiction to conclude that their theories, in many ways similar, explore diverse areas like reproduction of reality, plot, characterization, language and vision of life. She also contends that the worth of a novel depends on the novelists' sensibility in recreating reality, and a novel, as far as possible, should be a perfect work of art.

Among the Marxist critics of novel, Mikhail Bakhtin's literary theories stem from his humanist interpretation of creative works in their social context. Arnab Bhattacharya's careful and analytical study of Luckásian and Bakhtinian views on the epic and novel establishes that Lukács considers novel as a genre struggling to recapture the lost totality of life, whereas Bakhtin looks upon novel as a genre "carrying potential for defying stereotypical formulations". Formulating an interesting comparison between these two theoreticians' views on the novel and epic, Bhattacharya offers a clear explanation of their similarities and disagreements and an incisive overview of key areas like the epical past and the novelistic present as well as the role of heroes and language in these two literary genres. This well-knit article throws ample light on Lukács' and Bakhtin's originality in contradistinguishing the novel from the epic, but the topic invites a full-fledged treatment in future.

In his scholarly and analytical paper on *All About H. Hatterr,* Basavaraj Naikar explores another type of fiction which he terms as Philosophical Comedy. Not content with the *a priori* knowledge of things, Hatterr hurls himself into a series of experience for formulating *a posteriori* knowledge of life's truth but he continues to remain a comic figure similar to Cervantes' Don Quixote or Browning's Fra Lippo Lippi. His dependence on phenomenal experience drags him to the conflicting opposites of life in situations from which he comes out only when he becomes a monk to depend more on meditation and transcendentality. Thus, Naikar's paper turns out to be a celebrated novelist's fruitful study of a novel characterized by new modes of presentation both in content and style.

Another aspect of the bond of novel with philosophy colours Dr. Pande's article on Raja Rao's *The Cat and Shakespeare* demonstrating how the cat as mother symbolises the primordial cosmic mother—*paraskti*, while Shakespeare represents the world of everyday trivialities and the emotions of mundane existence. The phenomenal reality should go beyond the veil of *maya*. As the cat represents an impersonal principle, Shakespeare, as if, absorbs the cat and the two principles are finally united. Pande's exploration of the philosophic undertones of this novelette permeates his brief but revealing analysis offered in his article.

Families, nationhood and transnational indentities are the themes of many Indian English novels. Families, very often reflecting the power equations of the state, operate through the bonds of blood, race and religion. Arpa Ghosh studies the ways of families and nationhood as they are studied in Amitav

Ghosh's *The Shadow Lines*. The structure of family, like that of the nation, is erected on the principles of segregation and omission but this family pattern may be established at any time by event waves and memories, as they defy the logic of artificial boundaries or the shadow lines imposed by family and state structures. This paper lucidly exposes the vulnerability of the family and state structures.

In her paper on *The Namesake* and *Unaccustomed Earth*, Ketaki Datta succeeds in dissecting "otherness" and transnational identities in relation to the post-colonial theories of self, nationhood and cross-cultural identities. Nilofar Akhtar, on the other hand, studies the cross-cultural conflicts experienced by different generations of expatriates in their lives abroad, in her study of Jhumpa Lahiri's *The Namesake*. The issues of identity, nationality and belongingness characterize many fictions of the post-colonial era, and Akhtar aptly argues that the merit of *The Namesake* can be discerned in its attempt to understand different cultures and societies.

Intertextuality and intertextual reading of texts engage Shymasree Basu's attention in her paper on Barbara Kingsolver's *The Poisonwood Bible* and Joseph Conrad's *Heart of Darkness*. Referring to Graham Allen's views that intertextuality implies the relations among different texts, she examines Kingsolver's celebrated novel to find out her use of "motifs, images and tropes" which remind one of Conrad's *Heart of Darkness*. She finally observes that Kingsolver "implements presupposition in her text" and "for each of the prices Congo teaches them the value of life and like the Barthesque notion of the text, it keeps changing for ever." Shymasree's impressive paper dwells upon a current method of interpreting the text of a novel.

In her psychoanalytical study of Manju Kapur's *Difficult Daughters*, Sandhya Saxena refers to Freud's discussion of personality with a three-tier structure founded upon *id*, *ego* and *superego*. Man suffers when he neglects the "pleasure principle" of life but he has to suffer equally in social life when he flouts "the reality principle". In this novel, Virmati suffers as she neglects the reality principle of life, and consequently she has to oscillate between *id* and *superego*. Saxena also argues that the psychoanalytic criticism views desire in the context of language, and thus this novel, in the process of using a language medium of its own, constructs a sub-text. Saxena further observes that Virmati's defiance of the family and society results from her surrender to the pleasure principle of life, and her choice can also be interpreted in terms of the "structural unconscious" theory in currency now. Saxena's analytical paper explores the scope of studying novels from the angle of the psychoanalytic criticism.

Jaba Kusum Singh attempts to read Salman Rushdie's *Midnight's Children* in the light of Said's *Theory of Orientalism*. Rushdie's novel narrates the untold story of the neglected majority of people in India having no voice in the emerging money- and power-oriented structure of free India. Jaba Kusum contends that Rushdie's novel supports Said's argument that orientals can adequately talk about their class and creed.

Shirish Chindhade again takes up social problems in his article on Arvind Adiga's *The White Tiger*, arguing that though India's fast changing society is the immediate point of Adiga's attack, the novel shows "that the society that defies the sanctity of the means to achieve its end" degenerates only into self-annihilation and decay.

Debalina Banerjee explores another type of fiction—the science fiction, which she associates with myth and romance. Northrop Frye views science fiction as romance with strong mythological elements, and this mode of thinking is close to Levi Strauss' view that both myth and science adopt modes of 'structuring the universe'. Debalina concludes her article by pointing out that the science fiction projects an advanced reality which is rooted, as Frye holds, in the "poetic life of a story, not the homilectic life of some illustrated truism." Her paper illustrates how myth, romance and science can formulate a new branch of fiction popular in current time.

Bishnupada Ray, on the other hand, throws revealing light on the process of creativity in his well-knit paper on William Golding's *The Spire*, contending that this novel, with its suggestions of tyranny, architectural connotations, sexual metaphors and metaphysical ideas, is almost Coleridge's "Kubla Khan".

Tapati Talukdar offers an analytical discourse on James Joyce's *A Portrait of the Artist as a Young Man* to substantiate that Joyce's technical novelty is traceable in organizing chunks of language to articulate the growth of sensibilities in the hero's consciousness. This novel attains a cosmic dimension by embodying sensibilities that transcend the barrier of time.

My own article analyzes the roots, ideas and formal growth of the Romantic novel in the light of Germaine de Staël's' theory of fiction with its emphasis on the role of fiction in regenerating men, manners and society.

This book had its seed in my discussion of some cultural theories with Caroline Birch near a famous shrine in Kolkata, while it sprang to life by the encouragement I received from S.J. Peter Joseph, Mrs. Sumi Chatterjee and others. I am beholden to them. I record my utmost gratitude and thanks to the distinguished scholars and critics from different parts of the country who have imparted life to this anthology by their precious critical papers. I would also like to offer my grateful thanks to Dr. K.R. Gupta and other associates of the Atlantic Publishers and Distributors (P) Ltd. for their loving care and professional skill evinced in bringing out this book.

Partha Kumar Mukhopadhyay

1

Feminist Literary Theories and their Relation to Fictional Writings

Santwana Haldar

Feminist literary theories evolved out of the radical movements against patriarchal ideology that had shaped previous literary theories.[1] When the marginalized status of women is replaced by the central status, the issues of sharing the central status in the society with the men, who had so long grasped the central status ignoring the women, come forward. The right of suffrage or the right of education for women is not felt sufficient because, as said M.L. Carden, "The New Feminism is not about the elimination of differences between the sexes...it concerns the individual's right to find out the kind of person he or she is and to strive to become that person" (Carden 2). A total change of the system is required for fulfilling the purpose and this change includes different perspectives of approaching the women's problems the nature of which varies as vary the country, the race, the financial and social status of women. Hence the scope of feminist theories is ever expanding, as feminism is associated with post-modernism, post-colonialism, subaltern theories, eco-criticism, lesbianism and such other ideologies. Feminists is no more a monolithic term now and the various feminists share certain assumptions and concepts to explore the factor of sexual differences. These ideologies have brought a total change in literary activities. In its initial stage, feminist concern introduced specific feminine issues in fictional writings, projecting women as protagonists and depicting incidents from women's points of view. The old classics have also been rewritten, revealing the inherent gender discrimination much to the annoyance of the orthodox thinkers. The changes in the feminist theories—for example, women's equal status with men no more satisfies the feminists, as they want more—are continuously changing the mode of women's problems in fictional writings. The present paper intends to show how the different feminist theories are applicable in evaluating fictional writings and how fictional writings are used by the activists or the theorists in support of their movement or theory.

Post-modernism, Feminist Theories and Some Fictional Writings by Women

A serious philosophic discussion of gender discrimination started with the French existentialist philosopher Simone de Beauvoir who identified the woman as culturally "Other" to man (*The Second Sex,* 1949). She also exposed the false myths of women created by men. In her *Thinking about Women* (1968) Mary Ellman focused on the derogatory stereotypes of women in literature written by men and also pointed at some alternative views in some writings of women. Kate Millet's *Sexual Politics* (1969) is another important contribution towards the development of feminist theories based on philosophy. Millet attacked Freud's method of psychoanalysis which, she said, treated women as submissive sexual objects. These writers prepared the ground ready for an explosion of feminist theories related to other literary theories such as post-modernism and post-structuralism. Helen Cizous, Julia Kristeva, Luce Irigaray, Monique Witty and Gayatri Spivak are some post modern feminists, influenced by Derrida and Foucault. Derrida attacked the systematic, quasi-scientific pretensions of the strict form of structuralism by asserting that the notion of systematic structure, whether linguistic or other, presupposes a fixed center which does not exist. Michel Foucault and Jaques Lacan also sought to subvert, in their own ways, the claims for the existence of a self-evident foundation, or center, which assures the validity of all knowledge. This "antifoundationalism" (Abrams 247) gave a rude shock to all sorts of ideologies and theories including feminist theory.[2] If the existence of the 'center' is not confirmed, the change of woman's position from the marginalized condition to the 'center' hardly bears any meaning. The postmodern feminists, therefore, cannot reach a fixed point in regard to a woman's position in the society or in the family. A constant search for self identification in a surrounding that is lacking in fixed values characterizes the postmodern and poststructuralist feminist theories, and the protagonist's search for self identification is also the main theme of a good number of novels that ordinarily go by the name of feminist novels because of their choice of women characters as the protagonists. At its first stage 'feminist novel' was based on the theme of the various exploitations of women because of the gender discriminations in the society. Gradually, equal opportunities were not considered enough for women who are seriously engaged with a search for self identification and with proper opportunities to fulfill their potentiality. Let us consider Doris Lessing's *The Golden Notebook* (first published 1962) in this context. The novel is unique as it is lacking in a tight structure and comprises all sorts of ideas and experiences which, as the writer wrote in her Preface to the novel, she had not recognized as her own before their introduction in the novel. The novel includes a skeleton called 'Free Women' which is a conventional short novel that could stand by itself. Then there are four notebooks—Black, Red, Yellow and Blue—which are kept by Anna Wulf, a writer. She keeps the four notebooks separate, as she has to separate things off from one another out of fear of chaos. Throughout the notebooks several characters have discussed, theorized, dogmatized and labeled matters which appear incoherent. In the inner Golden Notebook, things have come together through the novelist's humanistic concerns. To quote from the Preface (June 1971 version): "Anna and Saul Green the American 'break down'. They are crazy, lunatic, mad.... They break down into each other, into other people, break through the false patterns they have made of their pasts.... They hear each other's thoughts, recognize each other in themselves. Saul Green the man who has been envious of Anna, now supports her, advises her, gives her the theme for her next book, *Free Women*—an ironic title.... And Anna who had been jealous of Saul to the point of insanity...gives Saul the pretty new notebook, The Golden Notebook, which she has refused to do earlier.... In the inner Golden Notebook, which is written by both of them, you can no longer distinguish between what is Saul and what is Anna, and between them and other people in the book.... The theme of 'break down'...is a way of self-healing, of the inner self's dismissing false dichotomies and diversions, has of course been written about by other people, as well as by me.... But nobody so much as noticed this central theme, because the book was instantly belittled by friendly reviewers as well as by hostile ones, as being about the sex war or was claimed by women as a useful weapon in the sex war" (http://thegoldennotebook org/book pp. 1-2). Here is an instance of how the feminist activists are sometimes reluctant to get at what the author intends to say through her book and instead impose their own meaning on some parts of the book without bothering about the whole. Lessing, however, was not against the ideas held by the feminist theorists and/or activists in regard to the liberation of women, but she maintained that the whole world is being shaken into a new pattern by the cataclysms we are living through. According to her, if we fail to accept it, the aims of Women's Liberation will look very small and quaint.[3] Lessing was so much concerned with the process of self realization—a process necessary both for man and woman—that her ideas about woman's emancipation far exceeded the limit prescribed by the theorists. Basically a postmodernist, she put emphasis on chaos and breaking up of relationship; but the humanist in her aspired for a unity through "the inner self's dismissing false dichotomies and diversions" which are hardly understood by others.

Post Colonialism, Feminism and Fictional Writings

The early feminist movements and theories were led predominantly by middleclass white women of North America and Europe. With the collapse of European colonialism in South Asia and Africa a new coinage 'post colonial feminism' came in vogue, challenging the views of the European and

American feminists who, it is argued, failed to notice the influence of colonial mindset behind the torture inflicted on women, doubly pressurized by patriarchy and colonialism. A prominent post colonial feminist Chandra Talpade Mohanty criticized western feminism as being ethnocentric. In her influential essay, "Under Western Eyes: Feminist Scholarship and Colonial Discourse" (1986) she argues that Western feminists have tended to gloss over the differences between Southern women and expresses her well-researched view that the nature of oppression of woman is diverse and contingent upon geography, history and culture. The book *Feminist Genealogies, Colonial Legacies, Democratic Future* (New York; Routledge: 1997) that she co-edited with M. Jacqui Alexander, reveals quite a new perspective of looking at feminist theories.[4] In 2003 (in *Feminism Without Border, Decolonizing Theory, Practicing Solidarity*) Mohanty elaborates her ideas in regard to the complex nature of the torture inflicted on women by men having a colonial mindset. She also argues for a bridging of theory and praxis. Black feminists such as Angela Davis and Alice Walker also shared this view.[5] In this context we may refer Manju Kapur's *Difficult Daughters,* Kiran Desai's Man Booker winning novel *The Inheritance of Loss* and Amitav Ghosh's *Sea of Poppies* in which the novelists have shown the nature of torture inflicted on women in colonial India by men with colonial mindset. Virmati, an educated girl in an enlightened family, is in the center of *Difficult Daughters,* a novel set in the backdrop of Indian Freedom Movement. Swarna, an activist and a friend of Virmati, indicates the change in woman's position in the Indian society as she says, "The war—the satyagraha movement—because of these things, women are coming out of their homes. Taking jobs, fighting, going to jail...here we are. Responsible for our own futures.... We are lucky we are living in times when women can do something else. Even in Europe women gain more respect during wartime. And here we have that war, and our satyagraha as well" (151-52). But this condition was not applicable to all women in India. Even Virmati, who managed to get an M.A. degree from Amritsar, suffered humiliation as the married professor Harish lured her to be used by him without thinking about her social status and her mental condition. His mood was off with any talk of marriage and Virmati was emotionally exploited by him, "Virmati felt trapped. What had she been talking, was it so unreasonable? Why was she looking so sad? How could she leave him like this? Slowly she moved towards Harish, and slowly she took him in her arms" (150). The professor being much older, more refined and civilized, Virmati was mesmerized by him. After facing a lot of humiliations and sufferings, she could somehow marry the professor and underwent another course of humiliation in the family, staying with his illiterate first wife under the same roof. She got a short relief as she started studying once again staying with another woman Leela in Lahore. But she was lacking in the courage to assert her individuality and remain free from his clutches. Thanks to the changing circumstances she got her educated, but only to be used by a man who needed an intelligent and well informed companion with whom he could talk about various national and international matters up to his satisfaction. He was much concerned with India's freedom but not with emancipation of women. As Virmati's daughter commented while making an analytical study on her mother's life after her death, "I play with the idea that she must have refused (to go to the professor's house during summer holidays). That she could have said, I'm my own mistress. I will relate to you with dignity or not at all. None of this hiding and whispering and keeping my voice down and struggle over who is going to wash your underwear and who is going to clean your shoes. None of this for me.... Perhaps the words were at the back of her mind, teasing her tongue with their shadowy sounds. She looked for an opening, but she looked timidly, for though she had escaped the marital home, an essential part of it, the marital bed she carried inside her head, and its burden was heavy.... In the end my mother could not have mentioned that she had more of a home with Leela than she did with him.... She could not have, because when I grew up I was very careful to tailor my needs to what I knew I could get. That is my female inheritance. That is what she tried to give me. Adjust, compromise, adapt" (255-56). Manju Kapur has vividly analyzed the differences in the status of Indian women in 1940s and 1950s: there were women like Virmati's cousin sister Shakuntala and her friend Swarna who could exercise their freedom due to the changing situations caused by war against the colonial rule, and at the same time most of the women tolerated humiliations like the illiterate first wife of Harish. And women like Virmati, thanks to the female inheritance they had, were used by the male as per their requirements.

Kiran Desai's *The Inheritance of Loss* equates colonial mindset to patriarchal one through the character of a native officer under the British government. The retired judge Jemubhai Patel belonged to a farmer's family in rural Gujrat. After his marriage his father-in-law had to bear the expenditure of his voyage to London as well as his higher studies there as part of the dowry. Jemubhai returned as an ICS officer and was posted as a judge. Along with his studies he also developed a colonial mindset—a firm faith that he was superior to his country men, the Others, who had not joined civil services—from his masters, the colonial rulers, who sincerely believed that they being "civilized" persons, had every right to oppress and thereby teach the "uncivilized" natives. After his return Jemubhai found his wife Nimi, then a young village girl of eighteen, not matching for his status and he had forgotten by now his thrilling experience of taking his newly wed bride on his bicycle for a ride together. After developing colonial mindset he behaved with his wife in a way a colonial ruler would have done with his subject. An insignificant mistake on Nimi's part who used his powder puff and kept it with her without telling him anything, generated hatred in him and he took revenge through sexual attack. "Jemubhai, his face a puff with anger, grabbed at his wife. She slipped from his grasp and his anger flew. She who had stolen.... This illiterate village girl. He grabbed at her again.... He came at her with a look of murder...he clamped down on her, tussled her to the floor...came filtering down, in a dense frustration of lust and fury...he stuffed his way ungracefully into her" (169). It was not the experience of one day. He repeatedly expressed his hatred and anger through such attack: "he repeated the gutter act again and again. Even in tedium, on and on, a habit he could not stand in himself. This distaste and his persistence made him angrier than ever and any cruelty to her became irresistible. He could teach her the same lessons of loneliness and shame he had learned himself.... She grew accustomed to his detached expression as he pushed into her, that gaze off into the middle distance, entirely involved with itself, the same blank look of a dog or monkey humping in the bazzar" (170). The judge left her in his quarter whenever he was on tour and Nimi could not even speak to anyone. Desai gives details of his torture thrown on her: "One day he found footprints on the toilet seat—*she was squatting on it, she was squatting on it!*—he could barely contain his courage, took her head and pushed it into the toilet bowl, and after a point Nimi, made invalid by her misery, grew very dull, began to fall asleep in heliographic sunshine and wake in the middle of the night" (173). Finally Jemubhai drove her out when one day after returning from tour he was summoned by the district commissioner and was given the astounding news that his wife had been a part of the Nehru welcoming committee at the railway station. He learnt that Mrs. Mohan, the wife of one of his colleagues, invited Nimi and almost compelled her to go to the station. But he could not tolerate that much audacity and gave her wife a final teaching after which she was sent to her parents' home for ever.... "He emptied his glass on her head...filled her ears with soda water. Then, when this was not enough to assuage his rage, he hammered down with his fists, raising his hands to bring them down on her again and again, rhythmically until his own hands were exhausted and his shoulders next day were strained sore as if from chopping wood" (304).

Deeti, the central woman character in Amitav Ghosh's *Sea of Poppies,* is one of the worst sufferers in colonial India. She was a victim of the colonial system of oppression in India when the farmers in the Gangetic belt were forced to cultivate poppies instead of paddy much to their inconvenience. Deeti's husband, an ex-serviceman and a crippled, was working in the opium factory while his land was used for producing poppy plant under Deeti's supervision. With their only daughter to feed at home, the couple could manage somehow to fill their stomachs but after Deeti's husband became ill inside the factory and she was summoned to bring him home, there was a total collapse. Much to her surprise Deeti learnt that her husband had already borrowed a big amount from the factory and that the opium she brought to the factory for sale was worth "just six dams". She had no other way but to go to the money lender who exploited her totally, compelling her to press her thumb impression on his account book in exchange for six months' worth of wheat, oil and 'gur'. When she learnt that her debt would double every six months, it was too late for her to do any thing. Besides financial oppression there was the physical one, specially designed for women. Deeti's brother-in-law Chandan Singh took the opportunity of his brother's illness to enter the house on the pretext of attending him. "But once past the door, he paid no attention to his brother and had eyes only for Deeti: even as he was entering he would brush his hand against his thigh. Sitting on his brother's bed, he would look at her and fondle himself through the folds of his dhoti; when Deeti knelt to feed Hukam Singh, he would lean so close as to brush her breasts with his knees and elbows. His advances became so aggressive that Deeti took to hiding a small knife in the folds of her sari, fearing that he might attack her, right on her husband's bed" (157). The assault, when it came, was in the form of argument. He directly said that only if she agreed to have physical relationship with him, she might conceive and give birth to a son and in that case she might protect her land and house which would otherwise pass to him after his brother's death that was imminent. He also reminded her that on the first night of her arrival in her husband's house it was he who impregnated her making her unconscious and that his brother was eunuch. It was clear to Deeti that there was hardly any way to escape and yet her loathing of her brother-in-law had reached such a pitch that she knew she would not be able to make her own body obey the terms of the bargain. She proclaimed that she would burn on her husband's pyre rather than give herself to him. She sent her daughter Kabutri to her brother's home as a preparation for self-immolation but in a most dramatic way she was saved from her husband's pyre by a lower class man Kalua who took her to the ship 'Ibis' aspiring to start a new life in Mauritius. When on board, they were detected by Bhyro Singh, an uncle of her husband, who knew all about her past and found her an easy target in the dark corner of the ship's store. "Bhyro Singh was wearing a langot and a banyan, ...he cupped his hands under his belly and moved it tenderly up and down, as though he were weighing it. Then, he picked a bit of lint out of the gaping mouth of his belly-button and examined it closely...Deeti felt herself choke and stuffed a fistful of her ghungata into her mouth.... Bhyro Singh reached for her ghungata.... Pulling her veil down, he tipped her head back with a finger and nodded with a satisfaction: I always said those are the eyes of a whore. Deeti tried to strike her hand away from her neck, but it stayed where it was.... He ran a finger up her neck and tweaked her ear-lobe. Don't you know, he said, that I'm the one who's in charge of your allotments? Don't you know it's me who decides who your master will be in Mareech? I've already set *your jora's* name down for a plantation up north. He'll never come out from there alive...for you I have other plans.... What does anyone want from a whore? His hand slipped through the neck of her choli and began to fumble for a handhold" (476-77). This time she escaped as others were attracted by her cry, but Kalua was severely beaten by Bhyro Singh who secured the Captain's approval after convincing the white man the gravity of Kalua's crime. On the pretext of supporting the existing rules of the land the colonial rulers supported the punishment inflicted on Kalua who being a lower class man, had dared to elope with a woman belonging to a higher class. Amitav Ghosh has thus described in detail how the colonial rulers contributed to the oppression of women, indirectly through the cultivation of opium and directly by supporting the existing social hierarchy in India. As Edward Said puts it, "post colonial authors attempt to connect experiences across the imperial divide".[6] This connecting of experiences enable the post colonial societies to have a clear self-image through which they could liberate themselves from imperialistic legacy.

Feminism, Subaltern Studies and Fictional Writings

The category of 'Otherness' made popular by the western feminist theorists is also applicable to the lower class people who are treated as the 'Other' by the upper class people. The mindset of the upper class in this respect claiming social supremacy is similar to the colonial and the patriarchal mindset. Hence, it is difficult to separate the issues of gender and the issues of class and race. In 1985 the "Marxist-feminist deconstructist", Gayatri Chakravarty Spivak, threw a challenge to the race and class blindness of the Western academy with her epoch-making article 'Can the Subaltern Speak?'.[7] By 'subaltern' Spivak meant the oppressed subject, the members of Antonio Gramsci's 'subaltern classics'.[8] A collective of intellectuals, now known as the Subaltern Studies Group, also started a systematic discussion of subaltern themes in South Asian Studies in early 80s. This group intended to study "the general attribute of subordination in South Asian society"[9] in terms of class, caste and gender. Its wide-ranging concerns are sketched out both with the visible collections of humanistic studies and the invisible system of culture based on confirmed beliefs and ideologies. Spivak's famous interrogation drew attention of the critics towards "an unrepresentable subaltern class", a class that has a lot of contribution to the building up of human history and yet has never been allowed to reveal its consciousness. She finds that both the women and the working class people have been marginalized by the dominant Western culture. Edward Said praised her capacity to introduce the theory of non-Western women. In fact, she has noted that the women as a class—to be precise, non-Western women—are denied the opportunity to express themselves. This theory has been picked up by many novelists who choose silent women for their protagonists, revealing how the torture inflicted on those women are aggravated because of their association with the lower class. Arundhati Roy's *The God of Small Things* may be an important example. The novel depicts how the ancient forms of oppressing the lower class people and the women in India merge with the legacy of colonialism. The central character in the novel is an upper class divorcee,

Ammu, who along with her twin issues, is compelled to stay in her father's family like an outsider, as she is denied any property of her father. Ammu's brother Chacko, who also had unsuccessful inter-religion marriage, enjoys all privileges in the family as well as society. It is reported in the novel that "They were a family of Anglophiles. Pointed in the wrong direction, trapped outside their own history, and unable to retrace their steps because their footprints had been swept away" (20). When Ammu came back to her father's home for good—her husband forced her to accompany his English boss to please him, and she fled—she had little idea about her position there. The family opposed her attempts to establish her as a singer. "On the days that the radio played Ammu's songs, everyone was a little wary of her. They sensed somehow that she lived in the penumbral shadows between two worlds, just beyond the grasps of their power. That a woman that they had already damned, now had little left to choose, and could therefore be dangerous" (44). It is clear that women have traditionally been treated in terms of reproduction while economic resources are male preserves. "Though Ammu did as much work in the factory as Chacko, whenever he was dealing with food inspectors or sanitary engineers, always referred to it as my factory, my pineapples, my pickles. Legally this was the case because Ammu, as a daughter, had no claim to the property" (57). In this rigid backdrop of gender patterns, Ammu's love relation with the untouchable Velutha—Ammu not only disobeys the love-laws prescribed by the society but also crosses the boundaries of ethnic or social groups—represents a threat for the community and it was obvious that the relationship would end in death. While Chacko's physical needs were appreciated in the society as natural, the love relation of Ammu and Velutha caused havoc in the house and in the society inviting beating, shutting up inside the house, police interference, false FIR, beating in police custody till death, strike, separation of the twins and what not. Chacko's foreign ex-wife and their daughter are the most welcome guests in the family and his casual relationships with the factory girls are also treated as natural; but Velutha the untouchable is the 'Other' and his relationship with an upper class woman is a transgression, the most unnatural thing that has to be suppressed even at the cost of his life. In *Sea of Poppies* also the torture inflicted on Deeti was sharpened after her association with the untouchable.

Gynocriticism, Ecofeminism and Fictional Writings by Women

Gynocriticism "concerns itself with developing a specifically female framework for dealing with works written by women, in all aspects of their production, motivation, analysis and interpretation..." (Abrams, 95). Dividing feminist criticism into two distinct varieties, 'Feminist critique' and 'Gynocritique', Elaine Showaiter speaks of two different roles of women—one, the role of consuming male produced literature and the other, that of producing texts. Gynocritics feel that postcolonial theorists do little to project the fact that colonialism, a hyper masculine construct, was a qualitatively different experience for women, from what it was for men. Colonized women were doubly colonized—first by patriarchy and then by imperialism—said Nilufer E. Bharucha ('From Commonwealth to Postcolonial Literatures: Old Wine in New Bottles'). With this extreme view, 'Gynocriticism' aims at a specialized discourse on female creativity as well as the female problem of using language. In *No Man's Land: The Place of the Women Writer in the Twentieth Century,* and *The War of the Words* (1988) Sandra Gilbert and Susan Gubar provide a theory of woman's relation to language specially refuting those of Jaques Lacan, Julia Kristeva and Nancy Chodorow. In *Bearing the Word: Language and Female Experience in Nineteenth Century Women's Writing* (1986), Margaret Homans observes, "Language is not a neutral medium but rather...its construction is based on presuppositions about gender that devalue women: the speaking or writing subject is constitutively masculine while the silent object is feminine" (22). Not only in its vocabulary and syntax but also in its rigorous rules of logic and tendency towards fixed classification, the language used by men—it is called 'phallogocentric' language—has been categorized as distinct from the language used by women. Helene Cixous speaks of an incipient feminine writing which has its source in the mother, in the stage of the mother-child relation before the child develops the male-centered language that is approved as genuine everywhere. All these concerns of the feminist theorists deeply affect the women writers and they try to experiment with the language of their female protagonists. Shashi Deshpande's *That Long Silence* is a case in point. Jaya, the protagonist in this novel, a writer whose realistic story on man-woman relationship was strongly criticized, among others, by her husband who argued that Jaya had crossed the limit of decorum through her realistic description in a language that is not befitting to her status as a married lady. Her husband was however happy when she started writing columns meant for women under the pseudonym Seeta. The language she now used was the sober language approved by the society for women's use. Seeta, the central woman figure in the great Indian epic *Ramayana,* is the mythical figure that stands for tolerance and perseverance. Choosing the column of 'Seeta', Jaya sought to identify herself as a spokesperson for the typical Indian woman who undergoes sufferings and humiliation silently and thus she could maintain peace in the family. Dissecting her creative self Jaya acknowledges later that her contribution to 'Seeta' column was simply an endeavor to evade reality and to take shelter in a make-believe world. She says, "Seeta had been the means through which I had shut the door firmly on all these women who had invaded my being, screaming for attention; women I had known I could not write about, because they might, it was just possible, resemble Mohan's mother or aunt or my mother or aunt (149). Deshpande makes it clear that Jaya's inability to encounter facts of life as a writer as well as her fear to disturb the comfort of a cozy life is camouflaged by the choice of the title 'Seeta'. Jaya's playing the role of 'Seeta' helps her find a corner in a woman's magazine and she becomes popular among sentimental readers much to her husband's satisfaction. She has to struggle hard for coming out of this camouflage of a popular woman writer who does not disturb the patriarchal society and is therefore appreciated by all. Deshpande reveals her protagonist's transcendence through a series of self-analysis. A gynocritic's concern for a woman writer's use of language while revealing matters from her perspective is clear in this novel.

Ecofeminism, or ecological feminism, is a term coined in 1974 by Francoise d'Eaubonne. It is a philosophy and also a movement born from the union of feminist and ecological thinking and the belief that the social mentality that leads to the domination and oppression of women is directly connected to the social mentality that leads to the abuse of the natural environment. It combines eco-anarchism or bioregional democracy with a strong ideal of feminism. It advocates the importance of interrelationships between human, non-human others and the earth. The influence of this ideology is visible in a good number of fictional writings where women are projected as natural friends of the environment. For example, Amitav Ghosh's *The Hungry Tide* (2004) projects women characters who are closely related to the environment, and try their best to protect it. The most prominent among them, Piya, has come from the States to the Sundarban area of South Bengal to make researches on Gangetic dolphins, a rare species. Finally, after some dramatic incidents took place, she decides to live in the area that has not yet been properly equipped for modern way of living. She is so much engrossed with the thought of the presence of a rare species of dolphin, the Irrawaddy dolphin, in the Sundarban area that she tells Kanai, a young man from Delhi, that she has gone "on a kind of cetacean pilgrimage". The writer has revealed her sincere sorrow when she found a dolphin lying dead with a huge gash behind the animal's blowhole. The shape of the injury suggested that the dolphin had been hit by the propeller of a fast-moving motorboat the kind of which is used by uniformed personnel, maybe from the coast guard or the police or even the Forest department. Piya's heart had leapt when she first saw the newborn surfacing beside his mother and now it was indeed difficult for her to look at the carcass. With the help of her companion-cum-boatman Fakir she heaved the animal out into the river with a faint hope that it would bob up again. The animal did not however bob up, but Piya had to face the severest shock when Fakir was also dead in the storm in his attempt to save her life. Piya's close relationship to the environment against the cruelty of the men who are responsible for the conservation of animal life is an instance of how modern literature projects ideas of ecofeminism. It is in fact impossible to discuss all the fictional writings that are influenced by feminist theories. Yet a few examples clarify the trend.

NOTES

1. The British philosopher Mary Wollstonecraft's *A Vindication of the Rights of Women* (1792) represents the beginning of feminism—that is, an intense awareness of identity as a woman (in the broadest sense of the term)—in the western world. She defined an outlook within which there was a scope for a theory to develop. But the first-wave feminist movement began at the Seneca Falls Convention (USA) of July 1948. At this convention prominent American feminists of the era authored a declaration of Sentiments which asserted fundamental rights to women including the right to vote. The first phase of feminist movement was over with the declaration of women's suffrage by the American government. The second phase of the feminist movement was associated with the Radical Movements against racial discrimination in America during the sixties. These radical feminists believed that the most oppressed group in the western societies was 'women', that patriarchy more than capitalism was responsible for social injustices. They upheld the process of socialization of women. In 1993 Rebecca Walker, a South African American and a Jewish, coined the term 'third wave feminism' that suggested creation of a more intense and comprehensive movement. While feminist movements seek liberation of women through political and social changes, feminist literary critics attempt to extend those changes into the domain of culture. Simone de Beauvoir, Mary Ellman, Kate Millet were among the famous feminist theorists.
2. Broadly speaking, feminism holds that the patriarchal society has curbed the freedom and autonomy of woman and that man has so far controlled the dominant institutions and the dominant ideologies. To realize their human potentiality the women have to transcend their femaleness thrown on them by the society, violating the norms of ideal womanhood. While feminist theories question "the adequacy of accepted

conceptual structures" (Elaine Showwalter, "Feminist Criticism in the Wilderness" in *Modern Literary Theory: A Reader,* ed. David Lodge, Longman: 2003, p. 210), feminist writers of fiction are concerned with the specific female problems within the sphere of the family as well as the larger background and their possible solutions in the changed circumstances.

3. Doris Lessing marked the differences between her approach and that of the feminists in an unequivocal way: "What the feminists want of me is something they haven't examined because it comes from religion. They want me to bear witness. What they would really like me to say is, 'Ha, sisters, I stand with you side by side in your struggle toward the golden dawn where all those beastly men are no more'. Do they really want people to make oversimplified statements about men and women? In fact they do. I've come with great regret to this conclusion" (*The New York Times,* 25 July, 1982). Lessing felt that in spite of being ill treated by men for ages the women have to come in terms with men somehow and the process requires acute self analysis for both.
4. Some other books that share M.J. Alexander and Mahanty's view are mentioned below: (a) Ashfar, Haleh, ed., *Women and Politics in the Third World* (Routledge, 1996); (b) Davies, Miranda, ed., *Third World Second Sex* (Prometheus Books, 1983); (c) Harding, Sandra, *Is Science Multicultural? Postcolonialisms, Feminisms and Epistemologies* (Indiana University Press, 1998); (d) Harding, Sundra and Uma Narayan, ed., *Border Crossings: Multicultural and Postcolonial Feminist Challenges and Philosophy* (Indiana University Press, 1998); (e) Jayawardhane, Kumari, *Feminism and Nationalism in the Third World* (Zed Books, 1986).
5. While discussing the common theoretical ground shared by postcolonial theory and feminist theory, Leela Gandhi makes an illuminating comment. She writes, "Both bodies of thought have concerned themselves with the study and defence of marginalized 'Others' within perspective structures of domination and, in so doing, both have followed a remarkably similar theoretical trajectory. Feminist and postcolonial theory alike began with an attempt to simply invert prevailing hierarchies of gender/culture/race, and they have progressively welcomed the poststructuralist invitation to refuse the binary oppositions upon which patriarchal/colonial authority

construct itself" (*Postcolonial Theory,* Edinburgh: Edinburgh University Press, 1988, pp. 82-83).

6. *Culture and Imperialism* (London: Vintage, 1994), p. 63.
7. Spivak's article was reprinted in *Marxist Interpretation of Culture,* eds. Cary Nelson and Lawrence Grossberg; Macmillan Education; Besingstoke, 1985, pp. 271-313. Spivak uses the contemporary cultural and critical theories to challenge the legacy of colonialism. She often focuses on cultural texts of those who are marginalized by dominant western culture: the working class, the women and the new immigrant. She carried out a series of historical studies and literary critiques of imperialism and international feminism. She strongly opposed the exclusion of the issues of the subaltern, especially subaltern women, in institutional and cultural discourses. In *A Critique of Postcolonial Reason* (1999) she explores how the major works of European metaphysics tend to exclude the subaltern (and also women) from their discussions.
8. *Selections from Political Writings 1921-26*; trs. Quentin Hoare; International Publishers, New York, 1978.
9. Preface, *Subaltern Studies,* Vol. 1. ed. R. Guha, OUP, Delhi, p. 7.

WORKS CITED

Abrams, M.H., *A Glossary of Literary Terms,* 8 edn. (Thomson Wadsworth; first reprint in India by Akash Press, Delhi; 2007).

Carden, M.L., *The New Feminist Movement* (Russell Stage Foundation; 1974).

Desai, Kiran, *The Inheritance of Loss* (Penguin Books; New Delhi; 2006).

Deshpande, Shashi, *That Long Silence* (Penguin Books; New Delhi; 1989).

Ghosh, Amitav, *Sea of Poppies* (Viking/Penguin; New Delhi; 2008).

Kapur, Manju, *Difficult Daughters* (Faber & Faber; London; 1998).

Lessing, Doris, *The Golden Notebook* (Harper-Collins; used from http://thegoldennotebook.org/book).

Roy, Arundhati, *God of Small Things* (Flamingo; London; 1998).

2

The Epic and the Novel: A Comparative Analysis of Lukácsian and Bakhtinian Views

Arnab Bhattacharya

Introduction

The novel as a literary genre has emerged vigorously in the 18th century Europe, though its origin looks back to the European Renaissance, Miguel Cervantes' *Don Quixote* being a case in point. The epic, on the other hand, is a product of ancient civilization. That is not to say that the epic is a thing of past which only is a matter of academic research today. Even in this modern world epics do exist. T.S. Eliot's *The Waste Land* is often described as 'an epic in a nutshell', whereas Seamus Heany's *Omeros* is regarded by many as a full-length modern epic. Voluminous novels like Leo Tolstoy's *War and Peace* or Vikram Seth's *A Suitable Boy* are said to be epical in structure. But my concern in this article will not be those literary constructions which are epical in spirit or in structure. Here I will concentrate exclusively on the classical epics which deal with mythological heroes' stupendous exploits, highlighting their physical prowess in the battle-fields. In this article my modest attempt will be to show how two great theoreticians of the genre of the novel, namely Georg Lukács and Mikhail Bakhtin, looked upon the novel as a logical literary development consequent upon the decline of the epic. Both of them viewed the novel as a natural outcome of the socio-historical development which marked the age of the novel radically out from the age of the epic. Their methods of contradistinguishing the novel from the epic are quite original, but a careful and perceptive analysis of their views can trace out certain parameters common to their theses, and facilitate a successful comparison.

Georg Lukács' *The Theory of the Novel* was written as a draft in the summer of 1914 and was revised into its final version in the winter of 1914-15. It first appeared in Max Dessoir's *Zeitschrift fur Aesthetik und Allgemeine Kunstwissenschaft* in 1916 and was published in book form by P. Cassirer, Berlin, in 1920. Lukács writes in its preface, "The immediate motive for writing was supplied by the outbreak of the First World War and the effect which its acclamation by the social-democratic parties had upon the European left." Lukács says that he had no objection to the downfall of Tsarism in Russia and the probable humiliation of Germany at the hand of the West, but his main concern was whether it was at all possible to thwart the suicidal tendencies lurking in the heart of Western civilization itself. He asks in no uncertain terms, "who was to save us from Western civilisation?" In fact, the Western civilization which was supposed to offer a viable model to the rest of the world, appeared deplorably defunct in ideology in the post First World War period to the Western intellectuals themselves. Oswal Spengler, in the introduction to his celebrated *The Decline of the West,* wrote:

> The decline of the West, which at first sight may appear, like the corresponding decline of the Classical Culture, a phenomenon limited in time and space, we now perceive to be a philosophical problem that, when comprehended in all its gravity, includes within itself every great question of Being. (Introduction, p. 3)

It appears that the 'great question of Being' occupied Lukács' mind too when he took upon himself the job of defining the origin and development of the novel. At the outset, as Lukács himself says, the book was intended to be written in a dialogue form, incorporating a series of dialogues among a group of individuals trying hard to get rid of their war psychosis, similar to the style adopted in Boccaccio's *Decameron* in which the people in flight from the Black Death tell stories to each other. Finally this initial plan was abandoned, and the book appeared in the form it is available in today.

It may well be questioned whether it is at all necessary to study social and psychological backdrop of a thesis which is supposed to be an objective one. The answer is that it is called-for, because Lukács himself insists on the particular frame of mind he was in during writing this book, saying "it was written in a mood of permanent despair over the state of the world. It was not until 1917 that I found an answer to the problems which, until then, had seemed to me insoluble" (*ibid.*). This was because his state of mind had a strong bearing on the methodology he adopted for his study. Admittedly, at that time Lukács was inclined to historical determinism, and was in a "process of turning from Kant to Hegel" (*ibid.*). This professed Hegelianism had a distinct bias towards a specific philosophy of historical process. This, along with his "youthful enthusiasm for the work of Dilthey, Simmel and Max Weber" made his work a typical product of "intellectual sciences" school. As for the distinguishing features of this school of thought, Lukács writes:

> ...It became the fashion to form general synthetic concepts on the basis of only a few characteristics—in most cases only intuitively grasped—of a school, a period, etc., then to proceed by deduction from these generalisations to the analysis of individual phenomena, and in that way to arrive at what we claimed to be a comprehensive overall view. (*ibid.*)

Lukács makes no bones about the limitations of this methodology, admitting that at that time he failed to observe that this method "scarcely succeeded in surmounting positivism, or that its syntheses were without objective foundation" (*ibid.*), and also that it was too generalised and too formulaic to successfully explain all the features of all kinds of novels. We must keep these things in mind when we will discuss his views on the epic and the novel.

It is these limitations that crept into Lukacsian theory due to historical reasons that Mikhail Bakhtin's views on the novel as a literary genre seek to rectify. It was in 1929 that Bakhtin's concept of 'dialogism' or 'polyphony' came to grab public attention with the publication of his magisterial *Problems of Dostoevsky's Art.* The book dismissed some of the shibboleths pertaining to the critical appreciation of art so much so that it came to be regarded as a political affront to the Communist regime in the USSR. The then Ministry of Education and the leading party intellectual Anatoly Lunacharsky found radical views expressed in the book 'politically incorrect' and exceptionable, and for this 'offence' Bakhtin was exiled to the wilds of Kazakhstan for six years. Bakhtin studied there as a bookkeeper in an obscure town of Kurstanaz, and during this time wrote some of his seminal essays including the famous "Discourse of the Novel", later included in his *The Dialogic Imagination.* In 1936 Bakhtin came back to teach in Moravian Pedagogical Institute in Saransk, and from 1940 to the end of the Second World War he lived in Moscow. It was in 1940 itself that Bakhtin submitted his dissertation on Rabelais' works, but it could not be defended until the war was over. From 1946 to 1949 there was a raging debate over the contents of the book which eventually split the city intellectuals into two camps. There were several stormy meetings (one lasting seven hours) between the warring camps to reach a consensus, but all went in vain. Eventually the government had to step in the result of which was that the State Accrediting Bureau denied him the doctorate. Thus *Rabelais and Folk Culture of the Middle Ages and Renaissance* had to wait nineteen long years before it was published in 1965. All these go on to show that Bakhtin's revolutionary discourses on the novel caused political flutter simply because those did not fit into the Communist cultural agenda propagated by Cultural Revolution. Bakhtin's thesis was as much part of political climate of his time and country as Lukács' was of his.

Though the novel came prominently to the limelight in the 19th century, it was a marginalised literary form until then, and its literary conventions were not rigorously formulated. It was more of a help than a hindrance to the practitioners of this genre, because they understandably enjoyed a lot more freedom than those of the other genres. Apart from Lukács' *The Theory of the Novel,* there have been some other seminal discourses on the novel like Ian Watt's *Rise of the Novel* (1957) and Lucien Goldmann's *Towards a Sociology of the Novel* (1964). All these are significant contributions to the understanding of the novel as a genre, but all these suffer more or less from the same limitation of sweeping generalisation based on insufficient objective datum. Bakhtin's theory is more comprehensive than those mentioned because he included more ancient texts in his critical purview, and also because, as the editor Holquist mentions in his introduction to *The Dialogic Imagination,* "he more than others perceives the novel as new. Not new when it is said to have 'arisen', but new *whenever* the kind of text made its appearance, as it has done since at least the ancient Greeks, a text that merely found its most comprehensive form in Cervantes and those who have come after" (Introduction to *TDI*, italics author's). The point is that the theoretical premise on which Bakhtin's thesis is founded is the recognition of a radical absence of an *a priori* notion in the construction of a novel, which goes on to valorize its fundamental heterogeneity. Holquist says that 'syncretic genres' like the ode, the lyric or the tragedy have a long history of evolution, and as such, have more or less rigid 'formal characterization' to conform to, which makes their subtle formal modulations fairly easily recognisable. This 'militantly protean' form which defies any patterned linear shape is a huge artistic advantage of the novel to Bakhtin's mind, because it allows it to accommodate an infinite interplay of languages or discourses which Bakhtin calls 'heteroglossia'. It is the same feature which, in Bakhtin's view, constitutes an intricate interrelationship between *what* is told and *how* it is told, i.e. the 'story' and the 'narrative' in a novel.

Now, we can proceed to compare Lukács' views about the epic and the novel in *The Theory of the Novel* with Bakhtin's in his *The Dialogic Imagination.* We can carry out this comparison on the basis of a few parameters which are immanent in both the theses. For this article I have chosen two parameters which are (1) the epical past and the novelistic present, and (2) the epic hero versus the novelistic hero/ characters.

1. *The epical past and the novelistic present*

In the very beginning of the section "The Epic and the Novel", Lukács points out:

> the epic and the novel, these two major forms of great epic literature, differ from one another not by their authors' fundamental intentions but by the given historico-philosophical realities with which the authors were confronted. The novel is the epic of an age in which the extensive totality of life is no longer directly given, in which the immanence of meaning in life has become a problem, yet which still thinks in terms of totality. It would be superficial—a matter of a mere artistic technicality—to look for the only and decisive genre-defining criterion in the question of whether a work is written in verse or prose.

Lukács clearly insists here on the historical distance which separates the age of the epic and that of the novel. But the stress is not so much on the historical distance *per se,* but on the *philosophical* one, which, to his mind, accounts for a radical difference between the two ages representing that of the epic and of the novel. Lukács holds that the epic age was one of 'extensive totality of life' with an 'immanent meaning' to be found in community living, whereas the novel came into being in an age when such a totality was already lost, but the longing for the totality was not. The novel's challenge was to construct a putative totality in place of an original one, to feign a presence in order to conceal an absence.

A little later, Lukács compares the epic verse with the tragic verse, and goes on to explain the kind of distance that the epic verse creates:

> Epic verse, too, creates distances, but in the sphere of the epic (which is the sphere of life) distance means happiness and lightness, a loosening of the bonds that tie

> men and objects to the ground, a lifting of the heaviness, the dullness, which are integral to life and which are dispersed only in scattered happy moments. The created distances of epic verse transform such moments into the true level of life. And so the effect of verse is here the opposite just because its immediate consequences—that of abolishing triviality and coming closer to the essence—is the same.

According to Lukács, apart from the historico-philosophical distance, the epic verse creates another distance—a distance which liberates from the 'trivialities' of life, and condenses the happy and magic moments of life within the epic structure. But Lukács is loath to credit the epic verse exclusively for creating such a distance because he thinks that this verse has been capable of creating such an effect only because it was produced in the epic age. Verse in which the epic is composed in is not at all *de rigueur* of epic literature, and can even be adverse to the creation of the epic totality, because, Lukács observes,

> verse can only weave a garland of freedom round something that has already been liberated from all fetters.... The lightness of great epic literature is only the concretely immanent Utopia of the historical hour, and the form-giving detachment which verse as a vehicle confers upon whatever it carries must, therefore, rob the epic of its great totality, its subjectlessness, and transform it into an idyll or a piece of playful lyricism. (*ibid.*)

Lukács says that even if verse was initially preferred as a medium of epic construction, in an age when it was deemed too light and too subjective, prose emerged to replace verse to communicate the 'epic totality'.

> It is no accident that the disintegration of a reality-become-song led, in Cervantes' prose, to the sorrowful lightness of a great epic, whereas the serene dance of Ariosto's verse remained mere lyrical play. (*ibid.*)

So, to Lukács' mind, epicality of an artistic construction depends on the content, and more importantly, on its ability to represent the totality of life which is a given in a specific age, and from this point of view, he considers even Dante's *La Divina Comedia* an epic despite its lyrical structure. The novel, on the other hand, Lukács holds, is a construction which emerged in an age when the, 'Immanent meaning' was lost, and, as such, had to devise ways to simulate a totality, or to unearth a 'concealed' totality. To quote Lukács once again,

> The epic gives form to a totality of life that is rounded from within; the novel seeks, by giving form, to *uncover and construct the concealed totality of life.* The given structure of the object (i.e. the search, which is only a way of expressing the subject's recognition that neither objective life nor its relationship to the subject is spontaneously harmonious in itself) supplies an indication of the form-giving intention. All the fissures and rents which are inherent in the historical situation must be drawn into the form-giving process and cannot nor should be disguised by compositional means. (*ibid.*, italics mine)

It is thus absolutely clear from Lukács' views that the main difference between the epic and the novel lies in the difference in their ages, the epic past being an age of 'immanent meaning' and the novelistic present being one of fissures and ruptures. For him, forms are only reflections of the 'reality of the being', and as long as such reflections are true, the question of media of expressions are immaterial.

When Mikhail Bakhtin takes up the comparison between the epic and the novel, he recognises the 'form-giving process' of the novelistic enterprise as an indication of its immense possibility of development. While Lukács views the novel as a struggling genre, trying hard to recapture a lost totality of life, Bakhtin views it as a flourishing genre, carrying immense potential for defying stereotypical formulations. In the very beginning of his essay "Epic and Novel" of his *The Dialogic Imagination,* Bakhtin says:

> The study of the novel as a genre is distinguished by peculiar difficulties. This is due to the unique nature of the object itself: the novel is the sole genre that continues

> to develop, that is as yet uncompleted. The forces that define it as a genre are at work before our very eyes: the birth and development of the novel as a genre takes place in the full light of the historical day. The genric skeleton of the novel is still far from being hardened, and we cannot foresee all its plastic possibilities. (*The Dialogic Imagination,* p. 1)

Bakhtin wrote this article in the mid-1930s; surely the novel has 'developed' a lot since then in the last 70 odd years, and its possibilities have already been manifested in great proportion. This not only justifies Bakhtin's anticipation, but also proves that his faith in the ability of the novel to become a vibrant genre adequately suited to the multi-coloured present. To Bakhtin, the epical past is *not* one of 'immanent meaning' as it is for Lukács, but one that is calcified and dead, representable only in highly stylised epic verse. Bakhtin writes:

> In an environment where the novel is the dominant genre, the conventional languages of strictly canonical genres begin to sound in new ways, which are quite different from the ways they sounded in those eras when the novel was *not* included in "high" literature. (*ibid.* p. 6, italics author's)

What is clearly visible here is that Bakhtin stresses the flexibility of style as a salient feature of the novelistic present while Lukács stresses its historico-philosophical core. This style, as the next quote from Bakhtin shows, is largely determined by its ability to parody itself in order to override any formulated stability:

> Throughout its entire history there is a consistent parodying or travestying of dominant and fashionable novels that attempt to become models for the genre: this ability of the novel to criticize itself is a remarkable feature of this ever-developing genre. (*ibid.*, p. 6)

One of the main reasons which Bakhtin points out for the novel's immense potential for development is its 'polyglossic' structure. By 'polyglossia' Bakhtin means interplay of many languages within a social unit. Unlike Lukács who defined the novelistic present as a philosophically different era of lost totality, Bakhtin steers clear of such a distinction even in terms of polyglossia, as the following excerpt shows:

> Polyglossia had always existed (it is more ancient than pure, canonical monoglossia), but it had not been a factor in the literary creation; an artistically conscious choice between languages did not serve as the creative center of literary and language process. Classical Greeks had the feeling both for "languages" and for the epochs of language, for the various Greek literary dialects (tragedy is a polyglot genre), but creative consciousness was realized as closed, pure languages (although in actual fact they were mixed). Polyglossia was appropriated and canonized among all genres. (*ibid.*, p. 12)

What is clearly noticeable here is that while Lukács views the novelistic present in terms of a lack or loss, Bakhtin views it in terms of a gain. Lukácsian philosophy makes the novel out to be a genre reaching out to the epical totality, whereas the Bakhtinian one projects it as a genre outreaching the epic and all the other genres in its polyglossic potential. In consonance with the tenor of his arguments, Bakhtin goes on to define the epical past which is in sharp contrast to Lukácsian understanding of it:

> The world of the epic is the national heroic past: it is a world of "beginnings" and "peak times" in national history, a world of fathers and of founders of families, a world of "firsts" and "bests". The important point here is not that the past constitutes the content of the epic. The formally constitutive feature of the epic as a genre is rather the transference of the represented world into the past, and the degree to which the world participated in the past. The epic is never a poem about the present, about its own time (one that became a poem about the past only for those who came later). The epic, as the specific genre known to us today, has been from the beginning a poem about the past, and the authorial position immanent in the epic and constitutive for it (that is, the position of the one who utters the epic word)

> is the environment of a man speaking about a past that is to him inaccessible, the reverent point of view of a descendent. (*ibid.*, p. 13)

It is difficult to miss the key point of the Bakhtinian analysis of the epic here. Bakhtin here is not concerned with the kind of philosophy that the epical past carries through; his focus is on the epical treatment of the past. He, unlike Lukács, does not deliberate on what content the epical past represents, but on how it orients itself in relation to the past. He points out that what the epic invariably does is to transfer the present in which it is being composed to a past which it can never be a part of, which will always be a far cry for it. For Bakhtin the epical past is more a function of authorial 'position' or attitude than of the fundamental philosophy of a specific historical time. A little later in the essay, he further qualifies the epical past thus:

> The epic past is called the "absolute past" for good reason: it is both monochronic and valorized (hierarchical); it lacks any relativity, that is, any gradual, purely temporal progressions that might connect it to the present. It is walled off absolutely from all subsequent times, and above all from times in which singer and the listeners are located. This boundary, consequently, is in the form of the epic itself and is felt and heard in its every word.
>
> To destroy this boundary is to destroy the form of the epic as a genre. But precisely it is walled from all subsequent times, the epic past is absolute and complete. It is as closed as a circle; inside it everything is finished, already over. There is no place in the epic world for any openendedness, indecision, indeterminacy. There are no loopholes in it through which we can glimpse the future; it suffices unto itself, neither supposing any continuation nor requiring it. Temporal and valorized definitions are here fused into a single and inseparable whole (as they are also fused in the semantic layers of ancient languages). (*ibid.*, pp. 15-16)

In this analysis of the content of the epical past Bakhtin comes close to Lukács, in that his qualification of the epical past as an 'absolute' one carries import similar to Lukácsian 'totality'. But, significantly enough, Bakhtin's viewpoint is cardinally different from Lukács', because Bakhtin views this 'absolutism' as a symptom of stagnancy, depriving it of any continuity into subsequent times, whereas Lukács views it as an indicator of self-sufficiency; while Bakhtin looks upon this past as moribund, Lukács as vital and full. In contrast to this epic world, the novelistic world, according to Bakhtin, is lively and dynamic, it reaches out to the future quite easily, without any inhibition. He writes:

> The novel, by contrast, is determined by experience, knowledge and practice (the future). In the era of Hellenism a closer contact with the heroes of the Trojan epic circle began to be felt; epic is already being transformed into novel. Epic material is transposed into novelistic material, into precisely that zone of contact that passes through the intermediate stages of familiarization and laughter. When the novel becomes the dominant genre, epistemology becomes the dominant discipline. (*ibid.*, p. 15)

Thus for Bakhtin, the novelistic present is characterised by 'epistemology', by knowledge and experience of the present, whereas for Lukács, it is characterised by a fractured totality.

Now, we will move to discuss the views of Lukács and Bakhtin in relation to the heroes/characters of the epic and the novel.

2. *The epic hero versus the novelistic hero/characters*

In Lukács' view, the epic hero is devoid of independence or autonomy, simply because he represents an age of an unproblematic community life which contains an internal homogeneity. He hails from a community whose values he embodies and whose aspirations he represents. He may be a few notches higher than other members of his community in terms of valour or physical prowess, but never posits himself in opposition to, or in distinction against, his community, and, as such, cannot claim to be an 'individual' in true sense of the term. To Lukács' mind, this non-interiority of the epic hero is purely symptomatic of the epic age, as he explains:

> The epic hero is, strictly speaking, never an individual, it is traditionally thought that one of the essential characteristics of the epic is the fact that its theme is not a personal destiny but the destiny of a community. And rightly so, for the completeness, the roundness of the value system which determines the epic cosmos creates a whole which is too organic for any part of it to become so enclosed within itself, so dependent upon itself, as to find itself as an interiority—i.e. to become a personality. The omnipotence of ethics, which posits every soul as autonomous and incomparable, is still unknown in such a world. (*The Theory of the Novel*)

A little later in his analysis, Lukács goes on to compare the tragic hero with the epic hero, throwing more light on the character of the epic hero:

> What is a symbol in tragedy becomes a reality in the epic: the weight of the bonds linking an individual destiny to a totality. World destiny, which in tragedy is merely the number of noughts that have to be added to it to transform it into a million, is what actually gives the events of the epic their content; the epic hero, as bearer of his destiny, is not lonely, for this destiny connects him by indissoluble threads to the community whose fate is crystallised in his own. (*ibid.*)

Lukács' point here is that the epic hero is not lonely even in his suffering or in his tragic destiny. The epic hero, Lukács holds, does not suffer for himself, but for his community; he epitomises the entire community in his own persona. The epic world for Lukács is characterised by a redoubtable centrifugal force which strongly binds whatever is external or peripheral to the centre, and, therefore, the relation between the part and the whole is always 'organic', and never a 'constructed' one. Lukács finds the first signs of transformation of the organic epic structure to architectural structure leading to the emergence of the novelistic hero in Dante. In Lukács' words:

> Dante is the only great example in which we see the architectural clearly conquering the organic, and therefore he represents a historico-philosophical transition from the pure epic to the novel. In Dante there is still the perfect immanent distancelessness and completeness of the true epic, but his figures are already individuals, consciously and energetically placing themselves in opposition to a reality that is becoming closed to them, individuals who, through this opposition, become real personalities. (*ibid.*)

Dante for Lukács represents a unique case of fusing the epical and novelistic content, resulting in a synthesis which Lukács calls '*epopoeia*'. Dante, Lukács holds, did not have to endow his hero with the tragic destiny which the community automatically and conditionally shares, rather the Dantean hero, through his very personal lived experience, attains such a transcendent status that he comes to symbolise not only the destiny of a community, but 'of humanity in general'. Dante's creation, for Lukács, is an intermediate stage between the epic and the novel, indicating the time which was already beginning to demand the novel. When the novel finally emerged, the 'immanent meaning' or the 'organic structure' of the epic world was totally lost, and so, naturally, Lukács shows, it had to resort to 'abstract systematization' to simulate a totality. In the chapter "The Inner Form of the Novel", Lukács defines this abstraction in the following manner:

> Such abstract systematisation is, it is true, the ultimate basis of the entire structure, but in the created reality of the novel all that becomes visible is the distance separating the systematisation from concrete life: a systematisation which emphasises the conventionality of the objective world and the interiority of the subjective one. Thus the elements of the novel are, in the Hegelian sense, entirely abstract; abstract, the nostalgia of the characters for Utopian perfection, a nostalgia that feels itself and its desires to be the only true reality; abstract, the existence of social structures based only upon their factual presence and their sheer ability to continue;

> abstract, finally, the form-giving intention which, instead of surmounting the distance between these two abstract groups of elements, allows it to subsist, which does not even attempt to surmount it but renders it sensuous as the lived experience of the novel's characters, uses it as a means of connecting the two groups and so turns it into an instrument of composition. (*ibid.*)

Lukács' clear insistence here is on Hegelian abstraction, which in novelistic terms translates itself into two sets of abstractions, namely, the abstraction between the nostalgia that the characters feel for a lost Utopian world, and that of the social structures. The characters of the novel are made to live through these two sets, and contribute to the development of the novelistic form. A little Jater, Lukács delves further into the subject:

> The novel is the art-form of virile maturity: this means that the completeness of the novel's world, if seen objectively; is an imperfection, and if subjectively experienced, it amounts to resignation. (*ibid.*)

Lukács evokes the image of a child's growth into adulthood, as he calls the epic form 'childlike' and the novel form 'mature', meaning that the novel, being an artistic product of a much later age, is like a child attaining maturity, for whom the world is no longer conceivable as a rounded whole, and this realization inevitably leads to a sense of defeat and dejection. This subjective experience is represented by the novel's characters.

Mikhail Bakhtin in his thesis does not dwell exclusively on the theme of the transformation of epic heroes to novelistic characters. But his analysis of the special features of the genre of the novel throws up certain clues to our understanding of what qualities are expected to characterise a novelistic hero or character. In his essay "Epic and Novel" of his book *The Dialogic Imagination,* he identifies the serio-comic elements, or more specifically, laughter as a dominant feature of the genre of the novel, whereas sobriety and grandeur characterise the epic. He qualifies the novelistic laughter in the following manner:

> Laughter demolishes fear and piety before an object, before a world, making of it an object of familiar contact, and thus clearing the ground for an absolutely free investigation of it. Laughter is a vital factor in laying down the prerequisite for fearlessness without which it would be impossible to approach the world realistically. As it draws an object to itself and makes it familiar, laughter delivers the object into the hands of investitive experiment—both scientific and artistic—and into the hands of free experimental fantasy. Familiarization of the world through laughter and popular speech is an extremely important and indispensable step in making possible free, scientifically knowable and artistically creative reality in European civilization. (*ibid.*, p. 23)

Bakhtin holds that the novel thrives on the familiarization of a world 'through laughter and popular speech', whereas Lukács stresses the point of abstraction in the novelistic expression. Naturally, while distinguishing the novelistic characters from the epical heroes, Bakhtin emphasises the ability of the novel's characters to embody this laughter, that is, their ability to laugh at themselves and at others, enabling them to adopt a critical view at things around them. Bakhtin analyses the wide range of critical perspectives that the comical stance of novelistic characters is capable of engendering in the narrative, as the following excerpt shows:

> One can play games with the comical (that is, contemporize it); serving as the objects of the game we have the primordial artistic symbols of space and time—above, below, in front of, behind, earlier, later, first, last, past, present, brief (momentary), long and so forth. What reigns supreme here is the artistic logic of analysis, dismemberment, turning things into dead objects. (*ibid.*, p. 24)

Alongside familiarization, it is this critical detachment, the objectification of all things visible in order to examine them critically is what, to Bakhtin's mind, characterises the novelistic narrative of which characters are the vehicles. These features come into the narrative due to its unflagging engagement with the dynamic present as a result of which, Bakhtin shows, the narrative space gets split into two authorial images. He writes:

> This is not merely a matter of the author's image appearing within his own field of representation—important is here the fact that the original, formal author (the author of the authorial image) appears in a new relationship with the represented world. Both find themselves now subject to the same temporally valorized measurements, for the "depicting" authorial language now lies on the same plane as "depicted" language of the hero, and may enter into dialogic relations and hybrid combinations with it (indeed, it cannot help but entering into such relations). (*ibid.*, pp. 27-28)

Like laughter and the comical, language is another very important criterion in the Bakhtinian theorisation of the difference between the epic and the novel. It is this language which, as the excerpt shows, clearly demonstrates where a novelistic hero is different from an epical hero. The language that this hero utters is very similar to the narrative language that the author uses, whereas in an epic the hero is made to communicate in grandiose terms. The images which appear in the novel, whether in the form of the authorial persona or of the novelistic hero, are characterised by the novel's relationship with the ever-changing present, by the altogether new sense of temporality that dominates the narrative space. Bakhtin elaborates:

> Through contact with the present, an object is attracted to the incomplete process of a world-in-the-making, and is stamped with the seal of inconclusiveness. No matter how distant the object is from us in time, it is connected to our incomplete, present-day, temporal transitions, it develops a relationship with our unpreparedness, with our present. But meanwhile our present has been moving into an inconclusive future. And in this inconclusive context, all the semantic stability of the object is lost: its sense and significance are renewed and grow as the context continues to unfold. This leads to the radical changes in the structuring of an artistic image. The

> image acquires a specific actual existence. It acquires a relationship—in one form or another, to one degree or another—to the ongoing event of current life in which we, the author and the readers, are intimately participating. This creates the radically new zone for structuring image in the novel, a zone of maximally close contact between the represented object and contemporary reality in all its inconclusiveness—and consequently a similarly close contact between the object and the future. (*ibid.*, pp. 30-31)

What comes out clearly from this analysis is that in Bakhtinian view the novel is characterised by a kind of fluid temporality which contrasts with the epic's 'absolute past'. Since the present (and also the past, for that matter) represented in the novel reaches out to the future, it is 'inconclusive', and never static or stagnant. Lukács too points out the lack of 'rounded totality' and the 'incompleteness' of the novelistic present, but to his mind it is the maturity of the age that produced the novel which makes the fragmentation of the artistic sensibility inevitable, and consequently makes the novel resort to abstractions. For Bakhtin this specific feature of the novelistic present is the source of its strength mainly because it destabilises the language opening it up to myriad possibilities. What Bakhtin calls "a zone of maximally close contact between the represented object and contemporary reality in all its inconclusiveness" is reflected not only in the narrative style of the novel, but also in the characters that the novelist portrays.

Conclusion

I am not too sure to what extent this longer than anticipated article of mine has been able to elucidate the points of departure and of concurrence of Lukácsian and Bakhtinian views on the epic and the novel. My aim has been to show how their views had political imports within them, and how they recognised the difference of ages between the epic and the novel, but differed radically in analysing the difference. In this article I have chosen only two parameters common to their theses to bring home this point. Maybe in some time in future I will have another opportunity to dwell on other parameters that their theses have in common.

REFERENCES

Bakhtin, Mikhail Mikhailovich, *The Dialogic Imagination: Four Essays*. Ed. by Michael Holquist (tr. by Caryl Emerson and Michael Holquist). Texas, USA: University of Texas Press, 1981.

Lukács, Georg, *The Theory of the Novel* (tr. by Anna Bostock), retrieved from www.ianzarotecaiiente.com

Spengler, Oswald, *The Decline of the West: Form and Actuality* (tr. by Charles Francis Atkinson). New York: Borzoi Books, 1926.

3

All About H. Hatterr: A Philosophical Comedy

Basavaraj Naikar

It is true that *All About H. Hatterr* has disturbed and irritated the naive reader and puzzled and unnerved the serious critic both by its thematic peculiarity and by its technical novelty and linguistic gallimaufry. In fact it has posed a real challenge to the analytical and explicatory powers of the critics. That is why critics have failed to designate and classify it confidently and define its boundaries clearly. There are also a number of critics, who want to solve such a critical problem by following the escapist method of never facing it. (The M.Phil., and Ph.D. students and their guides are rather afraid of choosing it for their research as they consider it a philosophical puzzle and a linguistic bugbear.) What is required in the critic in such a situation is an honest hesitation and willingness to offer an experimental explanation rather than the final appreciation or downright condemnation. It is this kind of honesty that T.S. Eliot reveals when he says, "In all my experience I have not met with anything quite like it. It is amazing that anyone should be able to sustain a piece of work in this style and tempo at such length." The responsibility of the critic increases in proportion to the complexity, novelty and peculiarity of the work of art. He has to interpret the pattern of meaning underlying the novel or any other work for that matter and help the common reader understand and enjoy it better than he generally would when left to himself. The present article is intended to offer such an explanation and inspire the other readers to come out with theirs.

All About H. Hatterr may be regarded as a philosophical comedy because the eponymous protagonist of the novel wants to seek Truth like a philosopher. His intention is to absorb the wide experience of life, to try to assimilate it and evolve a pattern of meaning or philosophy out of it. A pragmatist by temperament, H. Hatterr is not content with the *a priori* knowledge of the Truth of life, but intends to go through a series of experiences in an explorative manner and formulate an *a posteriori* knowledge of the truth of life. In this sense H. Hatterr is a kind of philosopher, who seeks after Truth through the pragmatic experience of life. But, in spite of such a serious mission, he does not rise to the height of a sage or saint or an epic hero, but, on the contrary, remains a comic figure. *All About H. Hatterr* may, therefore, be considered a philosophical comedy.

Who, then, is this comic figure called H. Hatterr? He is, as declared by himself, a hybrid product of colonial combination, of a Christian father and an Oriental mother. "Biologically, I am fifty-fifty of the species. One of my parents was a European, Christian-by-faith merchant merman (seaman).... The other was an Oriental, a Malay Peninsula-resident lady, a steady non-voyaging, non-Christian human (no mermaid)" (p. 31). H. Hatterr is thus a man, who combines the Eastern and the Western cultures in his sensibility and who wants to understand the meaning of life on his own. His name has a story behind it, and is suggested by the Rev the Head's too-large-for-him-hat. He was adopted by an English Missionary Society. He lives there in the sahib-society until his fourteenth year when he attains certain independence of thinking, feeling and acting. He, therefore, wants to look at life afresh and evolve his own *Weltanschauung* of life. That is why the novel is described by K.R. Srinivasa Iyengar as an account of "A journey and a struggle, a movement from innocence to experience, a growth in consciousness, education in the large school of life." It is because of the awakening of his consciousness that he finds the unsuitability to his temperament of the evangelical atmosphere of the English Missionary Society and decides to leave it for good. He, therefore, steals three books, i.e. an English Dictionary, a *Latin Self-Taught* and a *French Self-Taught* of Rev. the Head and the school's stereoscope and escapes from there. His decision to plunge into life makes it mandatory for him to choose a new name, i.e. Hindustaniwalla Hatterr, which serves as the new manifesto of his life to be. His escape from the evangelical institute easily reminds us of Fra Lippo Lippi's escape from the Carmelite Church in Browning's poem of that title. It is thus that H. Hatterr takes a bold decision to have a plurality of experiences in the manner in which Oscar Wilde wanted to lead a life of 'exquisite sensations'. His major ambition in life is to have the knowledge of Truth through the first-hand experience of life. He declares himself as "An Oriental gent, whose only assets in the world were a sable fur coat and a genuine delight in information and learning, spent the better half of his life digging up a pyramid" (p. 30). H. Hatterr's Anglo-Indian birth itself symbolizes his bicultural sensibility of the lowest order. As the novelist himself clarifies, "Hatterr was a portrait of man, the common vulgar species, found everywhere, both the east and the west" (p. 403). The comedy of the novel lies in this strange combination in the protagonist of the common vulgarity and the highly serious intention. Thus having decided to seek the Truth of life empirically, he visits the seven saints of India, who are repositories of knowledge, and tries to acquire the wealth of knowledge and experience of life. The number 'seven' is a significant one in the Hindu religion and suggests the *sapta rishis,* who are the seven saints converted into celestial stars. Besides, the number 'seven' connotes holiness or sacro-sanctity and quest for knowledge, of Truth and so on. (But the same number suggests evil, inauspiciousness and failure in a negative context. Thus 'seven' has an ambiguous meaning about it. H. Hatterr's meeting with these seven saints of India has, therefore, both the serious and the comic aspects about it.)

His meeting with seven saints one after another involves a spirit of adventure thereby making him a picaresque hero. His meeting with each saint enables him to learn a certain item of philosophy. The questions summarized in the 'digest' section, theoretically raised in the 'instruction' section of all the seven chapters of the novel, obviously, are the fundamental issues in the Eastern as well as the Western philosophies of the world. Hatterr's meeting with the first sage, i.e. Sage of Calcutta presupposes the philosophical question about the individual versus fate or Destiny. Whether the individual can shape his life according to his sweet will or should submit himself to the deterministic forces or powers beyond his control is the major question in all the philosophies, theologies and religions of the world. He learns from the Sage of Calcutta to be 'suspicious' in order to dispel the 'credible illusions'. In a way, Hatterr lays the foundation of his philosophical knowledge when he learns his formula of 'antithesis' of life in general. The second formula that he learns from the Sage of Rangoon is the irrationality of sexual urge in human life. "Cupid is blind, non-rational, anti-intelligent, sense-enemy; and so are his victims..." (p. 63). In his third encounter, he approaches the Sage of Madras, who thinks that his teaching is too abstract for the average mind of the former and directs him to a teacher of concrete instruction, Shaikh Eli Arabi, who teaches him the formula that "youth is an ugly age and characteristic" (p. 106). He learns his fourth formula from the Sage of Bombay that life is marked by the chance element or the unexpected and wonderful things, features and events. Hatterr becomes aware of the question, "In the affairs of man, gods and such-like foreign factors intervene? Is there any truth in the notion that paranormal interference is going on in the universe? Is a human feller a free agent? Is future tense a myth-joke?" (p. 160). His experience with the fifth sage, i.e. the Sage of Delhi teaches him "The oldest wonder in the world: The triumph of evil!" (p. 193). He comes to know the eternal conflict between appearance and reality and the triumph of the former over the latter. He learns from the sixth sage, i.e. the Sage of Mogalsarai-Varanasi the lesson of the unavoidability of the course of fate in human life. "'Kismet', or fate—if at all anything, and as potent as suspected for centuries—is a dam—baffling thing!" (p. 226). Similarly he learns from the seventh and last sage, i.e. the Sage of All-India the lesson about the inevitability of conflict among human beings and the defeat or destruction of the helpless by the mighty ones. The lesson also implies the attendant question as to whether Nature is "unsocial in intent? Is it Brute Force in motion or disguised Benevolence?" (p. 252). Thus all these encounters of H. Hatterr with the seven sages of India give him an awareness of the major issues, which are common to the Eastern and the Western philosophies and testify to Hatterr's quest for Truth.

The comedy of Hatterr's variegated experience consists in the conspicuous discordance between his individual expectations and the *a posteriori* knowledge, which itself is a confirmation of the *a priori* knowledge received from the saints. In other words, the comedy lies in the realization of the incongruence between dream and reality; expectation and actual happening; instinct and reason and so on. Hatterr's participation in diverse situations is symbolic of Man's quest for Truth and lends itself to psychological (especially Jungian) as well as philosophical religious interpretations.

His experience with a washerwoman helps him realize the formula taught by the Sage of Calcutta, "A wise man must master the craft of dispelling credible illusions" (p. 41). Hatterr's gullibility, which is in sharp contrast to the sage's ideal of 'suspiciousness', makes him accept the washerwoman as his beloved, and accept her on her words. Again the age-gap between Hatterr and the washerwoman is to be noted because of the comicality of it. The washerwoman is 'nearer sixty than fifty' and is obviously not a good match for him as far as age is concerned. Nevertheless Hatterr believes her because of his general faith in mankind. When the washerwoman is enamoured of Hatterr and therefore succeeds in making him go to bed with her, he begins to love her under the illusion that she also loves him. But this illusion is shattered when he is blackmailed by her and consequently loses his membership of the sahib-club and reputation. This shocking experience shows him the contrast between his illusion and the reality and naturally contributes to the comedy of the novel. This experience brings about a change in his behaviour by making him hate the woman he once loved.

Another experience of a similar kind confirms the incongruence between illusion and reality in a more elaborate manner. Introduced by his confidant friend Mr. Bannerji to a journalist Chari-Charier, Hatterr accepts an appointment as a 'reporter' and is immediately sent into a forest for bringing 'an interview' with the Sage of Wilderness. Hatterr goes to the Sage of Wilderness with the normal expectation of spending some time with a holy man. But again his 'illusion' is shattered when the actual experience turns out to be contrary to his expectation. As he goes there, he is embarrassed at his own plight of having to dance naked around a pile of clothes and of being ill-treated and even beaten by the younger brother of the Sage of Wilderness. Thus the Sage of Wilderness and his younger brother, whom Hatterr had taken to be holy men of high morality, turn out to be crafty and almost cruel merchants. As a result of his miserable failure to bring the 'write-up' about the Sage, he is dismissed from the job of a reporter. This experience enables him to formulate his own *a posteriori* philosophy of antithesis according to which the world is full of contrast and made up of hitters and crabs, the latter being further divided into two, i.e. courageous ones and docile ones.

His next experience again helps him realize the contrast between instinct and reason. He is instructed by the Sage of Rangoon that "Cupid is blind, non-rational, anti-intelligent, sense-enemy and so are his enemies" and therefore that "I command thee boy, desist! Extinguish the fires of passion with meditation! (p. 62). He is asked by the Sage of Rangoon to channelize his sexual instinct with the necessary discipline of mind. But average man as Hatterr is, he does not have the ability to do so. He says, "Meditation, didst say? It is so *extraordinary difficult* to meditate! It is so *extraordinary difficult* to extinguish the fires" (p. 62). But the powerful sexual urge in Hatterr is stimulated further by his pal Bannerji, who asks him not to suppress his libido and develop a complex. He, therefore, introduces Hatterr to the wife of a circus owner and asks him, "to make hay while the sun shines" (p. 68). Thus the dilemma in Hatterr between the need for sublimation and for submission to the urge of his libido is resolved in favour of the latter. He therefore falls in love with Rosie, a married lady and makes no bones about his intention to her. The comedy of the whole situation lies in the fact that in spite of his intense desire for sexual gratification he never gets anything except the peripheral one. When he asks her, "Rosie...will you allow me to kiss you, please?" (p. 72). She only makes "certain post-dated promises" (p. 73). The path of love being beset with innumerable hurdles, it demands a good deal of sacrifice on the part of the partners. But in the case of Hatterr, the sacrifice that he has to make for the possession of his lady is ridiculously greater than is necessary. He has got to act as a substitute lion-tamer in the Braganza shows in the absence of her husband. Forced by the basic sexual attraction for Rosie, he undergoes a traumatic experience in the show as a 'human plate' for the mutton piece, which is eaten by the lion. The forced encounter with the lion creates an anaesthesiac effect upon him. He, therefore, feels "my ego nearly suffers a separation from my anatomy, this earthly garb" (p. 87). Consequently he experiences a series of fantastic, wherein he sees the 'super masquerade', St. Paul's Church of London and the Surgical Ward Emergency Clinic. Thus, Hatterr is now completely disillusioned about his attraction for Rosie and realizes his folly. Again he becomes aware of the contrast between his expectation and his actual experience.

He, then, meets Sadanand or Always Happy XX, the Pope-Pontiff of the country of Behar and wants to extend the horizon of his knowledge of life. But there, in spite of Rialto's brother's dissuasion, Hatterr goes to Mysore, where a money-lender called Nighanteesrimahalingham Chety—Chety sends *halva* to him. Hatterr is both happy and surprised to have this pleasant experience. But the comedy of this situation will be complete when Hatterr receives a show-cause notice from the same man, who had sent him *halva*. Thus the contradictory experiences of receiving a pleasant gift of comfitures and a legal notice are as incongruous with each other as unexpected.

Again there is a contradiction between Hatterr's expectation and situational exigency. Later he returns to Always Happy, who wants to cure him of his libido or sex-mania and therefore recommends the remedies like ash-coating, dipping into the River Ganga, etc., during the night of nights. But Hatterr again finds it extremely difficult to suppress his libido. All these situations, which are quite comic, enable him to crystallize his philosophy of contrast in the manner of a serious philosopher. He says, "I am a mere nobody, but I have carried on some research on my own. And I say to posterity, in the Twentieth century, 'Life is contrast'. That is my *crux-Statement.* Damme, look at *life*! *Life* is ups and downs, light and shade, sun and cloud, opposites and opposites!" (p. 155).

Hatterr's acquaintance with the Sage of Bombay makes him realize the hypocritical basis of the so-called supernatural or paranormal happenings in the lives of nominal saints. His encounter with Anand Giri-Giri enables him to understand the contrast between expectation and actuality. Hatterr is unexpectedly forced to be confined into a room along with Anand Giri-Giri, who grows hysterical and is declared by his disciple Gangadhin to be haunted by a ghost. But the main comedy of this situation lies in the fact that Hatterr also pretends to be haunted by the ghost. When finally an exorcist is called in, the ghost is identified to be that of the late Heropal. When Bhata Govinda, the exorcist leads Hatterr to fire, the latter grows nervous and declares that he is leaving the body of Hatterr willingly and escapes from the ordeal of fire. But ironically enough, Anand Giri-Giri uses the same trick to escape from the same ordeal. Thus the exposure of the hypocrisy of the so-called saint and the contrast between the possibility of supernatural event and the hypocritical pretension of being possessed by the supernatural force on the part of Anand Giri-Giri heightens the comic effect of the situation.

The lesson of the triumph of evil that Hatterr has learnt from the Sage of Delhi is confirmed by him in his actual encounter with a Sadhu of the Naga Order, who asks him to be careful about his purse and says that he himself learnt it from his stay in Banaras. He, further, explains to Hatterr the operation of the law of causality in the world. The evils or sins react in a chain fashion. Desire for money is the root cause of many evils. All the money earned must be spent on charity. "If charity is not administered, know, money shall act upon them as poison. The poison shall cause hunger, insatiable hunger, for more money, more and more and they would spend their lives exchanging money, till they die, overloaded with wealth, their souls bloated with sin. Their souls would carry with them the accursed sin-load of *Karma*. That action—*Karma*—will set up evil tremors, from one birth to the next, for countless lives, till the souls are purged" (p. 211). Hatterr continues his practice of austerities with the Naga Sadhu, who tests him whether he has been following the lesson properly. But ironically enough, Hatterr's loincloth containing Rs. 200/- is snatched away by the Naga Sadhu, who has advised him so seriously against it. Thus the comedy of situation here lies in the contrast between the Guru's, i.e. Naga Sadhu's thieving his own disciple and his pretension of being an advisor against the same practice. The expectation of Hatterr is, as usual, falsified by actuality and hence the comicality of the whole scene.

The inevitability of the working of fate in human life taught by the Sage of Mogalsarai-Varanasi is realized empirically by Hatterr. Fate also creates an atmosphere of comedy by bringing together a good man like Hatterr and a wrong woman like Rialto. As Hatterr himself explains it, "All I know is that I wanted to raise a family; add to the world's vital statistics and legitimate; have a niche in the community, for my own kid, to hand out the wager till the end" (p. 226). It is this noble purpose, which has impelled him to marry the girl Rialto. But alas! There is no conjugal harmony at all between the two. On the contrary there is "between us all the temperamental difference in the world" (p. 226). Hatterr thinks that his marriage with Rialto is fatalistically determined. In spite of his repeated efforts he has not been able to understand her true nature, which proves the formula that "It is exceeding difficult to comprehend females..." (p. 225). Her interests seem to be diametrically opposed to his. When, for example, he is about to receive a title of 'Ocean of the Musical Art' (*Sangita Kala Sagara*) his wife Kiss-curl Rialto disperses the entire audience with her rifle and frustrates Hatterr's ambitious plan of possessing a prestigious title. Thus the yoking together of two consorts of contradictory tastes is realized by Hatterr to be the result of the irrefrangibility of the human fate and contributes to the comic atmosphere of the novel.

Hatterr's last encounter with the Sage of All-India, his reception of the lesson from the Sage and his disobedience of the Guru's instructions again heighten the comic effect. He, for example, is advised by the former to "Abscond from Charlatans and deceivers as thou wouldst from venomous snakes!" (p. 252). But this lesson of self-control prescribed by the Sage of All-India runs counter to Hatterr's nature. Hatterr believes in the formula that "all physical locomotion is due to the inborn will to search: food, sex, society" (p. 252). The same principle is reinstated by his friend Bannerji, who declares that "disappointments in life produce the craving for wine, woman and song" (p. 253). Thus stimulated by this sage he disobeys the instruction of the Sage of All-India and goes in search of new experiences. But again his expectations are all falsified by the strange events. Once when Hatterr is returning from a *Tamasha* show, he is beaten by a stranger. Here the fun that he had in the theatre is contrasted with the experience of being beaten and it is this discordance that evokes the comic sentiment in the reader. On another occasion, he is cheated by a shopkeeper, who uses false weights in selling the fried cakes to the former. On yet another occasion the bewitching beloved called Behari with whom Hatterr has fallen in love, is snatched away by a rival called Gopilal Gope. All these experiences shatter his illusions, enable him to realize his folly and evolve his philosophy of antithesis.

All these experiences of life enable Hatterr to translate the *a priori* knowledge into the *a posteriori* one and to crystallize his philosophy of contrast, subsequently summarized in eighty paragraphs of the appendix of the novel. The contrast between the mighty and the helpless; reason and instinct; participation and withdrawal; reward and punishment; appearance and reality; good and evil; fate and the individual effort; innocence and guilt or cunning is conspicuously noticed by Hatterr. The comedy of the novel consists in Hatterr's realization of the principle of antithesis in life. It is this realization again, which cures him of all his illusions and gives him a new awareness of life. His formulation of the philosophy of contrast might be attributed to the very exigency of his birth occasioned by the coming together of two diametrically opposed cultures—in other words his hybridity. His problems both in their theoretical and in practical aspect remind us of the major issues of religion, metaphysics, psychology, sociology, ethics and aesthetics, etc., raised by gigantic thinkers like Vedic seers, philosophers like Kant, Hegel, Libnitz and psychologists like C.C. Jung and Freud and so on.

But the main question about Hatterr seems to be with regard to the nature of his experience. There is no doubt about the sincerity of his thoughts and feelings. But the great philosophical issues of human life, which are reflected in his world, somehow, do not make him a serious philosopher. Why? What is it that makes him a comic hero rather than a religious or epic hero? He reminds us of the comic figures like Shakespeare's Falstaff, Ben Jonson's Bobadil, Cervantes' Don Quixote, Browning's Fra Lippo Lippi and *vidusaka* or court-jester of Sanskrit Drama and so on. The main reason for the comicality of his behaviour is ascribable to the hybridization of his very personality, which is made up of two diametrically opposed cultures like the Oriental and the Occidental. In his pursuit of Truth, Hatterr follows neither purely Western/ Christian path nor purely Eastern/Hindu path. Although he wants to know the total Truth of life by visiting all the seven sages of India, he never realizes the inadequacy and limitation of his empirical approach to life. He makes a vain attempt to combine the pragmatic experience with the transcendental one. He, for example, wants to allow a free play to his libido and yet be a respectable gentleman. The essential contradiction in him between the ideals and their falsification is externalized in the form of Mr. Bannerji and the seven sages of India respectively. Hatterr, thus, obviously becomes a battleground of the warring opposites of life. In so far as Mr. Hatterr sees only the external aspect of Truth and therefore sees only contrast, he may be said to be a comic figure, whose philosophy is based on his phenomenal vision. But he does not stagnate. After realizing the limitations of empirical approach and phenomenal experience with the seven sages of India, he becomes a Hindu monk, 504 Sri Yatim Rambeli under the supervision of Sri Sri Sri 1008 Guruji which enables him to reconcile the contradictions of the phenomenal world with the help of transcendental meditation.

REFERENCES

Desani, G.V., *All About H. Hatterr,* Harmondsworth: Penguin Books Ltd., 1972. (All the references are to this edition.)

Iyengar, K.R. Srinivasa, *Indian Writing in English,* Bombay: Asia Publishing House, p. 489.

4

Black Feminism and Novel: The American Context

Anita Myles

Amongst popular contemporary critical postulations, Feminism occupies a prominent place. While critics explore various forms and different stages of Feminism employing myriad metaphors such as Ecofeminism, Radical Feminism, waves of Feminism, one significant movement that attracted less attention of critics than it deserves is Black Feminism originating in America. The radix of modern feminist movement is tracked to French descent steadily spreading to other European and Asian countries including India, but the American Black Feminist Movement happens to be much older, more revolutionary and is a different assumption altogether. Gradually the black women writers have succeeded in arousing the interest of critics world wide by their bold and expressive exposure of the predicament of the exploited and neglected black women in America. In its widely accepted connotation, Feminism signifies an endeavour for attaining better understanding through action, speech or writing of women's rights and issues purposively for bringing them out of their erstwhile marginalized status. Phillip Rice and Patricia Waugh infer that,

> Feminism begins as enlightenment discourse founded in the Kantian idea of an autonomous and rational self who is free to choose; in the liberal concept of rights and ownership, and in the idea of citizenship and consensus

in the social contract tradition of Hobbes, Rousseau and Locke.[1]

Evidently, writers, sociologists, psychologists and philosophers consciously vindicated equal privileges for women through diverse epochs of history though the idea of Feminism gained momentum only in 1880 with awareness of women equability in France.

However, the subordination of women may be traced back to the origin of the universe beginning with the punishment and suffering of Eve in the Christian cycle. In Hindu mythology, the norms prescribed for women by Manu curtail their freedom immensely. The *Purdah* system of Islam may be interpreted as an extension of the same idea. Besides these, cultures too imposed restrictions on women granting them a lower status than men. Hence, Feminism surfaced as a reactionary response and rebellion against unequal pre-determined religious and cultural perceptions regarding women, though as a movement it emerged in different countries at different times.

The English Renaissance celebrated for its Humanism and rebirth of culture proved merely a platform for men, women being confined to limited roles of homemaking and reproduction. Ironically, one aspect of male chivalry was recognized by their ability to keep the women in subordination thereby proclaiming their masculinity. The seventeenth century witnessed some leniency shown to women who were permitted to articulate their thoughts. While Rachel Speght and Mary Fell favoured the education of women, the era also witnessed the emergence of women writers like Lady Mary Wroth, Mary Astell and Aphra Behn. Of these Astell may be considered as the mother of Feminist theory for her seminal work, *A Serious Proposal to the Ladies, for the Advancement of Their True and Greatest Interest* (1694) and *A Serious Proposal,* Part II (1697). In the eighteenth century Mary Wollstonecraft published her famous treatise *Vindication of the Rights of Women* (1792) which encouraged education among women and also provided impetus to feminist consciousness which took a definite shape through Barbara Smith, Bessie Raynes

Parke and Anne Jameson who formed the Society for Promoting the Employment of Women in 1859. Barbara Smith also initiated the *English Women's Journal* in 1858 in London to discuss employment and equality issues of women. These endeavours strengthened the position of women in the British society.

Different ages and different areas have their own ideas of Feminism but in literature, Feminism is mainly concerned with the representation of women in society and their corresponding position. These attempts to define what it is to be a woman assume a universal significance in that woman is considered more as a product of cultural norms and restraints rather than as a creation of Nature. Accepting that the inequality of the sexes is neither a biological construct nor a Divine proclamation but is a cultural reaction, women writers formulated two concerns. First of all they made efforts to demolish certain universal concepts about women as these served vested interests. Secondly, they endeavoured to restore a female point of view by popularizing knowledge about the experiences of women and highlighting their contribution to culture observing that any power or status granted to women only rates them down as the "second sex" still dominated by their male counterparts.

Literature has always been a handy tool in exploring the gender relations and sexual disparities. Feminist scholarship resorts to deconstruct the social construction of gender and all cultural postulations that support it. Feminine consciousness has certainly provided a fresh ardour and excitement to literary studies. A reasonably new perception of women in literature and the works by women writers have exposed some of the prejudices in the traditional approaches to literature so far dominated by a male perspective. A woman's experiences of life as a member of a gender-biased society formulate her psyche. Moreover, she is circumferenced by certain other factors such as her individual circumstances and society's expectation related to age, creed, class and race. The American Black Feminism also tends to be a corollary of the European model especially because the second grade position granted to women depended upon class inequality and racial discrimination. Thus the disillusionment of American women sowed the seeds of Black American Feminism.

The two day convention (July 19th and 20th, 1848) at Wesleyan Chapel in Seneca Falls created a substructure for Women's Movement in America stipulating the urgency for abolishing inequality between men and women. The Feminist Movement in America developed in three stages or Waves. The First Wave of Feminism (1848-1920) was supported by black women such as Maria Stewart (1803-79), Sojourner Truth (1797-1883) and Frances W. Harper (1812-1911) focusing on gender polarity proving the superiority of women over men. Later, the attention was shifted to equality between men and women thereby getting branded as Liberal Feminism. Concurrently, Socialist/Marxist Feminism combining the critical perceptions of Marxism and Feminism surfaced probing the causes of the inequalities in the social structures of the world in general and that of woman in particular.

The Second Wave of Feminism germinating around 1960 derived encouragement from two significant books, Virginia Woolf's *A Room of One's Own* (1929) and Simone de Beauvoir's *The Second Sex* (1949). Ultimately Betty Friedman's *The Feminine Mystique* (1963) inspired innumerable women to fight for their rights. The Movement acquired sufficient impetus from Mary Ellman's *Thinking About Women* (1968) which is a witty investigation into and at times a scathing analysis of the ways women are represented in literature by men. This was followed by Kate Millet's *Sexual Politics* (1969) which was considered as the core of the Radical Feminist Movement advocating women's rights to their own bodies and the freedom to take decisions regarding marriage and motherhood whereas Sheila Rowbottham's book, *Women Resistance and Revolutions* (1972) demanded equal pay for equal work and greater educational opportunities for women. Other branches of Feminism evolving around the 1980s instigated political action in favour of minority and marginalized groups of society, opening vistas for highlighting the predicament of African Americans.

The Third Wave Feminism expanded the horizon of the Movement by including in its agenda issues of race, gender and sexuality negotiating constructive policies for women such as maternity leave, laws against sexual harassment at work place, etc. This phase of Feminism emphasized upon the significance of race and class as essential constituents of human life thereby insisting that in the case of women it is not only sex that determines their social status but also their class and race. Consequently, epitomized as indispensable, Black Feminism attained recognition as an essential ingredient of the Feminist Movement.

The history of Black Feminism coincides with the chronicle of slavery in the United States of America. Black Feminism is distinguished from other Feminist Movements because it was impacted and enhanced by racial thralldom in America. As slaves the black women felt doubly exploited—first because they were slaves and secondly because they were black in a white country. The black women emphasized that barring these two differences they were women after all and hence demanded their due rights and privileges. In the Women's Rights Convention of 1950, Sojourner Truth, a black woman became the first black feminist to unveil the plight of black women when she boldly stated:

> Look at me! Look at my arm!..I have plowed, and planted and gathered into barns, and no man could head me—and ain't I a woman? I could work as much as any man (when I could get it.) and bear de lash as well—and ain't I a woman? I sold off into slavery, and when I cried out with a mother's grief, none but Jesus hear—and ain't I a woman?[2]

The statement instantly expounds a vivid comparison between the experiences of a privileged white woman on the one hand and a serf black woman on the other though proclaiming that both are the same biologically yet socially the status varies.

The torturous past of the black women instigated them to come together vouching to remain united for protecting themselves from getting destroyed by the cruel practices meted out to slavery, determined to understand as well as alleviate mutual pain and suffering. Consequently, in the 1790s the northern free black women formed a society for mutual relief, self education and the ultimate abolition of slavery followed by the formation of the Salem Colored Female Religious and Moral Society in 1816 and the Female Anti-Slavery Society of Salem in 1831.

Perceptively, Black Feminism basically evolved out of slavery and the color bar, that is racism and classism though another factor, sexism of the black men precipitated it. The prolonged saga of oppression knitted black men and women closely in the joint enterprise to reduce the harsh and ugly effects of servitude on the family by being united. Free black women in America played a wider role in buying freedom for husbands and children and women like Harriet Tubman helped slaves to escape through the Underground Rail Road. In 1870 the black men were enfranchised through the Fifteenth Amendment of the US Constitution but the women felt ignored and cheated though rejoicing in the victory of the black men offering constructive advice paving the path for the general upliftment of their race fearlessly in spite of bloodshed and lynching and other such violence by the Klu Klux Klan.

Instead of losing courage the black women stood firmly beside their men during critical moments. The Black Power Movement of the 1960s and the 1970s was a tangible effort for regulating the lives of the blacks on the right path but the fallout tended to be a sort of setback for black women when the black men began to dominate the activities of their women. The women felt betrayed as they were partners in the struggle for freedom so far but suddenly they encountered perpetual sexism in their liberation movement about apartheid. Their men were in the forefront clamouring for rights pushing the women behind the curtains. Such circumstances persuaded the black women to launch the Black Feminist Movement with the conviction that they were suppressed due to racism and sexism on the one hand and due to being women on the other.

To begin with, the black women in America refused to coordinate with the feminist movements initiated by the white women firmly believing that race and class tend to influence the lives of women because different women experience different degrees of exploitation and discrimination based on race and class. Further the black women felt enraged by the realization that the white women invariably exhibited keen interest in black men, an attraction reciprocated by their own men for the white women. This abnegation widened the chasm between both the black women and the white women as well as between the black women and the black men. Evidently, the Black Power Movement empowered black men more than black women, while the Women's Liberation Movement protected only white women ignoring the blacks.

Confronted by the complex dilemma created by the intersection of race, gender and slavery, the black women initially resorted to a life of silence—a quietitude which encompassed psychological, emotional and physical dimensions. While lack of education encouraged the silence of the blacks, a handful of educated black women tended to become one with the colonizers looking at fellow blacks from the point of view of the whites. Thus, the all round oppression of the black women resulted in the formation of the Black Feminist Movement which actually grew into adolescence in 1973 with the launching of the National Black Feminist Organization in New York. The movement readily gained momentum as a specific black woman programme because these women had comprehended the discrimination within their own race and realized that by offering no resistance initially they were responsible for encouraging sexism falling prey to perpetuating patriarchy within the black community. Thus the Black Feminist Movement came into existence. Conclusively Black Feminism originated from two movements: from racism in the Feminist Movement and from sexism in the Black Liberation Movement.

Literature played a fruitful role in spreading awareness amongst the black women making them realize the exigency of developing a critical feminist consciousness and to begin a dialogue directly expressing their experiences and connecting them to a larger socio-political system. In this context, Helen Cixous's statement is significant:

> I shall speak about women's writing: about what it will do. Woman must write herself: must write about women and bring women to writing, from which they have been driven away as violently as from their bodies.... Woman must put herself into the text—as into the world and into history—by her own movement.... Her libido is cosmic, just as her consciousness worldwide. Her writing can only keep going, without ever inscribing or discerning limits.... She lets the other language speak—the language of 1000 tongues which knows neither enclosure nor death.[3]

Though difficult, yet the black women articulated their agony through codes and symbols attempting to validate their existence as human beings encountering gigantic obstacles due to the hesitation of the American publishing companies in accepting writings by black women. This enigma was gradually resolved by perseverance and persistence.

Phillis Wheatley (1753-84), the earliest black woman poet, Harriot E. Wilson, the first African-American woman novelist and E.W. Harper, another novelist voiced the anguish of the suffering blacks though in a subdued tone. Frances Harper stepped further by employing colloquial Black English in her writings which added poignancy to the themes and strengthened her connectivity with the exploited race. Unfortunately, the voice of the blacks remained subdued and non-resonant due to the apathy of the publishers. Nevertheless, the black writers continued their efforts undeterred even though their creative imagination was harnessed. Eventually, Zora Neale Hurston (1891-1960) dared to create a heroine, Janie Crawford in her novel *Their Eyes Were Watching God* (1937) who was different from heroines of previous novels and became a predecessor in the true sense of Alice Walker's Shug Avery (*The Color Purple*, 1982), Toni Morrison's Sula (*Sula*, 1974), Shirley Ann Williams' Dessa Rosa (*Dessa Rosa*, 1986) and several others who claimed their true identity articulating openly against atrocities ruthlessly inflicted on them leading to a great transformation amongst black women who gradually shed off their roles as house workers and became successful writers. After a long and arduous cruise the recognition to black writing had been granted when in 1993 Toni Morrison was adjusted the Nobel Prize for Literature being the first black woman to receive this prestigious award considered to be a tremendous achievement for a black women writer as in the field of literature too, she encountered duel suppression: one, to make a space for herself in a world of white writers and secondly, the tendency to equate black literature with black men. It was evident that black writing in America was discriminatory against black women because enterprising writers like Anne Petry, Paule Marshall, and Anne Spencer were relegated and pushed to the wings.

With the publication of Alice Walker's *The Color Purple* and its film version in 1980 a revolt began sizzling against sexism encountered by the black women due to the men of their own community. *The Color Purple,* a slave narrative voiced the subjugation of blacks by blacks, a sort of neo-colonialism. Thus the reality of black women is transformed into Black Feminist writing. Several authors attempted to define the Black Feminist Movement. Alice Walker coined the term 'Womanist' to describe the movement. She emphasized the word Womanist rather than Feminist. For her Womanist meant self-determination, appreciation of all aspects of womanhood, and the commitment to the survival of both men and women. This definition is simultaneously affirming and challenging for it entails a woman to stretch her personal boundaries at the same time maintaining connection with the rest of humanity. Conforming to this view the writings of Alice Walker (novels, short stories and poems) focus stridently on the struggles of the blacks particularly, the women and their strife against a racist, sexist, and violent society. The writings of Alice Walker shed ample light on the role of women of color in culture and history.

Beginning with Phillis Wheatley, writers like Lucille Clifton, Allexis De Veaux, Rita Dove, Toni Cade Bombara and several others kept the flame alive. Their writings were recognized when awards were bestowed upon black writers. In 1949 Gwendolyn Brooks became the first African-American woman to receive the Pulitzer Prize for her second volume of poems, *Anne Allen* (1949); Lorraine Hansberry (1930-65) was the youngest and the only black woman to be conferred the New York Drama Critics Award for the Best Play of the Year for her play *A Raisin in the Sun* (1959); Margaret Walker was the only black person to get the Yale Younger Poets Award for her work *For My People* (1942); while Alice Walker won the Pulitzer Prize for her novel *The Color Purple* (1982). Later in 1993 Toni Morrison was declared a Nobel laureate.

Adjudged as a significant contribution to Black Feminism Paule Marshall's (b. 1929) first novel *Brown Girl Brownstones* (1959) explores the intersections of race, class and culture. It acted as a bridge between the novels of earlier writers such as Zora Neale Hurston's *Their Eyes Were Watching God* and writers of the seventies such as Alice Walker and Toni Morrison. Marshall's novels written over a period of thirty years are powerful narratives on the complexities of the power of black women. Simultaneously she is preoccupied with black cultural history insisting that the Africans should look back through time to understand the political, social and economic structures upon which contemporary societies are built. *Praisesong for the Widow* (1983) winner of the 1984 Columbus Foundation American Book Award once again charts a black woman's search for self identity. *Daughters* (1991) probes into the roles that black men and women play in each other's lives. In her writings Marshall advocates the view that confronting one's personal and historical past is the foundation for a genuine revolutionary process.

Toni Morrison (b. 1931) extended impetus and momentum to the Black Feminist Movement through her writings, being aware of the fact that sexism existed in the Black Liberation Movement while racism was the hallmark of the Women's Movement due to which the black woman faced the onslaughts of race, gender and class all at once finding herself in a disadvantageous position. Writers encountered tremendous difficulties in manifesting the manifold crippling effects of three hundred years of slavery of the blacks especially with the awareness of the psychic fragmentation that the black women underwent. Toni Morrison faced this challenge with fortitude, writing earnestly about the lives of African-American women, enumerating faithfully and truthfully their triumphs and tragedies, their humiliations, frustrations and joys. Her writings proclaim the cause of women of all ages: Pecola is eleven years old, Sula is in her twenties, Ruth, Pilate, Ondine and Sethe are middle aged women while Eva Peace and Baby Suggs are old black women. Morrison blatantly elucidates through these women that sexism and racism know no age. Nevertheless, Morrison reiterated the fact that women should stay connected with their roots in order to get the required strength and optimism for sustenance.

A lot of pioneering effort was made in this direction by black American women. Amongst these Gloria Jean Watkins (b. 1952), using the pen name Bell Hooks produced a ground breaking book *Ain't I a Woman: Black Women and Feminism* (1982) which explores the tense relationship between the racist and the patriarchal modes of oppression, with special reference to writings by and about black women in the late nineteenth and the early twentieth centuries. The treatise explores several recurring themes perpetuated firmly in her later works: the historical impact of sexism and racism on black women, devaluation of black womanhood, media roles and portrayal, the education system, the idea of a white supremacist—capitalist—patriarchy, the marginalization of black women, and the disregard for issues of race and class within Feminism. This work was largely influenced by Sojourner Truth's speech *Ain't I a Woman.*

With the rising percentage of educated and working class women and due to the global sharing of opinions, the Feminism Movement is gaining ground enormously and a greater number of writers, both men and women compete with each other to focus themes around female protagonists not only projecting their steady progression in life but also delving deep into their psyche attempting to understand their psyche and their psychological response in the context of the new roles expected of them in the transformed scenario. Feminist criticism is concerned with both the representation of women in literature and with the changing women's status in society thereby emancipating them from various oppressive restraints, the focus being on restrictions which ignore the existence of the ideas such as what it is to be a woman. These definitions assume that human nature is universal refusing to understand how culture plays a significant role in constructing and fixing identity. In this sense, Feminist Criticism may be indubitably accepted as one of the leading contemporary critical practices and the study of Black Feminism opens fresh vistas of explorations for this type of critical venture.

NOTES

1. *Modern Literary Theory,* Fourth Edition (London: Arnold; Co., Published in the USA by OUP Inc., New York, 1989), p. 143.
2. Elizabeth C. Stanton, S.B. Anthony, and Matilda J. Gage, *History of Women's Suffrage,* Volume 1 (Rochester, New York: Charles Mann, 1887), p. 116.
3. 'Le Rire de la Meduse', *L'Arc,* 61. Trans, as *The Laugh of the Medusa* in Marks and de Courtivron (1980), *New French Feminisms* (Amherst, Mass.: University of Massachusetts Press, Brighton: Harvester), pp. 245, 259-60.

5

The Archetypal Pattern: Science Fiction as Myth and Romance

Debalina Banerjee

Archetypal criticism advocated by the Canadian literary critic and theorist, Northrop Frye (July 14, 1912-January 23, 1991), believes that archetypes determine the nature and character of literary works and that a text's meaning is shaped by cultural and psychological myths. Archetypes are the inherent images, symbols and ideas that correspond to the primordial and elemental instincts in man. Archetypal criticism is an offshoot of the theory advocated by psychologist Carl Jung, who postulated that humankind has a "collective unconscious," a kind of universal psyche, which is manifested in dreams and myths and which harbors themes and images that we all inherit. The word "mythology" comes from the Greek word *mythos* meaning a narrative, and *logos*, meaning speech or argument literally meaning the oral retelling of myths, stories that a particular culture believes to be true and that use the supernatural to interpret natural events.[1] Northrop Frye defines "myth" as "A conception permeating many areas of contemporary thought: anthropology, psychology, comparative religion, sociology and several others" (*Myth, Fiction, and Displacement* 587).

The four *mythoi* namely comedy, romance, tragedy, and irony are all part of a central unifying myth. Since Frye's criticism is inclusive he points out that, "our five modes evidently go around in a circle as the god of one person is the *pharmakos* of another. Myths of gods merge into legends of heroes; legends of heroes merge into plots of tragedies and comedies; plots of tragedies and comedies merge into plots of more or less realistic fiction..." (*Anatomy* 43) but the principles of story-telling remain the same as the change is one of social context.

Northrop Frye defines science fiction as "a mode of romance with a strong tendency to myth" (*Anatomy* 49). According to him, "Science fiction frequently tries to imagine what life would be like on a plane as far above us as we are above savagery; its setting is often of a kind that appears to us technologically miraculous" (*Anatomy* 49). Frye observes that, "In romance the suspension of natural law and the individualizing of the heroes' exploits reduce nature largely to the animal and vegetable world..." (*Anatomy* 36). For Frye Man in a romance is still "half a god" (*Anatomy* 36). "Romance peoples the world with fantastic normally invisible personalities of powers: angels, demons, fairies, ghosts, enchanted animals, elemental spirits..." (*Anatomy* 64). "The romancer does not attempt to create real people but stylized figures which expand into psychological archetypes. It is in the romance that we find Jung's libido, anima and shadow reflected..." (*Anatomy* 304). All of these postulates are also true of science fiction.

> Both science fiction and myth deal primarily with beings of greater than ordinary power. Early myth presents semidivine beings who exhibit the quality of mana in their actions. Their source of power is something beyond the human. Since science fiction is being considered as the myth of technology, it is not surprising to find that man assumes the role of protagonist. His power, rather than being a suprahuman mana, is generally associated with superior knowledge, for knowledge is recognized as the motive force behind technological progress. (Sutton 236)

Fontentelle in *The Origin of Fables* (1724) remarks, that a myth is essentially a primitive science, the imperfect result of a conscious search for causes of observable events. Levi Strauss suggests that both myth and science can be considered as modes of structuring the universe.[2]

"A body of myth forms an autonomous universe which stands in metaphoric relation to the actual world" (Sutton 232). Science creates a universe peopled by the miracles of the human mind. In the words of Fred Saberhagen, a science fiction author and critic, "Science fiction gives a chance to impose different co-ordinate systems upon the human condition and try to see what will change and what will remain the same" (Sutton 233). This phenomenon can be best witnessed in Rudolph Bultmann, who attempts to apply scientific logic to the myth of Christianity and ends by "re-mythologizing" Christianity in the language of contemporary science rather than "de-mythologizing it" (Sutton 233).

In the late 19th century, the term "scientific romance" was used in Britain to describe much of this fiction. This produced additional offshoots, such as the 1884 novella *Flatland: A Romance of Many Dimensions* by Edwin Abbott the term would continue to be used into the early 20th century for writers such as Olaf Stapledon. Science Fiction connects with Mythology in its pursuit of meaning and order in an alien universe. Some of the precursors to science fiction as literature can be seen in Lucian's *True History* in the 2nd century, some of the *Arabian Nights* tales, *The Tale of the Bamboo Cutter* in the 10th century, Ibn al-Nafis' *Theologus Autodidactus* in the 13th century.[3]

Following the Age of Reason and the development of modern science itself, Jonathan Swift's *Gulliver's Travels* was one of the first true science fiction works, together with Voltaire's *Micromégas* and Kepler's *Somnium*. This latter work is considered by Carl Sagan and Isaac Asimov to be the first science fiction story. It depicts a journey to the Moon and how the Earth's motion is seen from there. Another example is Ludvig Holberg's novel *Nicolai Klimii iter subterraneum* (1741) (Translated into English as *Niels Klim's Underground Travels*).[4] Following the 18th century development of the novel as a literary form, in the early 19th century, Mary Shelley's *Frankenstein* and *The Last Man* were landmark novels defining the form of the science fiction novel. *Frankenstein* is about a scientist, Victor Frankenstein, who learns how to create life and creates a being in the likeness of man, but larger than average and more powerful while *The Last Man* tells the story of a future world that has been ravaged by a plague.[5] With the advent of new technologies and scientific discoveries such as electricity, the telegraph, and new forms of powered transportation, writers like Jules Verne and H.G. Wells, with their sci-fi narrative exploits captured the minds of the generation.

Herbert George Wells (21 September 1866-13 August 1946) was an English author, best known for his remarkable contribution in the science fiction genre. In Wells' *The Time Machine* the narrator is Hillyer, who discusses with his friends about theories of time travel. A week later their host has an incredible story to tell he has returned from the year 802701. The Time Traveler finds the Eloi, weak and little, who live above ground in a seemingly "Edenic paradise", and the Morlocks, bestial creatures that live below the ground, who eat the Eloi. As he flees into the far future, he encounters "crab-like creatures" and things "like a huge white butterfly", that have taken over the planet. In the year 30,000,000 he finds lichens, blood-red sea and a creature with tentacles. He returns horrified back to the present. "Much of the realistic atmosphere of the story was achieved by carefully studied technical details. The basic principles of the machine contained materials regarding time as the fourth dimension—years later Albert Einstein published his theory of the four dimensional continuum of space-time" (Liukkonen & Pesonen).

The Time Machine was followed by *The Island of Dr. Moreau* (1896), in which a mad scientist transforms animals into human creatures. The story is told in flashback by a man named Prendick. He travels with a biologist to a remote island, controlled by Dr. Moreau. In his laboratory he experiments with animals, and creates the Beast People. Moreau himself is killed by Puma-Woman. Prendick escapes from the island and returns to London, a changed man:

> Even then it seemed that I, too, was not a reasonable creature, but only an animal tormented with some strange disorder in its brain, that sent it to wander alone,

like as sheep stricken with the gid. (Liukkonen & Pesonen)

Isaac Asimov, the father of "robotics" in science fiction prophesied that with scientific advancement "not only man-made man is possible, but man-made superman" (Sutton 236). This idea is also conceivable in *The Invisible Man*, a similar Faustian story of a scientist who tampered with nature in pursuit of superhuman powers, and *The War of the Worlds*, a novel of an invasion of Martians. "The story appeared at a time when Giovanni Schiaparelli's discovery of Martian "canals" and Percival Lowell's book *Mars* (1895) stirred speculations that there could be life on the Red Planet" (Liukkonen & Pesonen). The narrator is an unnamed "philosophical writer" who tells about events that happened six years earlier. Martian cylinders land on earth outside London and the invaders, who have a "roundish bulk with tentacles" start to vaporize humans. The Martians build walking tripods which ruin towns. Panic spreads, London is evacuated. Martians release poisonous black smoke. However, Martians are slain "by the humblest things that God, in his wisdom, has put on this earth" (Liukkonen & Pesonen).

His novel, *In The Days of The Comet* (1906), is about a giant comet, that narrowly misses colliding with the Earth, but its tail gases cause changes in human behaviour. One of Wells's earlier stories, 'The Star' (1887), tells of a planet, that almost demolishes the world before hitting the sun. In *The Shape Of Things To Come* (1933), "Wells failed to anticipate the importance of atomic energy, although in *The World Set Free* (1914) a physicist manages to split the atom" (*Science Fiction*).

Jules Gabriel Verne (8 February 1828-24 March 1905) was a French author who helped pioneer the science-fiction genre. He is best known for his novels *A Journey to the Centre of the Earth* (1864), *From the Earth to the Moon* (1865), *Twenty Thousand Leagues Under the Sea* (1869-1870), *Around the World in Eighty Days* (1873) and *The Mysterious Island* (1875). Verne wrote about space, air, and underwater travel even before navigable aircrafts and submarines were invented, and before any means of space travel had been devised.

Consequently he is often referred to as the "Father of science fiction", along with H.G. Wells. Jules Verne's novels have been noted for their "startingly accurate anticipations of modern times. *Paris in the 20th Century* is an often cited example of this as it arguably describes air conditioning, automobiles, the Internet, television, even electricity, and other modern conveniences very similar to their real world counterparts" (Jules Verne).

Another example is *From the Earth to the Moon*, where;

> ...a space gun is used instead of a rocket, strangely similar to the real Apollo Program, and three astronauts are launched from the Florida peninsula and recovered through a splash landing. In the book, the spacecraft is launched from "Tampa Town" and ironically NASA is at a stone's throw distance from Tampa. In other works, Verne predicted the inventions of helicopters, submarines, projectors, jukeboxes, and other later devices. He also predicted the existence of underwater hydrothermal vents that were discovered many years after he wrote about them. (Jules Verne)

In *The Mysterious Island* Verne predicts the development of Hydrogen engines. A group of castaways speculate on what would happen when the world's coal reserves are exhausted:

> Water [will replace coal]. Water broken down into its component elements by electricity...the hydrogen and oxygen of which it is constituted will be used to furnish an inexhaustible source of heat and light. One day, the holds of steamships and the tenders of locomotives will be filled with those two compressed gases, powering their engines with an incalculable calorific force. (Jules Verne)

Jung considers the "living myth" of flying saucers as a golden opportunity to see "how in a dark and difficult time for humanity a miraculous tale grows up of an attempted intervention by extraterrestrial 'heavenly' powers—and at this very time when human fantasy is seriously considering the possibility of space travel and of visiting or even invading other planets" (*Flying Saucers*).

From the dawn of civilization humanity has tried to weave meaning into the innumerable marvels of the universe and as a means of establishing camaraderie with all that is alien has drawn patterns of familiarity in the vast unknown in the form of gods, demons and other inexplicable forces:

> In the area of scientific myth, the transcendent referent can no longer be the cosmos, since scientific research has shown that it is empirically knowable and as a consequence it is no longer entirely transcendent. As a referent, modern myth, especially science fiction, replaces the cosmos with the concept of space. Jung claims that it is the belief in this world and the power of man that is thrusting itself forward in the form of symbolic rumor and activating an archetype that has always expressed "order, deliverance, salvation, and wholeness". (Sutton 235)

According to Thomas C. Sutton and Marilyn Sutton, science fiction is a self-conscious form of myth in which man intentionally mythologizes scientific narrative. It is not unusual to find themes from mythologies serving as subplots for science fiction narratives. They cite the examples of Frank Herbert, who weaves a knowledge of ecology with allusions to Old Testament myths in his novel *Dune* (1965), and James Blish, who infuses shades of demonism in his creation theology *A Case of Conscience* (1958) "to produce a myth in which a priest-scientist confronts an alien world of complete perfection and, aware that it is a theological impossibility, is forced to acknowledge it as a demonic creation" (Sutton 236, 237). Another excellent example offered is Arthur C. Clarke's short story 'The Star' in which mythic material from Christianity furnishes the subplot.

> Clarke gives the mythology surrounding the star of Bethlehem and the birth of Christ a scientific explanation, proposing that the star was the result of the destruction of a completely idyllic race in a star system whose sun flared as a supernova at its death. Scientifically it is plausible that the star of Bethlehem, if there was one, was a supernova, but Clarke remythologizes extravagantly on this scientific basis. He

> suggests that God intentionally destroyed an entire people on the exploded star for His greater honor and glory. The underlying irony is made explicit by setting the narrative in Jesuit surroundings and playing on the Jesuit motto Ad maiorem Dei gloriam. In this particular myth, Clarke explodes a fiction concerning the star with scientific fact, and then goes on to mingle religion, psychology, and science to develop a mythopoeic vision. As myth, such a story is certainly much more conscious and literary than early myth, but it is not meant to be the myth of a tribe, rather it is the mythology concocted for the delight of technological man. (Sutton 237)

Northop Frye's estimate of literature as springing from a reservoir of imaginative resources, whether you call it a myth or the Jungian collective dream of mankind, is best exemplified by science fiction, which expresses the dreams of the mythopoeic man. And as literature for Frye is more flexible than a myth, hence science fiction peoples the universe with the promise of a better or a more advanced reality.

Again, myths are often used as allegories of science or religion or morality:

> They may arise in the first place to account for a ritual or a law, or they may be exempla or parables which illustrate a particular situation or argument. Unlike the myths in Plato or Achilles' myth of the two jars of Zeus at the end of the Iliad. Once established in their own right, they may then be interpreted dogmatically or allegorically, as all the standard myths have been for centuries, in innumerable ways. But because myths are stories, what they "mean" is inside them, in the implications of their incidents. No rendering of any myth into conceptual language can serve as a full equivalent of its meaning. A myth may be told and retold: it may be modified or elaborated, or different patterns may be discovered in it; and its life is always the poetic life of a story, not the homiletic life of some illustrated truism. (*Myth, Fiction, and Displacement* 599)

NOTES

1. http://www.newworldencyclopedia.org/entrv/MytholoRv
2. Thomas C. Sutton and Marilyn Sutton. "Science Fiction as Mythology".
3. http://en.wikipedia.org/wiki/Science_fiction
4. *Ibid.*
5. *Ibid.*

REFERENCES

Frye, Northrop. *Myth, Fiction, and Displacement: Daedalus.* 90: 3(2002). Web. JSTOR. 11 June, 2010.

——. *Anatomy of Criticism.* New Jersey: Princeton, Princeton University Press, 1973. Print.

Grewell, Greg. "Colonizing the Universe: Science Fictions Then, Now, and in the (Imagined) Future", *Rocky Mountain Review of Language and Literature.* 55: 2 (2001). Print.

Gunn, James E. "The New Encyclopedia of Science Fiction", New York: Viking, 1988. Print.

Jung, C.G. *Flying Saucers: A Modern Myth of Things Seen in the Skies.* London, New York. Routledge. 2001. Print.

Liukkonen, Petri and Ari Pesonen. *H.G. Wells.* Web. http://kiijasto.sci.fi/hgwells.htm. 5 July, 2008.

Schwartz, Sheila. "Science Fiction: Bridge between the Two Cultures". *The English Journal* (2007). Web. 26 March, 2010.

"Science Fiction". Web. http://en.wikipedia.org/wiki/Science_fiction, 30 June, 2010.

"Science Fiction". *Encyclopedia Britannica.* Web. http://www.britannica.com/eb/article-235714/science-fiction 12 Jan., 2010.

Sutton, Thomas C. and Marilyn Sutton. "Science Fiction as Mythology", *Western Folklore.* 28: 4 (Oct., 1969). 230-37. Web. 11 June, 2010.

Taormina, Agatha. "A History of Science Fiction". Web. Northern Virginia Community College. 16 Jan., 2010.

Verne, Jules. Web. http://en.wikipedia.org/wiki/Jules_Verne. 2 July 2010.

6

"The novel tells you a story, dear!"

V.M. Madge

Perhaps after publication of the Epic Theory of the novel by Henry Fielding in the 18th century, the art of fiction has not been discussed with that degree of artistic self-consciousness as we find in the late Victorian era and the early decades of 20th century. The credit for making this popular form so *discutable* must go to the American, Henry James. Alongside his theoretical formulations, we get Conrad's credo as an artist in his celebrated 'Preface' to *The Nigger of the Narcissus* (1897), Virginia Woolf's seminal essay 'The Modern Fiction' (1916), D.H. Lawrence's famous essays like 'Why the Novel Matters' and 'Morality and the Novel' and E.M. Forster's *Aspects of the Novel* (1925). This is only a random selection and does not take into account Trollope and H.G. Wells's protracted correspondence and exchange of views with James on the subject of the art of the novel. But even such a selection will serve to highlight how in those days the major practitioners of the form—for all the names mentioned were that—were preoccupied with making their theoretical considerations explicit.

This is rather unusual in the history of the English Novel. After Fielding we hardly find Jane Austen, the Brontë sisters, Dickens, Thackeray, George Eliot and Hardy waxing eloquent on their theory of the form. It is not that they had no 'theory' but they chose not to be explicit about it and went about their job of writing novels quietly. And as history is our witness, what a fine job they made. Their artistic success and, at the same time, their lack of theoretical explicitness puzzled James who had come to England to carve a niche for himself in the world of letters. The pronouncements of novelists like Trollope who assured his readers that he could give his tale any turn they wanted simply horrified James, the stickler for artistic integrity of a work, and stung him into polemics. The very earnestness of the Americans' essays forced the contemporaries like Wells to spell out their assumptions about novel writing and inspired the new generation of English novelists to take a look at the theoretical reticence which was beginning to be seen almost as a national characteristic. Perhaps that may explain the spate of essays dealing with the art and form of the novel.

The present paper seeks to examine this phenomenon by taking into special consideration, specifically Henry James's 'The Art of Fiction', Lawrence's 'Why the Novel Matters' and E.M. Forster's *Aspects of the Novel*—and in that order—and to show how the Jamesian aesthetic because of its extreme preoccupation with technique did not produce any striking results, whereas the English novelists despite their 'cavalier' attitude to their art—or because of it—knew their job better and produced memorable results.

Henry James's essay 'The Art of Fiction' was published in *Longman's Magazine* (September 1884) and reprinted in his *Partial Portraits* (1888). The essay was James's reaction to Walter Besant's lecture-pamphlet published under the same title a year before. Its nature, therefore, is, quite expectedly, highly polemical, and the tone equally pontifical. Taking up the organic unity of a novel or, for that matter, any work of art as his point of attack, James snipes at the theoretical nayvet of English novelists and critics and at their cavalier attitude to their art.

The theoretical nayvet is something that passes under the name of British solid common-sense. James questions those very assumptions underlying their views on the art of fiction. For instance, he fails to understand what he calls the 'apologetic' attitude of British novelists. On the one hand, they claim their writing to be 'realistic' and on the other they do not tire of reminding their readers that after all what they are writing is 'fiction'. Such an apologetic attitude is not found on the Continent. If the novel is a realistic mode of writing, it is, in James's eyes, hardly distinguishable from history. As he says in *Partial Portraits,*

> It is impossible to imagine what a novelist takes himself to be unless he regards himself as an historian and his narrative as history. It is only as an historian that he has the smallest *locus standi.* As a narrator of fictitious events he is nowhere,...[1]

He wonders whether Gibbon and Macaulay would have been ever apologetic about their writing!

James finds the British attitude to the art of fiction not merely apologetic but at times even cavalier. And here Anthony Trollope with his frequent authorial intrusions is his *bete noir.* He cites an example from Trollope's best known novel.

> Had she given way and sobbed aloud, as in such cases a woman should do, he would have melted at once, implored her pardon, perhaps knelt at her feet and declared his love. Everything would have been explained, and Eleanor would have gone back to Barchester with a contented mind—But then where would have been my novel? She did not cry and Mr. Arabian did not melt.[2]

James regards this as an implicit admission by Trollope that he can give his narrative any turn the reader may like best. He is greatly annoyed by 'these little slaps at credulity'[3] for they not only destroy the whole artistic illusion but blow up the very concept of integrity of a work of art.

Similarly, Besant's remarks on the 'story' bring forth James's ire. Understandably so. Taking umbrage at Besant's comments, James points to the integrity of a work of art.

> I cannot see what is meant by talking as if there were a part of a novel which is the story and part of it which for mystical reason is not the story represents the subject, the idea, the data of the novel,...[4]

With such a highly abstract notion of story, James takes up cudgels with 'the writer in the *Pall Mall*' who asserted that "the story is the thing". He also takes up issue with Besant about what constitutes a story. According to James, even the states of consciousness of a 'Bostonian nymph who rejects an English duke for psychological reasons' can be a matter of adventure and hence of story.

D.H. Lawrence in his comparatively short essay 'Why the Novel Matters' brings out the uniqueness of the novel as a form of writing and hence its importance. He compares it with other kinds of writing like philosophy and science. The latter are abstract and schematic and view man from their specific field as a biological species, a physical object, an amalgam of certain chemicals or as God's creature and so on. But it is only in the novel that we see man in totality and in a far more tangible and concrete way. The novel with its formal flexibility is eminently suited to represent all minutiae of being alive in the world. "The novel is one bright book of life", Lawrence says. It includes life in all its internal and external details. Whereas sciences, both actual and social, deal with man in the abstract and from their narrow point of observation and interest, the whole of man, indeed of life, is the province of the novel and that life in its entirety is presented in a concrete way. To use the famous phrase, in the novel one gets the 'felt life' in all its totality. Lawrence's observations also remind one of the 'task' of the writer that Conrad described in such memorable terms.

> My task which I am trying to achieve is, by the power of the written word to make you hear, to make you feel—it is, before all, to make you *see*. That—and no more, and it is everything. If I succeed, you shall find there according to your deserts: encouragement, consolation, fear, charm—all you demand—and perhaps, also that glimpse of truth for which you have forgotten to ask.[5]

A piece of writing aiming at such extraordinary accentuation of sensory powers has its own significance in a world dominated by scientific categorization. It is the novel that not only aims at heightened sensitization but by its elasticity of form is supremely and singularly qualified to accommodate within itself the very pulse of the ever-changing life. That is why the novel matters.

In 1925 E.M. Forster was invited to give a series of talks on the art of fiction in the Clark Lectures in Cambridge, which later on were turned into a book *Aspects of the Novel* which in its turn has now become a classic in the study of fiction. The informal tone may be due to the original form of lectures being retained. But despite the chattiness, Forster's comments are by no means superficial and they show the much-maligned British common sense at its best. His perceptive and subtle yet clear distinction between story and plot, between flat and round characters, between the autobiographical and omniscient point-of-view—a term he borrows ironically from Percy Lubbock, an admirer of Henry James,—have now become common currency in any discussion of the novel form.

Now if anything stands out from these theoretical formulations by these three practitioners of the form, it is that it is one thing to theorize about the novel but quite another to write one.

This appears to be the case especially with Henry James in spite of—or is it because of?—his greater theoretical sophistication. When one looks at their fictional achievements, James's performance does not compare at all well with that of Lawrence and Forster. The reasons—and there are many—are not far to seek.

Firstly, the difference between the theoretical musings of Lawrence and Forster on the one hand and the theorization of James on the other is that the English novelists spoke explicitly about theory at the end of their career whereas the American theorized while he wrote, if not before. Lawrence's essay was published posthumously in 1936 and by 1925 Forster had written his last novel *A Passage to India.* Consequently, with Lawrence and Forster theory emerges out of their practice while with James the picture is exactly the opposite. F.R. Leavis pointed out the deleterious effect James's obsession with theory had on his novels, which show a remarkable atrophy of sensibility and divorce from the roots of life.[6]

Even an admirer of James like Dorothea Krook begins her study by citing a none too flattering, almost a left-handed compliment by T.S. Eliot according to whom Henry James is a difficult writer for English readers because he is an American, for Americans because he deals with European subjects and for Europeans because he writes in English![7] The reference to Eliot is helpful for several reasons. In the first place, it tells the reasons for James's universal obscurity and secondly and far more importantly it serves to bring out the difference between the literary careers of these two Americans. T.S. Eliot came to England following the footsteps of his senior fellow countryman to make his name in the literary world. Both rebelled against the literary practice of their time. But whereas Eliot located his rebellion within the framework of the English poetic tradition, James did not ally himself to any English novelistic predecessor. The result was that James always remained an alienated American whereas Eliot became the denizen of both the literary hemispheres one by birth and the other by 'naturalization'.

Further, his reformist earnestness seems to have misguided James in coping with the bantering tone of the British novelists whenever they chose to talk about their craft. For instance, what James took to be their 'apologetic' attitude was actually a sound sense of what they were doing when they wrote novels. To say that after all what they were writing was but a fiction and not history was not being 'apologetic' but merely asserting the true nature of their work despite the pretence of realism. And that art can never be 'true' in the sense history was conclusively shown by Laurence Sterne in his hilarious *Tristram Shandy*. Surprisingly James seldom speaks about that 18th century predecessor. In narrating his myriad problems in beginning the account of his life according to Aristotle's concept of the 'beginning' and the Horatian injunction of starting the work *ab ovo,* Sterne had brilliantly underscored the essential fictionality of all fiction. What the contemporaries of James like Trollope were doing was merely to elaborate on that in their own way. To draw attention to this essential fictionality, to break the illusion of reality later on became the credo of the Brechtian Epic Theatre and also a salient feature of the self-reflexive postmodernist fiction.

The frequent reminder that they were writing fiction might have saved the British novelists from confusing fiction with history. From the earlier quotation it will be clear that James's theory of fiction contains precisely this confusion. Long back in time Aristotle in the ninth chapter of his *Poetics* had clearly distinguished between poetry and history. The latter narrates events as they have *actually* occurred and the former as they may occur in accordance with the laws of necessity (*ananke*) and probability (*eikos*). The identification of the novel with history by James, who carried a notebook in his pocket to record material for his novels, shows the closing of the American's mind to the Classical wisdom and sanity.

James seems to misread completely Trollope's novelistic strategy in the latter's authorial intrusions. It is possible to argue that far from destroying the pretence of realism and the aesthetic integrity, they display Trollope's confidence in himself as an author. Indeed Wayne Booth in his comments on the earlier quoted passage from *Barchester Towers* implies this when he talks of the inviolability of Eleanor's character and the relationship that Trollope has managed to establish with his readers.[8] That James completely missed the complexities in Trollope's creation of illusion due to his view of the novel as history is brought out by Kincaid, when he says,

> The venerable analogy that James here ignores and tries to dismiss to the realm of irresponsibility is provided by the image of artist as maker.[9]

If authorial intrusions in Trollope are a sign of his casual attitude, what is one to make of James's own in his novels? For instance, in *The Portrait of a Lady*,

> Smile not, however, I venture to repeat, at this simple, young woman from Albany who debated whether she should accept an English peer before he had offered himself....[10]

In what way is James's intrusion different from that of Trollope unless the latter one's were more candid in acknowledging the fact of fictionality?

It is in James's pontification with Besant over the nature of the story that he appears most vulnerable both as a theorist of fiction and as a novelist despite his comparative relativism in attitude seen in 'Art of Fiction'. Stung by Besant's derisive comments on the 'romance' of a Bostonian nymph who rejects an English duke—an obvious reference to *The Portrait of a Lady*—James harangues him over the story aspect of the novel and asks as to what constitutes a story, and what exactly is meant by 'adventure'. Even the stages of psychological development can form a story and the way in which a girl looks at you across the table can be an 'adventure'. Both these terms are thus relative, according to James.

Indeed these terms *are* relative. But thanks to the enlightened critical opinion and the popular taste of generations of readers, the conceptual contours of 'story' are not as fuzzy as James tries to make them. Forster defines story as a chain of events arranged in sequence of time and plot as events arranged in terms of causality. The 'events' mentioned by James can become story depending upon the skill of the novelist who can take this apparent inaction to the level of action. For as once again Aristotle points out, 'men in action' are the objects of artistic imitation. And action with Aristotle is a technical term implying not physical activity but a process of change in fortune; the protagonist goes from happiness to misery and *vice versa*. The story and the plot are the embodiment of that action. Now James or for that matter any novelist is free to show how a narrative of the mental stages a Bostonian nymph passes through reflects that process of change or how the way a girl looks at you across the table brings out a change in your fortune one way or the other.

Any novel becomes 'interesting' or, shall we say, 'readable' by the way its story describes that process of change from one state to another. Forster regrets that the story is totally and only concerned with 'life by clock-time' for the novel can do and often does many other 'valuable' things. But unfortunately those valuable things cannot go to make a novel by themselves. And hence Forster's rather rueful reply to the question what does a novel do: the novel tells you a story, dear!

A look at the history of the stream of consciousness novel —largely a product of the Jamesian aesthetic—will bring out the inevitability of the story aspect. Even these novels while rejecting a well-made plot had to have a story no matter how threadbare of a family visit to the lighthouse, or the hosting of a garden party or the meeting of spiritual father and son in their metropolitan peregrinations. It will explain why the experiment was a shortlived affair and also why writers like Virginia Woolf and Faulkner did not write all their novels in that mode. No doubt, the experiment did give a new dimension to the art writing novels but it did not replace the traditional mode of plot and story. In fact, a contemporary novelist like Muriel Spark wishes she would like to write novels like H.G. Wells!

The lesson to be learnt here by any theorist of fiction is not to discount story from his considerations. It may be an evil but it is a necessary one. And the novelist in his turn has to be a good storyteller. If he tells his story-well, everything else he crams into it will be forgiven. Unfortunately, James both as theorist and practitioner of fiction forgot that. H.G. Wells' comments to him after reading the bulky *The Golden Bowl* and *The Wings of Dove* are appropriately chastening. He says that the impression he got of James after wading through those tomes was that of a mighty hippo trapped in a small cave and trying to pick up a small pea on the floor![11]

On the other hand, the novels of Tolstoy and Dostoevsky, bulkier than James's, which he dismissed as 'loose baggy monsters' continue to be masterpieces of world-fiction precisely because they do their primary job of storytelling so well. In his interview with the *Time* magazine, Alexandre Solzhenitsyn who regarded himself as the inheritor of the 19th century tradition of Russian fiction, as opposed to the Soviet fiction of the Bolshevik Era, was asked as to what he thought of Henry James's comment on the novels of the Russian masters. His was a slap of a riposte when he said that in Russia novel writing is taken seriously, that novelists are often looked upon as interpreters of life, indeed as prophets and, hence, Tolstoy and Dostoevsky talk responsibility about life and do not indulge in mere verbal games![12]

NOTES

1. Henry James, *Partial Portraits* (London: Macmillan, 1888), pp. 116-17.
2. Anthony Trollope, *Barchester Towers,* Vol. 3, Chapter 12 (London: OUP, 1980), p. 32.
3. Henry James, *Partial Portraits,* pp. 116-17.
4. *Ibid.*, p. 120.
5. Joseph Conrad, *Four Tales* (London: OUP, 1949), p. 6.
6. F.R. Leavis, *The Common Pursuit* (London: Chatto & Windus, 1952), p. 140.
7. Dorothea Krook, *The Ordeal of Consciousness in Henry James* (Cambridge, 1962), p. 1.
8. Wayne Booth, *The Rhetoric of Fiction* (Chicago and London: 1961), p. 206.
9. James Kincaid, *The Novels of Anthony Trollope* (Oxford, 1977), p. 33.
10. Henry James, *The Portrait of a Lady* (1947, London: OUP, 1964), pp. 117-18.
11. Nicholas Delbanco, *Group Portrait* (London: Faber and Faber, 1982), p. 145.
12. *Time,* Sept., 1985, pp. 7-8.

7

Embodiment of Vision in William Golding's *The Spire*

Bishnupada Ray

In *The Spire,* William Golding tries to express something which Coleridge the visionary saw in a momentary flash of dream vision in 'Kubla Khan', but could not possibly grasp its full significance. A troubled genius that he was, Coleridge salvaged only Kubla's stately pleasure dome, the sacred river, the romantic chasm, the Abyssinian maid and the poet-prophet from his dream and rendered them into a poem which bears a far-reaching significance. The first half of the poem is a tourist's description of Kubla's pleasure dome and its surroundings, derived mainly, as various critics have pointed out, from Coleridge's reading of several well-known travelogues. The second half is a pure vision of a singing maid and a divinely inspired poet wishing to build Kubla's dome in the air. The beauty of Kubla's dome, suggested through its reflection in water as 'a miracle of rare device', is combined with the symphony of the singing of paradise by the Abyssinian maid. Interpreted as a vision of Eden, the poem definitely bristles with the religious experience of a visionary, but not without the subterranean tension that makes the experience complex and uncertain. The power and glory of Kubla Khan lies in his decree to build the pleasure dome, but the poem is silent about how it is built or what Kubla felt about it. It is left to the imagination that the gorgeous dome, like the Taj Mahal, is built upon the oppression of a tyrant. However, the dome stands as a symbol of pleasure, its garden is a mini-Eden complete with the ominous presence of sexual energy. It is certain that the female body is used as a subtext in the poem. Humphry House gives the lead saying that the dome "is an agreed emblem of fulfillment and satisfaction, it is breast-like, full of touch and eye, rounded and complete" (House, 118). This may look a little far-fetched, but the landscape unmistakably contains strong imagery of the female anatomy—

> But oh! that deep romantic chasm which slanted
> Down the green hill athwart a cedem cover!
> A strange place! as holy and enchanted
> As ever beneath a waning moon was haunted
> By woman wailing for her demon-lover!
> And from this chasm, with ceaseless turmoil seething,
> As if this earth in fast thick pants were breathing
> A mighty fountain momently was forced. (ll. 12-17)

Thus a clear outline of a faceless female body emerges as an embodiment of the vision of creativity itself, to be fulfilled through an orgasmic process. The romantic chasm is the female principle; the sacred river Alph is the power of fertility, earthed to the 'sunless' and 'lifeless' ocean, thus completing the full circuit of vital energy. The poem not only sings about the divine spirit, but takes into account the infernal force of the body as well. The material dome of Kubla and its spiritual counterpart, the song of the Abyssinian maid are the logos of reason, order and harmony; the savage romantic chasm and the pagan Dionysian figure are the logos of imagination, chaos, wildness and even madness. The domelike upward joy in the divine creation and the divine music is suddenly revealed to the visionary as resting on the savage and seething underside, it's 'tumult' beneath counterpointing the 'mingled measure' above. Humphry House thinks that "there seems a strong likelihood that he [Coleridge] was hampered by problems which belong to the psychological borderland where matters of religion overlap with matters of sex" (House, 130). There is no doubt that the poem is open to the problematic and paradoxical nature of both creativity and spirituality. *The Spire* is Golding's 'Kubla Khan' with all the implications of tyranny, architectural feat, the disruptive sexual tension of the body and the romantic view of creative energy as essentially a marriage of heaven and hell. Golding begins exactly where Coleridge ends; the wishful thinking of the poet-prophet in 'Kubla Khan'—'I would build the dome in air' is translated into an act of will in *The Spire*. His selection of a Dean of a cathedral as the protagonist of his novel gives him ample scope to explore the problematic nature of spirituality and creativity as part of the essential human condition.

In Golding's novel, the building of the spire becomes synonymous with the process of giving body to a vision. The corporeality of the spire is underlined by the body imagery, especially its phallic connotation and the symbolic identification of the protagonist with its physicality especially its precarious condition with his own spinal disease. The very model of the cathedral on which the spire is to be built appears to Jocelin:

> like a man lying on his back. The nave was his legs placed together, the transepts on either side were his arms outspread. The choir was his body; and the Lady Chapel [...] was his head. And now also, springing, projecting, bursting, erupting from the heart of the building, there was its crown and majesty, the new spire. (8)

The vision of the spire was conceived by Dean Jocelin as an act of God's will and God's glory, but his cathedral lacks foundation and even Rachel, the wife of master builder Roger Mason, knows "'that there has to be as much weight under a building as there is over it'" (43). Jocelin's faith in vision is thus made problematic by the voice of reason coming from all around him, almost confirming his occasional doubt that it is an act of willfulness. He gradually comes to realize the price he has to pay for building the spire, his personal holiness, the sanctity of the cathedral, his reputation and the overriding human cost—the destruction of four people as sacrifices to his vision. The body of the cathedral must be supported by the pillars of human bodies. "Nearer to him than the floor were the people, the four of them—and his body shuddered again—

Roger and Rachel Mason, Pangall and his Goody, like four pillars at the crossways of the building" (62). And when the spire is built, Jocelin thinks that he has "traded a stone hammer for four people" (222). Although he often shudders at his folly, he is too strong-minded to resist even Satan, and becomes Satanic himself. The building of the spire, his 'bible in stone' (51) is carried out with satanic energy, like Kubla's tyrannical decree or Captain Ahab's demonic pursuit of the white whale. "Energy", Blake argues in *Marriage of Heaven and Hell,* "is the only life, and is from the Body; and Reason is the bound or outward circumference of Energy. Energy is the Eternal Delight" (Blake, xvi). What is remarkable here is the realization that "The Eternal Delight is at the same time the Eternal Awakening. It is perhaps the Hell which Heaven could never truly reject" (Bataille, 72). Both in "Kubla Khan" and *The Spire* creative energy is inextricably mixed with sexual energy. The body of the cathedral becomes his own body in pain and frustration as if

> he was lying on his back in the marshes, crucified and his arms were the transepts [...] Only Satan himself, rising out the west, clad in nothing but blazing hair stood over his nave and worked at the building, tormenting him so that he writhed on the marsh in the warm water, and cried out loud. (64-65)

The identification of Satan working at the nave of the building with the image of naked Goody Pangall with her blazing red hair lying on his body in his dream is really the sexual identification of the erection of the spire, the fulfillment of which is orgasmic bliss and the repression of which means sexual tension and crucifixion. The physicality of the spire compels Jocelin to have dual vision of spirituality and demonism; consequently he develops two centers of his own body—the spine which is looked after by his angel and the loins which is taken over by Satan, one is tiring, another is tormenting.

> Often, his angel stood at his back; and this exhausted him, for the angel was a great weight of glory to bear, and bent his spine [...] Satan was given leave to torment

> him, seizing him by the loins, so that it became indeed an unruly member. (138)

It is obvious that the spire symbolizes the sublimation of Jocelin's repressed sexual desire for the red-haired Goody, the Abyssinian maid of Coleridge's poem, who is his inspiration and also the means of fulfillment. Her body becomes the bait to trap Roger Mason, the only person who can perform the miracle of building the spire on a cathedral that cannot support its weight, a seemingly impossible task—the genius Jocelin badly needs to materialize his vision. However, Jocelin's symbolical orgasms remain mostly masturbatory and coitus interrupts. When he is unceremoniously withdrawn from cathedral service by the Visitor, he experiences troubled orgasm and rushes to work in the night's storm to fix the spire with a holy Nail to prevent it from premature falling, and thus from failing. And true to the nature of his creative energy, he finally has two alternate visions of the spire. First, the spire as a sublimation of his repressed sexual desire, "there was a tangle of hair, blazing among the stars; and the great club of his spire lifted towards it" (221). Second, the spire as the perfect spiritual orgasmic fulfillment.

> It was slim as a girl, translucent. It had grown from some seed of rosecolored substance that glittered like a waterfall, an upward waterfall. The substance was one thing that broke all the way to infinity in cascades of exultation that nothing could trammel. (223)

By means of his exultation, he enters Eden. He cannot recapture the great moment of vision, the kingfisher "was gone, an arrow shot once" (205) like the divine song of the Abyssinian maid of Coleridge's poem, but the spire stands "beyond the wall, bursting up with cloud and scatter, laying hold of the earth and the air, a fountain, a marvel, an appletree" (205). He gains the final insight into the very nature of existence before his death.

> Heaven and hell and purgatory are small and bright as a jewel in someone's pocket only to be taken out and worn on feast days. This is a grey, successive day for dying on.

> And what is heaven to me unless I go in holding him by one hand and her by the other? (222)

What Jocelin effects through his spire is the marriage of heaven and hell. The cathedral with its heavenly spire upward and the hellish dark pit downward is Jocelin's own psychological reality, "'I'm a building with a vast cellarage where the rats live'" (210). As Kubla's beautiful dome is balanced by the chaotic chasm, so Jocelin's spire is balanced by the chaotic pit, the cellarage of his mind (166). Is not this the eternal condition of creativity itself? In admitting the cellarage of his mind, Jocelin voices the romantic bearing on the modernist view of creativity in the same way Yeats in "The Circus Animals' Desertion" calls his creative mind as 'the foul rag-and-bone shop of the heart' from where all visions start.

WORKS CITED

Bataille, Georges, *Literature and Evil* (Trans. Alastair Hamilton), London: Calder & Boyars, 1973.

Blake, William, *The Marriage of Heaven and Hell,* London: O.U.P., 1975.

Golding, William, *The Spire,* London: Faber and Faber, 1986.

House, Humphry, *Coleridge: The Clark Lectures, 1951-52,* Indian Reprint, New Delhi: Kalyani Publishers, 1988.

8

The Romantic Novel: An Assessment in the Light of Germaine de Staël's Theory of Fiction

Partha Kumar Mukhopadhyay

From a historical perspective, the Romantic Age extended from the colonial wars to the accession of Queen Victoria to the throne of England. During that period the social unrest caused by political and economic agitations and the long-lasting battles left as deep scars on people's lives as the intellectual ferments stirred by the French Revolution. In England, however, the movement for liberty and the threat of revolution gradually faded through the enactments of several bills like the reform bill of 1832 and the initiation of several other measures like the manhood suffrage and the abolition of slavery in English Colonies.

Romanticism cannot be explained and categorized within a single formula. The urge for democracy, agitation and protest, quest for fresh values and new avenues of life, attachment to nature and past characterize Romantic literature which also vigorously assert the rights and claims of common man in social and political life. Hence, the often used epithet like the 'Renaissance of wonder' (Watts-Dunton) fails in explaining in full measure the elusive and multifaced character of the Romantic Age. Wellek argues that Romanticism is a loose term incorporating imagination, symbol and nature whereas Prof. Bateson contends that the French Revolution, Industrial Revolution, Nationalism and Romanticism 'were the concurrent cosequences of a single cause, a sudden mutation, as it were, in the European social organism'.[1] He further points out 'the evasion and relaxation of social pressures which recommenced...was all pervasive.'[2] Consequently, in the Romantic Age, the middle class people ventured to rediscover their identities in their own ways. Within the fast changing social framework, the novelists record in their works their responses to the complicated social mechanism facing changes. Thus, the early nineteenth century fiction chronicles individuals' response to and interaction with society.

In this context we may review the thoughts of some eminent philosophers who influenced many spheres of Romantic literature. Immanual Kant's (1724-1804) thoughts, even though they are not directly related to any genre of literature, had already given shape to the philosophical foundation of Enlightenment and also influenced the literary activities of the early nineteenth century. He exposes the limitations of knowledge in metaphysics in his *Critique of Pure Reason* (1781), and in *The Critique of Judgment* (1790) he examines the nature of aesthetic judgment in relation to the role of teleology or purposiveness functioning in nature. As the mind in knowing does not conform to things, things Kant argues, conform to mind. G.W. Friedrich Hegel's (1770-1831) thoughts representing the strongest phase of Post-Kantian idealism, views human beings to operate within a dialectical scheme moving around thesis, antithesis and synthesis, and he holds everything from history to culture as the outcome of this one dynamic process. Hegel's main concern is with the Absolute spirit's quest for and conquest of its own self. Hegel's works like *Phenomenology of Mind* (1807) and *Philosophy of Rights* (1821) introduced changes in the literary and critical thoughts of the nineteenth century.

Hegel's thoughts along with Jean Jacques Rousseau's (1712-78) accounted for some major changes in the literary and socio-cultural ways of the Romantic Age. In *Social*

Contract (1763) Rousseau observes that civil society formed by a genuine social contract can properly safeguard people's freedom and liberty and such a contract implies people's obedience to a self-regulated laws enforced by the general will. Rousseau's thoughts inspired the French Revolution and many aspects of the Romantic literature, including novels.

Thus novels of the Romantic Age are the products of the philosophical and socio-historical forces of the time. More than the ideas of philosophers discussed here, Germaine de Staël's' (1766-1817) famous discourse on novel in her celebrated "Essay on Fiction" helps one in discerning the mode of the Romantic fiction. Staël, an eminent literary figure of France during her time, was both the product of Enlightenment and the new intellectual movements coming after it. In her famous theory on fiction, she elaborates on man's two basic faculties—reason and imagination. As reason has limited functions in catering to the needs of human beings, fiction, the product of imagination, according to Madame Staël, apart from providing us with pleasure, also influences man's moral ideas, enhancing simultaneously his enlightenment.

She classifies novels into three types—allegorical, historical, and realistic—imaginative which does not depict reality as it is but as coloured by imagination of the novelist. She excludes tragedies from the novel category as the elevated character of tragedies and their morality remain beyond the reach of ordinary people. Comedy, she further argues, cannot be incorporated within the novel category as the novel genre is above the limitations of the artificial conventions comedy usually follows and can depict easily the habitual flow of man's feelings.

History, Staël argues, offers lessons of public life and are about nations and national events which do not exert, 'a sustained moral influence upon us'.[3] History, not alive to private happiness and misery, offers lessons which are usually unclear and limited. Hence, Staël thinks that 'History, in a word, cannot make its lesson perfectly clear'.[4]

The morality of novel stirs the inner emotions of man:

> Novels, on the contrary, can portray personalities and feelings with such intensity and detail that no other kind of literature can produce so profound an aversion to vice and love of virtue. The morality of novels depends more upon the unfolding of the inner emotions of the heart than upon the events they relate. A practical lesson may be drawn not from the arbitrary event the author invents to avenge crime; rather, indelible impressions remain of the truth of the pictures drawn, the gradual unfolding of a chain of errors, the willingness to sacrifice, and the sympathy for misfortune. Everything is so believable in these novels that one is easily convinced it could very well have happened just that way. A novel is not a story of the past but often seems to be one of the future.[5]

Staël dwells on the usefulness of *Tom Jones* to show the limitations of judgments structured on appearances and exhibit superiority of natural and instinctive qualities, which ignore 'superficial conventionality'.[6] Staël thus argues 'All novels ought to be philosophical since they all should have a moral goal.'[7]

Staël further examines the role of love which is a major nourshing emotion men experience mainly in youth. The true function of novel becomes narrow and the vision of novelists restricted if novels depict love emotions only. Hence, Staël contends, the novelists should describe the passions and emotions of man's life in ripe stages. Though bad novels distort reality, good novels offer an intimate understanding of reality as represented in the feelings and emotions of human heart. A novel's representation of reality should be truthful and unified, and the truth of fiction is inherent in the impression it produces on others, 'when it reaches only the reader's eyes, it can do nothing but abuse, but when it moves the heart, it can have a great influence upon all human conceptions.[8]

Novels, moreover, fashion moral truths by showing them in actions which can move and win the reader. The impression a novel creates has more unity than any other literary work because reality offers broken and disconnected picture of events offering no moral lesson, whereas the novel leaves a powerful impression on mind by offering moving examples of vice and virtue. Thus Staël lays emphasis on the specific role of novel in depicting human emotions with all their colourful aspects and imparting moral lessons to mankind—lessons which history or any other branch of literature fails to deliver in proper ways.

In her another famous discourse *Our Literature Considered in its Relationship to Social Institutions,* Staël argues in favour of women's education, enlightenment and literary career though the public prejudice, the social system and monarchy are against them. She is also eager to restrict the social inhibitions on women. She sees the fair sex as occupying a pivotal social position which, with its voice of conscience, may smoothen the social process.

Morroe Berger thinks that she 'spoke for rationality and also for feeling. She saw European civilization as a whole.'[9] The importance of Staël's theory of fiction is discernible in her emphasis on the dual role of fiction in depicting reality, and at the same time rising above it and illustrating moral lessens which only become disconnected pictures in the actual events of daily life. Berger takes care in noting, 'In his famous introduction of 1842 to the Human comedy, Balzac said much the same thing.'[10]

The Romantic fiction may be assessed in the light of Staël's theory of fiction. After the rise of novel and its increasing popularity ensured by Daniel Defoe (1660-1731), Samuel Richardson (1689-1761). Henry Fielding (1707-54), and Tobias Smollett (1721-71) in the Eighteenth Century, novel writing further matured in Goldsmith's *The Vicar of Wakefied* (1766), Fanny Burney's *Evelina* (1778). The 'terror' novels employing supernatural elements in a remote setting found powerful exponents in Mrs. Ann Radcliffe (1764-1823). In the Romantic Age, Sir Walter Scott (1771-1832), a prolific author and a man with vivid imagination, takes refuge in the colourful life of by-gone ages to offer his famous historical novels. Some aspects of romanticism—love for past and exercise of imagination—find eloquent voice in Scott. Jane Austen's (1775-1817) world represents a cosy subjectivity in the sense that she is keen on depicting the homely domestic comedy of a world familiar to her. Thomas Love Peacock (1785-1866) was also a notable novelist of the Age. Thus in the beginning of the early nineteenth century, novel-writing became a powerful literary mode of expression, owning its specific style and characteristics.

Jane Austen's novels intimately portray the life pattern of people living in Hampshire of the Southern part of England. *Sense and Sensibility* (1811), *Pride and Prejudice* (1813), *Mansfield Park* (1814), *Emma* (1816), *Northanger Abbey* and *Persuasion* (1818) are her six novels which, apart from some short stories and literary fragments, span her literary career. In her novels, Austen never deviates from the social code of her time in depicting the love and marriage relationship between the sexes. In *Persuasion* the lovers are united when they slowly work out a bond of love between them. In *Pride and Prejudice* Elizabeth finally overcomes her prejudices to accept Darcy who appears to be a proud man. Austen's moral awareness never fails in considering the issues of money and wealth, social status and family inhibitions, sensibility and sociability, social conventions and revolutionary impulses when she sketches the conflicts arising in the minds of lovers but with subtle touches and detached irony, she exposes the social pretensions to espouse the cause of prudence and tolerance in life.

Austen's moral values are evident in *Sense and Sensibility* in which two sisters of contrasting characters experience desertion by the men they love. The conventional Elinor is sensible and capable of detachment but Marianne, the other sister, is sentimental and represents the emotional fever of the Romantic Age. Their pangs in love transform their characters, and it is only when sense gives way to sensibility and sensibility to sense that true love wins. Austen's narrative method is simple but alive to the dissection of feelings with ample reference to time sequences:

> When at last she returned to the unconscious Marianne, she found her just awaking refreshed by so long and sweet a sleep to the extent of hopes. Elinor's heart was full. The past, the present, the future, Willoughby's visit,

> Marianne's safety and her mother's expected arrival, threw her altogether into an agitation of spirits which kept off every indication of fatigue, and made only fearful of betraying herself to her sister.[11]

Austen thus reacted against the Gothic novels by representing the placid way of provincial life and exposing in an enlivening manner the bourgeois morality and hypocrisy. With a root in her provincial surroundings, Austen can adroitly measure the rhythm and ways of her class and time.

Mansfield Park explores the situation of a poor girl Fanny Price living as being adopted in a wealthy family of Bertram and finally becoming united in marriage with Edmund. Emma Woodhouse in *Emma,* anxious for the happiness of others, comes to realise how wrong and foolish can be any intervention with the outside world and other people's way of life. Moreover, in the *Pride and Prejudice,* Austen's social awareness asserts itself in her fictionalizing the contingency of marriageable women in the late eighteenth century.[12] The dire need for immediate marriage sometimes induces them to wrong choice of partners as is found in the *Pride and Prejudice* where the eldest daughter's courtship fails in yielding the desired results and Lydia also runs away with a wicked man. Thus Austen exemplifies the issue of the ill-mated marriages of her time occasioned by the prevailing social conditions.

Jane Austen was not a theoretician of fiction but in *Northanger Abbey,* and also in some of her letters, she illustrates her idea of what a well written novel should be:

> Although our productions have afforded more extensive and unaffected pleasure than those of any other literary corporation in the world no species of composition has been so much derided. From pride, ignorance, or fashion, our foes are almost as many as our readers. And while the abilities of the nine-hundredth abridger of the History of England or of the man who collects and publishes in a volume some dozen lines of Milton, Pope, and Prior, with a Paper from the Spectator, and a chapter from Sterne, are eulogized by a thousand pens, there seems almost a general wish of decrying the

> capacity and undervaluing the labour of the novelist, and of slighting the performances which have only genius, wit, and taste to recommend them.[13]

Here Austen is critical of the cheap sentimental novels of her time, pointing out that a good work of art should offer a thorough knowledge of human nature in all its varieties along with command over wit and humour. In her disapproval of the Gothic and sentimental fiction, Austen displays her faith in the serious functions of novel-writing. She firmly holds that a novel should display the greatest powers of the mind. The high-seriousness involved in the process of fiction writing also engages Staël's attention in her theory of fiction.

James Staneir Clarke writes to Austen on the 16 Nov. 1815:

> Your late works, Madam, and in particular *Mansfield Park* reflect the highest honour on your Genius & your principles; in every new work your mind seems to increase its energy and powers of discrimination. The Regent has read & admired all your publications.
>
> Accept my sincere thanks for the pleasure your volumes have given me.[14]

A sense of morality enriches Austen's novels which show how it is only after their attaining of self-knowledge that his heroines can properly interact with others and the reality of the external world. Giving up her fruitless attempt of arranging matches for others, Emma Woodhouse awakens up to a broader understanding of others and ends by marrying knightley as she deeply loves him. Elizabeth Bennet, an independent minded lady, holding to her prejudices against Darcy, finally discovers her true self to detect the lovable qualities in the apparently proud Darcy whom she finally marries. Thus Austen probes into the minds and hearts of different characters to detail how their attainment of self-knowledge helps them to live happily in a world crossed by mere shows and appearances only. Austen's novels thus come close to Madame De Staël's concept of the power of fiction in transforming people.

Walter Scott (1771-1832), with his antiquarian knowledge of the by-gone ages with its colourful society, men of varied occupations and thrilling episodes of history, embraced the past to win European reputation. In his *Waverly* (1814) novels, he selects the Eighteenth Century England and the Seventeenth Century Scotland comes to life in *The Bride of Lammermoor* (1819) in which he juxtaposes history with imaginary tales to narrate his minute study of characters and social manners. Scotland became a part of European romanticism in Scott. England of Elizabeth I breathes in *Kenilworth* (1821) and the reign of James I in *The Fortunes of Nigel* (1822). From England he moves to France in *Quentin Durward* (1823). Thus his sense of history, antiquarianism, Tory sentiment going against revolutionary enthusiasm and love for chivalry and romance produce a range of fictional works where historical accuracy and characters and situations of imaginative creation mingle together. In picturesque details, he can easily draw so many ages of the past with minute observation of men, manners and morals.

Consequently, in Scott one finds intense imagination with realistic details. In his novels, Lords and Ladies, soldiers and Knights, Pirates and gypsies become integral parts of a procession of living men and women. Scott enjoyed European reputation because his tales of knights taking part in tournaments or protecting the honour of chaste ladies in distress captured the imagination of Europe in love with a rosy picture of the ages of chivalry and romance. What Scott offers are tales of heroic actions and an orderly loyalty of people to the chiefs of their class and clan.[15] A nationalistic pride glows throughout his novels.[16]

Sir Walter, like Staël, lays stress on the moral responsibility of fiction. He further thinks that the story of a fiction should be a well-knit one and consistent in its parts, 'the more closely and happily the story is combined, and the more and felicitous the catastrophe, the nearer such a composition, will approach the perfection of the novelist's art'.[17] Williams takes care in pointing out that Scott simply echoes Dr. Johnson's elevation of moral criticism when he praises Richardson's works and censures, the 'moral depravity' evident in Smollett's *Count Fathom.*[18]

Scott writes:

> It may perhaps be added, that although the composition of these works [well-written novels] admits of being exalted and decorated by the higher exertions of genius; yet such is the universal charm of the narrative, that the worst novel ever written will find some gentle reader content to yawn over it, rather than to open the page of the historian, moralist, or poet.[19]

Scott's views on fiction is similar to Staël's theory of fiction with its emphasis on the elevated role of fiction in influencing men and society.

Thus the Romantic critics were framing new theories of novel which catered to their needs of self-expression in proper content and style. The self-expression of the Romantic novelists incorporates also the moral responsibility of reforming the social life though David Aers thinks that Jane Austen's art, religion, 'her morality and community quite fail to transcend the narrow limitations of her historical class.'[20] Gillian Russell and Clara Tuite, while dwelling upon the Romantic Sociability, show that the sensibility represented in Marianne Dashwood is anti-sociable and Austen never approves of 'the counter-Revolutionary perception of sensibility'[21] as it threatens social stability. The Romantic theoreticians of novel expect the novelist to be a creative and moral genius who can properly assess the contradictions between form and matter, individual and society, social conventions and revolutionary urges to 'transcend the supposed limitations of conventional form'.[22] The novels of the Romantic age are responsive to the emerging socio-economic trends of the time and several other theories of fiction as framed by the eminent critics and novelists of the age.

The Romantic self's throbing search for an existence free from the oppression of mundane reality has yet to operate within the pressing framework of the real social process. Consequently, the Romantic literature stages a duality of mind and matter, the physical and metaphysical world, conventionality and revolutionary urges. Even in its escapist flights, the writer's self has to cross the bondage of the physical world. The Romantic fiction intimately depicts different phases of that conflict.

Germaine de Staël's "Essay on Fiction" helps us a lot in assessing the Romantic fiction. Staël's argument that novel offers an intimate representation of reality as framed in the perception of the novelist and can uphold moral values which can effectively influence people is exemplified in Jane Austen's delineation of men and women moving within a narrow social boundary but having minds and feelings that can guide and control others' lives. Even Scott's colourful imagination, love for past ages and his tales of romance and chivalry expounds moral lessons which are of all ages. The importance of Madame de Staël's theory of fiction is evident in her moralistic assessment of the role of fiction in purifying and transforming people and society—a process which echoes the romantic idea of reforming the ugly reality by a creative process which narrows the gulf between the individual ego and the demands of the external world. In her emphasis on the role of fiction in regeneration of society and people because of its more potent power than history, Madame de Staël elevates fiction more than any theorist of this genre writing before her. The Romantic self with its reformative urges is properly voiced in Staël's theory of fiction.

Romantic subjectivity, individualism, revolutionary jeal and love for nature—all have their voices in the novels of the Romantic Age. The interaction between mind and intellect, feeling and emotion and the subtle threads of the internal and external world characterize these fictions. Plots, techniques of presentation, characters, dialogues and visions of life are as important here as the demonstration of virtue and vice pointed out by Staël. Moreover, Staël's categorization of novels into historical and realistic finds adequate expressions in Walter Scott and Jane Austen's novels. Following M.H. Abrams we may conclude that the British Romantic novel propounds that works of art, including fiction, follow dual symbol systems pointing in two directions, ostensibly representing the outer world but indirectly voicing the novelist and his feelings. These dual symbol systems permeating the English novels of the Romantic Age very often accommodate a high seriousness and moralistic vision of life which can redeem and transform a fallen society as elaborated in Madame de Staël's theory of fiction.

NOTES

1. E.W. Bateson and H.T. Messrole, *A Guide To English and American Literature* (Longman: London, 1976), 141.
2. *Ibid.*
3. Madame de Staël, *On Politics, Literature and National Character,* Transl. and ed. Morroe Berger (Sidgwick and Jackson: London, 1964), 205.
4. *Ibid.,* 206.
5. *Ibid.*
6. *Ibid.,* 208.
7. *Ibid.,* 204.
8. *Ibid.,* 203.
9. *Ibid.,* 69.
10. *Ibid.,* 38.
11. Jane Austen, *Sense and Sensibility* (Peacock Books: New Delhi, 1994), 292.
12. Claudia Durst Johnson and Verson Johnson, *The Social Impact of the Novel: A Reference Guide* (Greenwood Press: Westport, Connecticut, 2002).
13. Jane Austen, *Northanger Abbey* (Peacock Books: New Delhi, 2002), 21-22.
14. *Jane Austen's Letters to her Sister Cassandra and Others,* ed. R.W. Chapman (Oxford University Press: Oxford, 1979), 113a.
15. Claudia Durst Johnson and Verson Johnson, *The Social Impact of the Novel: A Reference Guide,* 82.
16. Katie Turmpener, *Bardie Nationalism: The Romantic Novel and the British Empire* (Princeton University Press: Princeton, NJ, 1997).
17. *Sir Walter Scott on Novelists and Fiction,* ed. Ian Williams (Routledge and Kegan Paul; London, 1968), 446.

18. Ian Williams, *Sir Walter Scott on Novelists and Fiction*, 3.
19. *Ibid.*, 226
20. David Aers, Janathan Cook and David Punter, *Romanticism and Ideology Studies in English Writing 1765-1830* (Routledge and Kegan Paul: London, 1981), 136.
21. *Romantic Sociability: Social Networks and Literary Culture in Britain 1770-1840* eds. Gillian Russell and Clara Tuite (Cambridge University Press: Cambridge, 2002), 8.
22. Clifford Siskin, *The Historicity of Romantic Discourse* (Oxford University Press: Oxford, 1988), 27.

9

Families and Nationhood: A Study of Amitav Ghosh's *The Shadow Lines*

Arpa Ghosh

The family often simulates the nation in its power equations and patterns of growth and development. The pyramid-like structure of the traditional patriarchal family with the father in the apex and the servants, serfs and hangers—on in the bottom-level, often reflects the pattern of the state with its power equations. The State usually denotes a geo-political territory rather than an imagined piece of land. The traditional dendritic family is also anchored in a focal patriarchal point that commands nodal importance in terms of ideological power and influence.

Patriarchy perpetuates itself through family. Blood and male kinship are the binding agents. The family draws its boundaries in the lines of kinship, race and religion. The women's and children's roles are problematic. At times, they are victims of patriarchy, solemnized into role-playing. At other times, women are often to be found in the role of panders and power-brokers of patriarchy using their clout within the family to legitimize patriarchal rule. Notable examples of women as victims and power-brokers are the daughters-in-law and mothers-in-law (respectively) in Ashapurna Debi's groundbreaking novels *Prothomprotisruti* and *Subornolata.*

In significant ways, the family replicates the oppressive powers of state. Patriarchy functions through the physical and psychological oppression of weaker rudiments like women, children and slaves. A means of psychological mind bend is erasure and suppression of memory. All untoward, threatening and seditious occurrences are sought to be erased from the family memory and by default from national memory. These occurrences threaten to fissure the smooth, linear master-text constructed by the family. As in the nation, so too in the family, whenever seditious elements raise their heads, they are normally counted as battle and rebellion to be quenched and doused in order to ensure the health of the state. These elements, however, are often that part of the familial and national memory that defies the erasure tactics of patriarchy and remembers oppressive and criminal acts perpetrated against certain subordinate elements. Remembrance therefore is a way of uncovering the erasure tactics of the family.

Related to the issue is the debate between history and fiction. If history is the official, state record (nation) or the popular anecdotes handed down from generation to generation, usually by patriarchs and patriarchal agencies (family), fiction often comprises of tales overlapping truth and fantasy, tales precariously hinged on flawed personal memory and imaginative wish-fulfillment. The difference between fiction and history is, fiction does not make truth claims as history does. Also, fiction lays open the fissures whereas history seeks to conceal and layer over, drawing popular attention to 'forgotten' and 'trivial' occurrences.

Like the nation, family too is a structure, often fragile, oppressive, erected on the principles of omission and segregation. Amitav Ghosh's *The Shadow Lines* and *The Glass Palace* are novels that try to understand the evolution and functioning of nations through the medium or vehicle of family. Creditably, Ghosh brings to his fiction, his knowledge of history and anthropology and investigates certain fault-lines of history.

In *The Shadow Lines* a time-span of forty years 1939 to 1979 is studied through Ghosh's depiction of three families;

Mayadebi family comprising of her husband the Shaheb and their three sons, Jiten, Tridib and Robi, the narrator's family of Tha'mma, his parents and himself; and the Price family in the UK, friends of Mayadebi, consisting of the widowed Mrs Price, and her children Nick and May.

While the latter two families are based in Kolkata and London respectively, Mayadebi and her diplomat husband travel all over the world and do not have a single home to speak of. The sisters, Tha'mma and Mayadebi, lead vastly different lives. Tha'mma is the matriarch of her family, ruling her household with an iron hand. She has fixed traditional and hidebound opinions about time, freedom, and nationhood. She is conservative and bigoted in most of her opinions, believing in stability and national boundaries drawn in blood. According to Tha'mma one has to be bound to a nation with ties of blood or violence in order to belong to that nation. Expressing her anger regarding her grandniece Ila's decision to live in England, Tha'mma says:

> Ila has no right to live there (in England).... She doesn't belong there. It took people a long time to build that country; hundreds of years, years and years of war and bloodshed. Everyone who lives there has earned his right to be there with blood: with their brother's blood and their father's blood and their son's blood. They know they are a nation because they have drawn their borders with blood.... War is their religion. That is what takes to make a country. Once that happens people forget they were born this or that, Muslim or Hindu, Bengali or Punjabi: they become a family born of the same pool of blood. That is what you have to achieve for India, don't you see?[1]

Tha'mma condemns Ila's decision to live in England while remaining silent on the topic of an alternate address for Ila, who has been shuttling over the major part of the globe throughout childhood and adolescent years without ever being afforded a scope to sink her roots in one particular town or city. As a woman, Ila is expected to toe the line by the patriarchal Tha'mma, the traditional Robi and the chauvinist

Nick (after her marriage). Ila's personal insecurity engendered by a lifestyle imposed on her by her parents is not taken into consideration. As an only child of rich, influential parents, she is indulged, but not afforded a space that bespeaks equality with the patriarchal forces of the family, namely Tha'mma, Robi and later her husband Nick. From early girlhood Ila learns to suppress and render her vicarious experiences as victim of racism. When as a child she relates one such experience to her cousin the narrator, she narrates it in the form of a children's tale, where her doll Magda, rather than she herself is the victim of racial enmity and violence among British school-children (73-75).

Tha'mma's statement (quoted above) also negates Mayadebi's and Jiten's globetrotting way of life as well as Tridib's detached stance regarding nationhood. In fact, Tha'mma's statement is at odds with her own situation. She is an East Bengali married to a Bengali businessman stationed in Burma. It is only later as a widow that she starts living in West Bengal. Her experience and her statement are at odds with each other. Tha'mma embodies the dominant ideology of nationhood that repudiates and excludes the kind of loop-holed ideology that is sustained through an oppressive, domineering personality rather than logical reasoning.

Finally, as in Tha'mma case, such ideology does more harm than good. In a foolhardy bid to 'rescue' her uncle from his Bangladeshi 'enemies' (the uncle in fact had accepted his position and was peacefully sharing his ancestral house in Khulna with Muslim squatters), Tha'mma becomes the cause of twin murder; that of her ninety-year old uncle and her nephew Tridib. In a bid to stanch the instinctive sexual love the narrator feels for his cousin Ila, Tha'mma almost gets him rusticated from his university. The self-alienation and megalomania (playing god) instinct in nations and nation-building is depicted in the powerful persona of Tha'mma whose lifelong aim is to protect and cherish her family, and who in the process inflicts irreparable damage on the same family.

Tha'mma's conservatism is further encouraged by her submissive son and daughter-in-law, the narrator's parents, who accept her domination. Tha'mma's is a small, exclusive, patriarchal set-up. As a woman she is a power-broker of patriarchy, domineering mother, mother-in-law and grandmother, seeking to instill discipline and fear in her familial subordinates. Her concepts about nationhood, blood ties and female conduct reflect an age-old narrow-mindedness. When in the final count her notions crumble like dust in the face of reality, instead of accepting more liberal concepts, Tha'mma collapses in a fit of violent hysteria, unable to come to terms with her disillusion and sorrow.

The Price family, friends of Mayadebi, is a typical, middle-class, lily-white British family. The very stability of this family attracts Ila, the narrator's cousin and Mayadebi's grandniece, who wishes to ignore her Indianness and get assimilated into British society. A route to this aspiration is Ila's marriage to Nick. Ila attempts to use marriage as a means of cooption and assimilation, switching families and loyalties. The stability that eluded her in her father's home, Ila seeks to obtain by marrying Nick Price. Ila wishes to be free, but confuses freedom with recklessness. Her marriage places her in a subordinate position. Gradually disillusioned by her husband Nick's twin betrayal—marital infidelity and viewing her more as an exotic than his soulmate—Ila sinks into a self-delusory state. In her last telephone call to the narrator before his return to India, she denies her previous tear-filled confession about her erring, unrepentant husband:

> You mustn't pay any attention to what I said the other day.... I was just overwrought and it made me suspicious. Nick wouldn't dream of doing anything that might upset me, really, believe me. You mustn't believe a word I said. I made it all up. Thai's what I sis, I made it all up. That's the truth of it. I talked to him later, and he showed me how silly I was being. It's all fine now. We need a little holiday, that's all. (248)

Ila is a woman who desperately wishes to enter, through marriage, the dominant power group in London. Having failed to achieve personal happiness, her self-respect severely dented, she chooses to forget and ignore her husband's shortcomings as this is the only way to maintain the fragile makeup of her 'family'. This strategy of self-delusory erasure is an integral part of nation-building that *The Shadow Lines* as a novel interrogates and dismantles.

Mayadebi's set-up is apparently a stark contrast to the other families. Apparently, she enjoys more space, freedom, variety of experience than her widowed sister Tha'mma or her widowed friend Mrs Price. Mayadebi travels all over the world with her husband, shunting her children into hostels and ancestral house. In that sense she is richer and freer than her widowed sister. Her eldest son Jiten grows up to be a diplomat like his father and has the same lifestyle. The other two sons Tridib and Robi mostly live away from their parents, and are left to mature on their own. Compared to the docile, sedentary set-up of the narrator's family, Mayadebi and her son Jiten appear to lead non-conventional lives. But, Mayadebi's family differs from Tha'mma's, only in degree and not in kind. Her son Tridib's death, unnecessary as it is violent, is hushed up so that her husband's career remains unharmed. Taking the narrator to Kalighat Temple, his father makes him promise, he will henceforth remain silent about Tridib's death, an incident the father refers to as an 'accident':

> Listen, you have to promise me something. Remember you are holding Ma Kali's flowers in your hands, so you can't ever go back on your word. Promise me that you'll never talk about this anywhere—never, not in school, not to Montu, not to your friends in the pard. You know that Meshomoshai—Tridib's father—is a very important man in the *government? He* doesn't want people to hear about this—it has to be kept secret, so you mustn't talk about it. Most of all, you mustn't ask your Tha'mma any questions about what happened. She's already very upset, and it would only get worse if you make her talk about it. (239)

Mayadebi's husband's concern about his status and professional security and the son's concern about Tha'mma's comfort override the enormity of Tridib's death, so much so that the narrator is ordered to suppress and if possible erase the memory of the incident.

In the novel, Tridib's death is the point at which personal memory clashes with official and family history. The death is a classic combination of private tragedy and public aberration. For as long as the narrator can remember, his immediate family has remained silent on the issue. The confusion resulting from the silence provokes the narrator to mistakenly think that the riots in Khulna that take Tridib's life are part of the partition violence of the sixties. He nurses this belief for a long time, chiefly because he is never afforded a scope to discuss the death with any of the senior members of his family. It is only much later in 1979 when he is a student of Delhi University, entering into an argument with his friends regarding important public events in their childhood, and later looking up old newspapers in the university library, the narrator realizes that Tridib's death was a freak accident, offshoot of a theft of a saint's relic that took place in Hazratbal Mosque in Kashmir. When the relic got stolen, Hindus, Muslims and Sikhs in a rare show of solidarity took to the streets in Srinagar to protest against the crime. Strangely, not a single incident of religious animosity or public disturbance was recorded at this time of collective grief. Yet strangely enough, not a single incident of religious violence occurred during this difficult time (225). On 4th November 1964, the relic was 'recovered' by the officials of the CBL. 'There were not explanations; indeed to this day nobody really knows what happened to the Hazratbal relic' (226). Without naming names, the laconic comment hints at state machinations. The celebrations in response to the news of the recovery were countrywide. Only, in Khulna, a crowd marching in protest against the theft erupted in a violence that burnt down shops and killed a few people (226).

The narrator's detection of this paradoxical fact of lack of information was properly percolating to the edges of empire (the news of recovery failing to travel from Srinagar to Khulna, East Pakistan in time, where the violence was triggered off as protest against the theft at a time when the relic had already been restored) and resulting in the unnecessary waste of fine human possibility as in Tridib's death.

The narrator rues the fact that newspapers have a way of prioritizing certain items to the suppression and neglect of others. The initiation of the riots in Khulna had not been thought important enough by news agencies. As a result Tridib and Tha'mma have been allowed to leave for Khulna by their Indian relatives.

> And yet he knew, and they must have known too, all the canny journalists; everyone must have known in some voiceless part of themselves—for events on that scale cannot happen without portents. It they knew, why couldn't they speak of it? They were speaking of so much else, of the Congress conference, of the impending split in the Communist Party, or wards and revolutions: what is it that makes all those things called 'politics' so eloquent and these other unnameable things so silent? (227-28)

The national silence reflects the silence in the narrator's family regarding an incident that is on one hand stray and superfluous, and on the other, deeply symptomatic of the riven, cleft nature of the Indian sub-continent, where passions ride high and shadow lines often lack the substantiality of concrete boundaries.

Tha'mma considers her set-up to be very different from Mayadebi's. She dislikes her grandniece Ila's defiant ways, calls her a greedy slut, is wary of her nephew Tridibs (loafer and wastrel in her view) influence on her grandson the narrator and openly disdains Mayadebi's husband for his profession and drinking habits. Tha'mma refers to her brother-in-law as Shaheb, a slur pointing to his imitation of British habits. Also, the fact that his grandmother is called Tha'mma, while his grandaunt is referred to as Mayadebi indicates the narrator's quiet demarcation of the different lives led by the two sisters. The first name indicates individualism, while the common noun suggests strong family bonds. Tha'mma's family is for her a fiefdom to be guarded against subversive, threatening elements who might challenge her belief-system.

If Tha'mma quests for stability and a replication of the bounded, fenced-off nation in her family, Ila, a victim of peregrinating childhood and adolescence—her parents cart her all over the globe without ever allowing her to settle in any one stable address and quests for stability. Suffocated by bigoted, intolerant Indian morality, Ila looks for 'freedom' in London, hoping at last to find it by marrying her childhood sweetheart Nick and getting assimilated into London society. In her own way, Ila seeks to exclude the burden of history, childhood memories and family feelings when she sets up her family. Instead of evolving a healthy multiculturalism, Ila is anxious to disown her Indianness, often ignoring her Indian relatives. Like Tha'mma, Ila too draws her own borders and erects her own fragile nation in the formation of her family. The families in *The Shadow Lines* are constructed along traditional patriarchal lines. Yet they are riven by subversive elements that destabilize them. One subversive element is the narrative method with its complete confounding of a linear time mode. The narrator's memory is sole reference point, and he, in spite of Tha'mma's determined attempts to inculcate in him divisiveness, is an integral part of all three families. Even at the outset the emotional conflict is noticeable.

> I remember trying very hard to imagine him (Tridib) back to my age.... It wasn't easy.... In the end since I had nothing to go on, I had decided that he had looked like me. But my grandmother, when I asked her, was very quick to contradict me. She shook her head firmly, looking up from her schoolbooks and said: No, he looked completely different—not at all like you. (3)

The narrator loves his Tha'mma, but at the same time is deeply and permanently marked by his interactions with his uncle Tridib who teaches him to see beyond the artifice of nations and territories. Also, he experiences a keen sexual love for his cousin Ila regarding her much traveled, stylish, female self as alter-ego to his sedentary, male self. Robi, his youngest uncle he trusts and respects implicitly, while Mrs Price and May inspire in him a trust and family feeling when he is in the UK. Tha'mma's determination to draw lines between her family and that of Mayadebi's in the way lines were drawn between the families of her father and uncle in their house in Dhaka, fails.

Tha'mma is a woman whose address is messily at odds with her nationality. This anomaly never ceases to irk her. Possibly, her love for discipline arises out of an existentialist insecurity regarding her identity as erstwhile East Bengali now permanently settled in West Bengal.

> It had suddenly occurred to her then that she would have to fill in 'Dhaka' as her place of birth in that form, and that the prospect of this had worried her in the same way that dirty schoolbooks worried her—because she liked things to be neat and in place—and at that moment she had not been able to quite understand how her place of birth had come to be so messily at odds with her nationality. (152)

At variance with Tha'mma bigotry is her uncle's willing compromise with changing circumstances. When Muslim refugees occupy his ancestral house in Dhaka, the uncle stays back and lives with them instead of fleeing to his sons:

> It's not safe for you here, my grandmother said urgently. I know these people look after you well, but it's not the same thing. You don't understand.
>
> I understand very well, the old man muttered. I know everything. Once you start moving you never stop. That's what I told my sons when they took the trains. I said: I don't believe in this India-Shindia. It's all very well, you're going away now, but suppose when you get there they decide to draw another line somewhere? What will you do then? Where will you move to? No one will have you anywhere. As for me, I was born here, and I'll die here. (*SL*, 215)

In an e-mail sent to Dipesh Chakrabarty, Amitav Ghosh says:

> Two of my novels, (*The Shadow Lines* and most recently *The Glass Palace*) are centred on families. I know that for myself this is a way of displacing the nation.... In

> other words I would like to suggest that writing about families is one way of not writing about the nation (or other restrictively imagined collectivities). I think there is a long tradition of this, going back at the least to Proust—and it's something that Jameson, Anderson (and even Bhaba) never seem to take into account.[2]

For Ghosh, the nation is a restrictively imagined collectivity working by means of boundaries, fences, cut off points, including and excluding races, religions, economic groups and so on. Family tries to function by segregation and self-definition, but is never quite successful, as Ghosh shows in his novel. One reason could be, suppression of individual memory is often an abortive project when compared to suppression of collective memory which yields more success.

Individual memory knows no restrictions. It tends to flit back and forth in time, collating and juxtaposing related incidents. Temporally and spatially, memory works in a manner that defies and confuses the concept of nationhood. In *The Shadow Lines* memory is a tool deployed to register similitudes rather than diversities. A war in China recalls a riot in Calcutta which actually reflects a more violent and bloody riot in Dhaka. An act of violent slaughter and self-sacrifice (Tridib's) is a mirror-image of another violent carnage in another moment in time (Tresawsen's). Memory links and relates, forging a meaning out of this joining, while nations distance, sever and exclude, engendering confusion, angst and madness in the people it includes and excludes.

Ghosh is a postmodern novelist in that he challenges the basic family-oriented ethos of the classic realist novel. *The Shadow Lines* has elements of a psychomachia; a battle fought for the soul of the narrator. The two major contenders are Tridib and Tha'mma. Tha'mma embodies a strict patriarchal code of conduct. Her love for the narrator borders on oppression: 'I was so shaken by the sight of her resurrected hand, reaching out to me after her death, as it had all through my childhood.' (93)

Tridib is on the other end of the spectrum that anchors Tha'mma at one end;

> And so, fifteen years after his death, Tridib watched over me, as I tried to learn the meaning of distance. His atlas showed me, for example, that within the tidy ordering of Euclidean space, Chiang Mai in Thailand was much nearer Calcutta than Delhi is; that Chengdu in China is nearer than Srinagar is (242). Tridib stands for everything that Tha'mma resists, and everything that defines a nation. Apparently, he is a layabout and a braggart who lives in the world of his imagination. He wastes his time gossiping in road corners. He does not belong to any particular familial set-up, coming and going as he wishes, and comfortable in 'neutral' spaces rather than family gatherings.

However, Tridib is an archeologist who understands the frangible nature of nations; the flimsy, often hypocritical basis on which nations are erected, and how easily they can crumble. He inculcates in the narrator, a sense of the past, past wars, past instances of nation-building, and past friendships that have defied the divisive, separatist logic of nation-formation. Tridib lovingly tutors the boy in the basic lesson of humanitarianism that rises above and beyond blood-thirsty nation-building.

Tresawsen's story—a story—that the narrator is told by Tridib long before his voyage to the West, is a case in point. Tresawsen's household set-up, where Tresawsen and his friends peacefully cohabit with a German girl they all love, a set-up that is tragically demolished by the blanket bombing of the Second World War, is an alternative arrangement that defies the patriarchal strictures of conventional family. Tresawsen's sister, Mrs Price, wishes to rationalize the arrangement and bring it within the purview of a traditional family, but the fact is the arrangement remains a miracle and a mystery. Instead of neglecting these almost-forgotten details, Tridib encourages the narrator to remember and take into account such alternative arrangements, as possibly the only hope towards defying and flouting the barbaric exclusivity of nationhood.

> Mrs Price has often speculated about Francesca to Mayadebi: she knows that Francesca shares that house in Brink Lane with the three men. But the trouble, as she puts it, is that she doesn't know which of them exactly Francesca shares it with. It ought by rights be Alan (Mrs Price's brother, Alan Tresawsen), she thinks, because she is convinced now that Alan injured himself trying to smuggle her out of Germany. But at the same time Francesca seems to be very familiar with Mike.... (64-65)

Instead of being influenced by gossip, Tridib trusts his own perception.

> Two days later, when Tridib came to Brick lane...to collect Tresawsen's things, he found a picture of the four of them together, stuck on the kitchen wall: it had been taken in a park, and all of them were laughing, Dan standing a little apart, and Mike with his arms around Tresawsen and Francesca. (103)

The novel advocates vigilance when it comes to analyzing and studying the different and competing forms of human communes within and outside nationhood. In Tresawsen's arrangement, Ila finds a resemblance to her own closeness to her British 'brothers'. 'We live like that too, in Stockwell' (103), she informs the narrator. But her statement proves to be a bluff when the narrator sees how the white students of Stockwell exoticize Ila, calling her 'our own upper-class Asian Marxist', tolerating rather than accepting her. (97)

In Ila's Stockwell commune there are invisible lines drawn on the basis of race, religion and colour, though these lines are a more devious than the harsh communal lines drawn elsewhere.

If Tresawsen's household is an unconventional arrangement, Tha'mma uncle's peaceful cohabitation with the Muslim squatters who have peopled his Khulna mansion in the wake of partition is another instance. Tha'mma's uncle after devoting a lifetime to fighting wasteful property cases against kin realizes in his old age that compromise is the only way of survival. If friendship and love are the basic elements of

Tresawsen's home, geographical location is the basic of the uncle's 'home'. He refuses to return to Calcutta with Tha'mma, fearing Calcutta for its strangeness. Driven by an idée fixe of 'we' (Hindus) and 'they' (Muslims), Tha'mma pays no attention to his fears and courts disaster by forcibly dragging him away from his age-old Khulna home.

These two instances show how the conventional family drawn in lines of racial, religious, patriarchal and class hierarchy is not the only sociological unit. There are other unconventional but more flexible, survival and growth-oriented structures which if fostered, could lead to less conflict-ridden ways of life. Tridib honours and cherishes the memory of such arrangements (Tresawsen's) while Tha'mma rejects them (her uncle's way of life), stubbornly sticking to her own reactionary concepts of kinship and family.

The other instance of Tridib's nonconformism is the pornographic letter he sends to May Price (137). In his letter Tridib describes a lewd sexual encounter he witnessed in his childhood in the ruins of a bombed cinema-hall in London, between a woman and a man 'in a uniform'; an encounter that stands outside the spatial limits of history. The man for the crucial period of the encounter is oblivious of his State-imposed duties; the woman remains nameless; and the encounter takes place in an intermediary twilight space neither private nor public, neither confined nor open. The encounter is borne out of mutual need, greed and pleasure, in other words pure human instinct working at variance with the strictures of propriety and decorum imposed by the State.

For Tridib, the experience is central to his belief that such encounters are possible and desirable. State-imposed strictures cannot do away with the basic human urge to fulfill one's personal destiny.

> That is how he wanted to meet her, May—as a stranger in a ruin. He wanted them to meet as the completest of strangers—strangers-across-the-sea—all the more strangers because they knew each other already. He wanted them to meet far from their friends and relatives—in a place without a past, without history, free, really

> free, two people coming together with the utter freedom of strangers. (144)

Tridib alludes to the love story of Tristan and Isolde more than once, a tale handed down to him by none other than Tresawsen and one he cherishes as the love that flouted natural and man-made boundaries.

> Where did it happen? I asked. Which country?
>
> Ah, said Tridib. That's the trick, you see. It happened everywhere, wherever you wish it. It was an old story, the best story in Europe, told when Europe was a better place without borders and countries—it was a German story in what we call Germany, Nordic in the north, French in France, Welsh in Wales, Cornish in Cornwall, it was the story of a hero called Tristan, a very say story, about a man without a country, who fell in love with a woman across the seas. (186)

Tridib's death is more of a textual rupture than an apologia; an instance of suppressed memory later excavated by the narrator in an attempt to understand family and national politics. The death shocks precisely because it is unnecessary, accidental and eminently avoidable (had State and family machinery been more sensitive to nascent issues of brewing communalism). The death, though resolved within the text, by May and the narrator, who come to terms with it in ways that the grieving, hysterical Tha'mma cannot (239)—in fact May defies it by calling it a 'sacrifice' on Tridib's part—all textual markers point to the massive irrationality of Tridib's death. May's assessment of the death makes Tridib a tragic character, whereas Tridib is essentially a man who defies State-related indices, tragic heroism being one such index. The hero's position is defiance and rebellion, whereas Tridib is essentially an impartial, disinterested observer. May's endeavour to resolve Tridib's death arises possibly from her romantic attachment to him. The text and the narrator bifurcate in the last instance. The narrator identifies himself in the last reckoning as Tridib's bereaved nephew who wishes desperately to find some kind of meaning in Tridib's death. The text however seeks throughout to uncover seemingly irrational, inexplicable, 'meaningless' caesuras like Tridib and the uncles' deaths, Ila's childhood victimization in the hands of her white schoolmates, the happiness that animates Tresawsen's amoral home—caesuras that have the power to dismantle the seamless narrative of family-formation and nation-building.

NOTES AND REFERENCES

1. Amitabh Ghosh, *The Shadow Lines*, New Delhi: OUP, 1995. First published Ravi Dayal Publisher, 1988, pp. 77-78. (All quotations are taken to this edition.)
2. Amitav Ghosh, e-mail correspondence with Dipesh Chakrabarty, circulated by the author via e-mail and also carried on www.AmitavGhosh.com. Message dated December 14, 2000.

   My insight into *The Shadow Lines* has been enhanced by my reading of the following texts:

   (i) Amitav Ghosh, *The Shadow Lines* with critical essays by AN Kaul, Suvir Kaid, Meenakshi Mukherjee and Rajesware Sunder Rajan, New Delhi. OUP, 1995.

   (ii) Amitav Ghosh, *Critical Perspectives*, Delhi: Pencraft International, 2003.

10

James Joyce's *A Portrait of the Artist as a Young Man*: A Landmark of the Twentieth Century

Tapati Talukdar

It would perhaps be no exaggeration to attribute 'landmark' status to James Joyce's debut novel *A Portrait of the Artist as a Young Man*, published in 1916, which is the consummate version of *Stephen Hero*. He left the initial version incomplete presumably for the manifest immaturity he had discovered on writing part of it. What makes the final version a work of the highest artistic excellence is the deployment of innovative techniques and style to narrate it abandoning the obsolete novelistic strategies that are too apparent in the fragmented version posthumously published as *Stephen Hero*. The contemporary critical world was vehemently stirred to read a novel that sent shock waves to the artistic world at large. The initial reception of the novel betrays the bewilderment of the writers and critics, some were effusive, some bitterly critical, but none could ignore the artistic merit of Joyce whose collection of short stories titled *Dubliners*, published in 1914, has already shaken the literary world. But Joyce's contemporaries like Yeats and Pound appreciated the depth of Joyce's maiden attempt at writing a novel. Pound, who deserves the credit of establishing him as a genius by serially publishing A *Portrait*, hailed the book as a "hard, perfect stuff". In his letter to Joyce written on 7 September,

1915 he went to the extent of prophetically attributing a "permanent" status to the novel like those of Flaubert and Stendhal, effusively starting the letter "...I have just read the splendid end of *A Portrait of the Artist*.... I think you must soon, or at least sooner or later, get your recognition...we don't get prose books that a man can reread. We don't get prose that gives us pleasure paragraph by paragraph" (*L Il*, 364).

The enduring appeal of Joyce's work lies not only in his employment of diverse innovative strategies in narrative techniques, but also in his introduction of mundane details of everyday life into the realm of art. The unprecedented explicitness with which he depicts the trivialities of the lives lived by ordinary people of Dublin in *Dubliners* gives a foretaste of the matter and manner of his unique presentation of the fictional world. But the explicitness is only apparent as critics and readers are left bewildered by the use of dented discourses in the stories, more so, as nothing of consequence happens in the stories. And *A Portrait of the Artist as a Young Man* provides him a broader spectrum to show his skills and talent in the novelistic art and paves the way for the consummation of his techniques in *Ulysses* and *Finnegan's Wake*.

What urges us to study Joyce is, as Attridge emphasizes in his introductory article on Joyce, the "pleasures" that we derive from reading him. The pleasures emanate, as he traces them, from the "...qualities of inexplicability, unpredictability, inexhaustibility..." that Joyce's texts have inherent in them eluding "...a satisfying feeling of completion and finality" in readers (2). The reason appears to be that Joyce's texts are built on the principle of openness that allows readers to interpret them in diverse ways. As the stories of *Dubliners* are marked for their open-endedness, *A Portrait* and *Ulysses* too yield to varying explications, as attested to by the voluminous critical responses they have evoked for almost a century.

It is Joyce's cult of objectivity that he practises in his work with unwavering consistency that ushers in a fresh air in the fictional world he constructs. His verbal twisting along with the use of narrated monologues and stream of consciousness technique to render the mental working of characters makes his fiction amenable to myriad readings. The critical consensus that elevates him almost to the Olympian heights like Shakespeare is that he is perhaps only next to his illustrious predecessor in his manipulation of language. His untiring experimentation with the structure and texture of language that his aborted attempt at writing *Stephen Hero* conforming to the traversed tradition gave an impetus to and firmly establishes him as a modernist writer at the second half of the twentieth century. His fiction hardly satisfies the traditional expectation of reading a well-knit plot with its strong story elements.

But Kershner destabilizes the critical consensus on objectivity that Joyce's equating the artist with God leads to by making Stephen assert in *A Portrait* that "The artist, like the God of the creation, remains within or behind or beyond or above his handiwork, invisible, refined out of existence, indifferent, paring his fingernails" (233). Following M.M. Bakhtin's celebrated terms he makes use of in *Rabelais and His World,* Kershner applies the term 'dialogical' to Joyce's technique of presentation of various voices in his fiction. He is struck by Bakhtin's silence on Joyce as *Ulysses* and *Finnegan's Wake* are, according to him, "...outstanding illustrations..." of dialogism for which Bakhtin appears to substitute two other terms, namely 'polyphony' and 'heteroglossia'. He detects the presence of dialogism in "embryonic form" in Joyce's *Dubliners* and *A Portrait.* Kershner elaborates on the application of this technique in Joyce's early work in the following lines:

> The more intensive our examination of *Dubliners* and *A Portrait*, the more we are struck by the fully realized, wholly distinctive qualities of the characters' voices, each of them held in dialogical tension with the narrative voice of the author. In the case of *Portrait*, Joyce's exploration of voice goes even further, in the direction of an analysis of the competing elements within Stephen's

> own inner monologue and of his indebtedness to the voices of his society. (18)

Joyce's predominant use of 'free indirect discourse' creates the stance that the narrative narrates itself but the very structure of the discourses implies the penetration of the authorial voice into those of Stephen in the novel. The pronominal 'he' occupies the subject-position and the tense of narration is invariably past in the 'free indirect discourses' which can be changed to direct discourses by changing the subject and tense. Hence, we cannot describe the discourses as totally objective. It is Joyce's deft deployment of the technique of thought—presentation of the protagonist in *A Portrait* that creates the stance that the words Stephen uses to construct his portrait as a young man are his own by imparting to them his attitudinal colourings. He is shown adapting the words he culls from his memory and collects from his surroundings to express himself in different phases and situations of his life. The whole narrative of *A Portrait* can be viewed as a manifestation of the growth of language in his consciousness. The novelty of Joyce's technique consists in organizing chunks of language to register the development of artistic sensibilities in his consciousness exposed to the discordant voices of the society he belongs to. Stephen of both the versions of the novel dwells on his fascination with words he hears in mundane locales he frequents and reads in diverse contexts. Stephen's adolescent attraction for words which provide him access to the real world is recorded by his consciousness in Chapter 11 of *A Portrait* in the following sentences:

> Words which he did not understand he said over and over to himself till he had learned them by heart: and through them he had glimpses of the real world about him. The hour when he too would take part in the life of that world seemed drawing near and in secret he began to make ready for the great part which he felt awaited him, the nature of which he only dimly apprehended. (64)

The cited lines betray cognitive and aesthetic development in the protagonist's consciousness and also his conscious endeavour to correlate words and worldly activities which appear to be missing in the opening part of the novel. Again in the fourth chapter we hear Stephen who is now much more mature for his wider literary exposure enabling him to quote a phrase by Hugh Miller "A day of dappled seaborne clouds". Though he substitutes Miller's 'breeze-borne' by 'seaborne' (Deane, 306), intentionally or otherwise, he dwells on his fascination with words: "Words. Was it their colours? He allowed them to glow and fade, hue after hue: sunrise gold.... No, it was not their colours; it was the poise and balance of the period itself. Did he then love the rhythmic rise and fall of words better than their associations of legend and colour?" Stephen goes on giving vent to his carping doubts whether he derives more pleasure "...from the contemplation of an inner world of individual emotions mirrored perfectly in a lucid supple periodic prose..." (180-81). The musical prose that marks the style of particularly the second part of the closing chapter appears to embody his streams of emotions in a prose akin to that of Pater who may be the inspiration behind his developing 'a lucid supple periodic prose'. But we cannot help wondering if it is lucid enough, but we are captivated by the musical refrains and resonances he is able to create by the poetic rendering of his language. The style of his linguistic growth seems to show a linear progression, though the episodes of each section of each chapter appear to be discontinuous.

The oft-quoted sentences that start off the narrative posit Stephen in the innocent linguistic consciousness that befits a child who nostalgically renders:

> Once upon a time and a very good time it was there was a moocow coming down along the road and this moocow that was coming down along the road met a nicens little boy named baby tuckoo...
>
> His father told him that story: his father looked at him through a glass: he had a hairy face.
>
> He was baby tuckoo.... (3)

The sentences that open *A Portrait* sound like the song of innocence of a child who renders his childlike consciousness when language flows as naturally and spontaneously as a river. The time spoken of belongs to, what Kershner describes as, following Bakhtinian terminology, "...'absolute past', the infinitely distant time of earliest narrative. There is no separation between this narrative event and Stephen himself: 'He was baby tuckoo'..." (155). The fairy tale resonance gives way to Stephen's appropriation of terms in a song that he sings and asserts it as "...his song". The narrative goes on representing the intrusion of the outside artistic rhythms to which he dances and his exposure to the sharp divide between Protestantism and Catholicism that invades his consciousness. He appears to recollect the dictates of his mother and Dante, a member of his extended family, not to mix with the Protestant Eileen and he has to "apologise" for his intimacy with her. The expository beginning of the novel shows his exposure to the divisive political world dominated by two hostile leaders, one is Michael Davitt and the other being Charles Stuart Parnell. Stephen's awakening sense organs give him an access to the labyrinth of the world he is posited in.

The unusual opening of the novel rendered in what Burgess calls "opaque" language which is, in his words, "self-referring", in contrast to the "transparent" language used by most of the conventional novelists (16), proclaims Joyce's modernism. It is the opacity of his linguistic exploitation that makes Joyce's texts open to inexhaustible investigations by readers and critics. Joyce intentionally builds dented discourses in his short stories as well as novels to make readers active participants in his fictional world that defies a straightforward and conclusive interpretation.

The narrative proceeds showing Stephen grappling with an alien vocabulary when he is in the boarding of Clongowes Wood College, an elite Jesuit school at the age of six. In the wide playgrounds, his fragile body compels him to keep on the "fringe of his line...out of the reach of the rude feet". His physical weakness appears to sharpen his cognitive skills in listening to words and applying them to other contexts. He is capable of perceiving the new world he is placed in and assessing his fellows by applying discriminatory epithets to them: "Rody Kickham was a decent fellow but Nasty Roche was a stink" (4). He is exposed to the slang usage of a simple word like "belt" and asked by his father "...never to peach on a fellow" (5-6). Joyce tries to capture his protagonist's intellectual and emotional growth through his acute sensibility of language. He imparts immediacy to Stephen's perceptive abilities by using sentences and fragmented assertions that appear to be unmediated. The insertion of punctuations like exclamation and interrogation marks makes us feel as if we hear Stephen speaking his intimate thoughts to us: "Nice mother!... She was a nice mother but she was not so nice when she cried" (5). Incremental repetition marks the discourses of Stephen as his narrated monologues follow a chain of association leading him from one recollected incident to another. The memory of one of his boarding mates, Wells, who shouldered him into the square ditch recurs in the opening chapter eliciting from him the exclamatory assertion: "...how cold and slimy the water had been!" (11). He goes on spinning words and contextualizing them manifold and discovering affinities between unlike things. When he feels himself inferior to the big boys, he regretfully asks himself: "When would he be like the fellows in poetry and rhetoric?" He finds out the answer:

> That was very far away. First came the vacation and then the next term and then vacation again and then again another term and then again vacation. It was like a train going in and out of tunnels and that was like the noise of the boys eating in the refectory when you opened and closed the flaps of the ears. Term, vacation; tunnel, out; noise, stop. How far away it was! (14)

Thus Stephen grapples with the wide world with the aid of language that lulls him with sound and sense enabling him to develop his own discourses at the close of the novel. Even words devoid of denotation enact their sense on his growing consciousness—"the sound of the cricket bats: pick, pack, pock, puck" create the soothing effect like "drops of water in a fountain falling softly in the brimming bowl" (61). The use of this image indicates the overflowing happiness that fills his aggrieved mind at the end of the opening chapter when he succeeds in redressing his grievances by reporting to the Rector against Father Dolan for unjustly pandying him for not writing as his spectacles were broken. This is the first occasion in the opening section when Stephen emerges as an active participant to register his vehement protest against injustice. It seems he has moved to the centre stage from his usual position on the fringe. He becomes a performer from a passive onlooker and this incident prepares us for his eventual rebellion against all institutions of his country. The language rendering his victory and its aftermath betrays a qualitative difference from the childlike monologues that dominate the second section of the first chapter. It captures his intellectual, spiritual and linguistic growth at the same time as he takes the vow not to show his pride to Father Dolan for whom he "wished he could do something kind..." (61).

Joyce's objectivity is most pronounced in linguistically capturing the intensity of Stephen's sensation of acute physical pain when he is beaten mercilessly by Father Dolan by withholding any comments on the atrocity perpetrated on a too young boy like Stephen:

> A hot burning stinging tingling blow like the loud crack of a broken stick made his trembling hand crumple together like a leaf in the fire and at the sound and the pain scalding tears were driven into his eyes. His whole body was shaking with fright, his arm was shaking and his crumpled burning livid hand shook like a loose leaf in the air. A cry sprang to his lips, a prayer to be let off. But though the tears scalded his eyes and his limbs quivered with pain and fright he held back the hot tears and the cry that scalded his throat. (51)

Burgess highly acclaims Joyce's impersonality in transmitting through language the severity of the merciless assault made by one in the religious hierarchy and his observation is cited below:

> ...one ought to observe that much of the excruciating effect springs from objectivity, from an unwillingness to allow the author's own indignation to intrude. Then there is the elemental simplicity of the vocabulary, which emphasizes the elemental shock of pain. There is no finicking attempt to vary the words used: 'scald' appears three times, an apt word worthy to be repeated, since it combines the elements of fire and water. Stephen's passivity is pointed by the two references to his hand as a leaf—once in the fire, once in the third element, air.... The passivity is present in his tears: he does not cry...the tears are 'driven into his eyes'...the cry springs to his lips. (66-67)

The cited sentences from the text that draw such effusive comments from Burgess show Joyce's narrative art of foregrounding the young Stephen's agony by using passive constructions and mundane images to add to the impact of the scene. His repetition of words betrays his attitude despite his utmost objectivity in narrating such an inhuman act performed by a Father entrusted with the noble duty of supervising studies. This episode leaves a lingering impression on the developing consciousness of Stephen whose disillusionment with a Jesuit Institute along with the bitter experience at home during the Christmas dinner paves the way for his ultimate decision to renounce religion.

The Christmas dinner episode that opens the third part of the opening chapter is remarkable both for its thematic impact on the budding artist and also for the changed narrative technique that Joyce adopts to represent it. The monologic perceptions of Stephen rendered through his free indirect discourses give way to a dramatized narration with minimal narration. Stephen is exposed to the heated debate that shows him the wide division among his family members. The discussion veers from the topic of the Church's meddling in politics to the theme of betrayal of Parnell by the Church and his countrymen. He discovers his father Simon Dedalus and Mr. Casey condemning the priests for Parnell's downfall and premature death and Dante calling Parnell "a public sinner"

(31). Stephen hears the indecent language that his father uses against the votaries of the Church calling them "Sons of bitches!" and "Lowlived dogs..." (33). Though the conflicting religious persuasions leave Stephen momentarily confused to think who is right—his father or Dante, who is some sort of a surrogate mother to him, the preceding section represents a vision of the corpse of Parnell that Stephen sees in his sickbed. He discovers himself wailing with the mourning crowd when his dead body is brought aboard a ship. Joyce seems to highlight the impact of the betrayal of a patriotic leader who fought for Ireland's independence from the shackle of the British dominion on the formative phase of his protagonist. This incident along with many others has a strong autobiographical ring and the motif of betrayal that characterizes Joyce's *Dubliners* in his short stories is woven into the narrative fabric of *A Portrait* as well.

The four sections of the opening chapter show in microcosm the narrative strategies to be deployed in the other parts of the novel and also signal the evolutionary trend of the language to be manipulated in the chapters that follow.

The lyrical repetition of words and phrases that marks the close of the first chapter referred to earlier in my discussion hints at the growth of artistic sensibilities in Stephen who suddenly renders the soothing sight, smell and sound he experiences in a different language.

The second chapter is rendered in a much more mature language than the preceding one. Complex syntactic structures mark the discourses emanating mostly from Stephen's consciousness. The poetic close of the opening chapter stands in sharp contrast to the down-to-earth reference to the "black twist", annotated by Seamus Deane, the editor of *A Portrait of the Artist as a Young Man*, as "tobacco twisted in a chord" (290). Joyce makes use of double temporal perspectives in both the versions of the novel. This is what Requelme observes in this connection:

> In both *Stephen Hero* and *A Portrait*, Stephen alternates between allegiances to the visionary and to the material, between internal fantasy and external reality.... In

> *Stephen Hero* Joyce portrays Stephen as both ruthlessly analytical and visionary.... In *A Portrait*, by contrast, Joyce presents the two perspectives of realism and fantasy not primarily as aspects of character but fundamentally as aspects of style.... The realistic and visionary components become much more complexly intertwined than in *Stephen Hero*, for they begin to become elements in a style that emphasizes memory. (104-05)

Stephen's life in his home at Blackrock is realistically described and we hear a coherent account of Uncle Charles who, we are told, is his "constant companion" (62). He visits the park, accompanied by Uncle Charles, and meets an old friend of his father. His assessment of the person surprises us as it is couched in a much more mature discourse which markedly differs from the spontaneous flow of the streams of thought that come out of his childlike consciousness. This is how he evaluates Mike Flynn who supervises Stephen's run:

> Though he had heard his father say that Mike Flynn had put some of the best runners of modern times through his hands Stephen often glanced with mistrust at his trainer's flabby stublecovered face, as it bent over the long stained fingers through he rolled his cigarette, and with pity at the mild lusterless blue eyes which would look up suddenly from the task and gaze vaguely into the distance while the long swollen fingers ceased their rolling and grains and fibres of tobacco fell back into the pouch. (63)

The winding sentence with its complicated structuring realistically renders Stephen's close observation of his trainer. We see him through Stephen's eyes, but the speaker appears to be somebody other than Stephen as the words 'often', 'mistrust' and 'pity' indicate. In the opening chapter, the discourses almost always appear to emanate from Stephen's consciousness without the mediation of the narrator, excepting, of course, the Christmas dinner episode and the narrated dialogues. His intimate and informal rendering of the world he is exposed to through a chain of words that depict how his elemental senses are awakened in him imparts immediacy to his perceptions in the first chapter. But the narrative technique employed in the second chapter focuses on his growth represented through the formal construction of his utterances that capture a wider contour of his consciousness. His vocabulary now embraces abstractions replacing the concrete sensations of seeing, smelling, hearing, touching and feeling raw emotions.

Burgess traces the abstractions in his developing consciousness to his reading nineteenth century fiction. This is corroborated by what we are told about Stephen's literary interest in poring over a "ragged translation" of Alexandre Dumas's *The Count of Monte Cristo*, published in 1844. The story has such a deep impact on his evolving consciousness that it gives rise to a longing for love in his adolescent mind. The narrative alternates now between his visionary impulses that the tale of adventure evokes in him and the harsh realities that bite him when he vaguely understands the financial constraints that his father faces leading to some changes in his house. The contrary impulses are thus juxtaposed: "...these changes in what he had deemed unchangeable were so many slight shocks to his boyish conception of the world. The ambition which he felt astir at times in the darkness of his soul sought no outlet. A dusk like that of the outer world obscured his mind...." But the world of imagination gains transcendence over that of reality when the image of Mercedes, the beloved of Edmond Dantes in *The Count of Monte Cristo*, possesses his mind making him feel a "strange unrest". Like the adolescent boy in "Araby", he feels he is "different from others" and prefers brooding over the "unsubstantial image" to playing with children. The first section of the second chapter comes to a close showing Stephen once again in a visionary mood nurturing the conviction, termed by the speaker "a premonition", that this image would "encounter him" in reality and, as a result "...he would be transfigured" (67).

But the second section opens on a starkly realistic tone echoing the noise that the dismantling of their residence creates by rendering in detail how two caravans halt before their house with men "tramping into the house" and how the furniture is "hustled out" and Stephen sees them move "lumbering heavily..." (68). Here, as in the opening chapter, sounds enact sense, but in a different way. It is not the surprise of discovering music in sounds, but they hint at the bitterness and heaviness that the change of residence creates on the still adolescent Stephen. Joyce's own experience of frequent change of house in his youth, like many other details of the novel, lends to the description an authentic touch. Chunks of his own experience have been used, to such an extent, to portray Stephen that it becomes difficult to read Joyce's attitude to his fictitious self. However, Stephen's mood of "embittered silence" lingers in his mind and he is able to trace the causes as we hear him confessing that

> He was angry with himself for being young and the prey of foolish impulses, angry also with the change of fortune which was reshaping the world about him into a vision of squalor and insincerity. Yet his anger lent nothing to his vision. He chronicled with patience what he saw, detaching himself from it and tasting its mortifying flavour in secret. (69-70)

This introspection that enables Stephen to study himself more precisely than before betrays his comparative maturity by making him give up momentarily his vagueness in his resort to abstractions in his terminology. The mode of his chronicling his experience appears to mimic his author's portraiture of himself. But the juxtaposition of the contrastive impulses here shows us Stephen's character no less than Joyce's style of representation of the dual mode. Hence we cannot wholly accept Requelme's reductive assessment of the dual perspectives propelling Stephen throughout the narrative to aspects of style only. This is not to refute what Requelme establishes in his seminal discussion on the "Oscillations in Style and Narrative" in *A Portrait*, which certainly helps us to find a definite direction in the labyrinth of Joyce's text, but to add a minor point. What appears striking in the second chapter is that the language does not always emanate unmediated from the consciousness of Stephen, as in most of the sections of the opening chapter, and the presence of another voice is often felt in the structuring of his thoughts.

Stephen's restless mind is soothed when he notices Emma Clery (who is not named) fixing her glance at him "...flattering, taunting, searching, exciting his heart". What surprises us is Joyce's anonymous introduction of Stephen's visionary image whom we have already met in *Stephen Hero*. The earlier Stephen's irresistible physical attraction for Emma is narrated in detail in *Stephen Hero*. But the tranquil and cautious response of Stephen in *A Portrait* is a clear indicator that Joyce wants to project his protagonist as much more mature than his earlier self. Purged of the raw emotions, Stephen does not succumb to her flirting language conveyed through her eyes viewing her not as an individual but as a representative figure of the women. It seems he subscribes to what Shakespeare says in *Hamlet* "Frailty, thy name is woman". A voice within him warns him and he disappoints her by not holding her hands when she comes to his step on the tram. Instead of pursuing her madly, like the Stephen of *Stephen Hero,* with the proposal to spend a night of lovemaking with him, the refined and restrained Stephen is seen standing "...listlessly in his place, seemingly a tranquil watcher of the scene before him" (73). Peake aptly sums up the conflict and struggle in the later Stephen "between the natural human desire and the strange withdrawal of his temperament" (87). The detachment that Stephen appears to attain is practiced by him in his calculated indifference to the physical charm exuded by Emma who gets abbreviated in the verse titled "To E—C". The verse seems to embody the stylistic strategy that Joyce exploits in drawing the portrait of the artist in the making by deleting many episodes and experiences culled from Joyce's own life in the fragmented version and reshaping and refining them to recreate Stephen in *A Portrait*. Though the poem is not mentioned, the content that he sieves from his experience of the encounter with Emma is recorded by him in the following sentences:

> During this process all these elements which he deemed common and insignificant fell out of the scene. There remained no trace of the tram itself...nor did he or she

> appear vividly. The verses told only of the night and the balmy breeze and the maiden luster of the moon. Some undefined sorrow was hidden in the hearts of the protagonists.... (74)

It appears to be an amalgam of modernism and romanticism that Stephen tries to make in the sketchy literary output penned by the budding artist. But the apparent detachment gives way to 'stasis' much later in the narrative when he appears to be purged of kinetic emotions and tells Lynch, one of his few friends, about his aesthetic theory focusing on the dictum of impersonality of the artist cited above. He quotes profusely from Aquinas and many other great minds of antiquity and also refers to Shelley's *Defense of Poesy*. Stephen goes to the extent of pointing out the incompletion in Aristotle's *Poetics*. The abundance of allusive references confuses us to discover who his real model is. We may extend the contrary textual rendering in each chapter to the formulation of his aesthetic theory which also betrays the assimilation of classical tenets, imperatives of modernism and romantic inclinations he cannot shed. Seamus Deane also contends in this connection in his notes on the text of *A Portrait* that "Stephen's theory is a conflation of various ideas and is not at all closely modeled on Aquinas..." (319). The novel poses innumerable stumbling blocks to make a proper assessment of Stephen and, by extension, of Joyce's attitude to his young artist who shares so much of his creator that it becomes difficult to differentiate their point of view.

As Stephen goes on registering, to use Deane's perceptive phrase, "the myriad subtle sensations" (xxvii), throughout the narrative, the cult of impersonality he propounds appears to be somewhat contradictory. It seems likely that Joyce makes his protagonist undergo diverse phases of his experiences which have an orienting pattern for growth from kinesis to stasis. His attitude to Emma for whom he writes a villanelle, a nineteen line poem, after a gap of ten years shows rapid fluctuations in his mood. He ecstatically discovers that in the "virgin womb of imagination the word was made flesh" enabling him to compose the poem (236). But "rude brutal anger routed the last lingering instant of ecstasy from his soul" (239) after a while. He feels angry with her and jealous of the "priested peasant" she has chosen as her paramour, though he is aware that his anger is homage to her perennial physical attraction. She is "the temptress of his villanelle" of whose dark eyes he writes in it "Your eyes have set men's heart ablaze". Emma's rejection of Stephen, who claims himself to be "a priest of eternal imagination, transmuting the daily bread of experience into the radiant body of everlasting life" (240) fills his mind with rancour. But the mood of bitterness gives way to a feeling of repentance in him for his unjust treatment of her as shortly "he began to feel that he had wronged her. A sense of her innocence moved him almost to pity her...and a tender compassion filled his heart as he remembered her frail pallor and her eyes..." (241-42). Stephen emerges as a memoirist in *A Portrait* culling from his memory his first meeting with her and then the night he was on the tram with Emma, referred to above. Memory provides a thread to unify the discontinuous narrative to depict the curve of his emotive growth.

It is Stephen's strong aural sense that hones his artistic sensibilities by his exploration of the vast realms of literature and philosophy. It comes to his aid in detecting ultimately the utter hollowness characterizing the religious discourses he is exposed to in the third chapter of *A Portrait*. He gets momentarily shaken, particularly remembering his close encounter with a prostitute which convinces him that he is steeped in sins. He confesses of his guilt and practises a masochistic regime to purify himself. He is assailed by a host of voices from his parents, from religious fathers and friends who compete to draw allegiance from him to his family, to the Church and to the country. He even gets an offer of priesthood. His protracted dilemma and confusion get resolved by the sight of a wading bird-girl working on his sensitive mind as an 'Epiphany', a sudden spiritual realization, that dispels the cloud of indecision as to his choice of vocation. To him, the girl "seemed like one whom magic had changed into the likeness of a strange and beautiful sea-bird" (185). Joyce depicts the impact of her image on Stephen's soul which had already "...arisen from the grave of boyhood, spurning her graveclothes" (184): "Her image had passed into his soul for ever and no word had broken the holy silence of his ecstasy. Her eyes had called him and his soul had leaped at the call. To live, to err, to fall, to triumph, to recreate life out of life!" (186).

The word 'Epiphany', explained in detail in *Stephen Hero*, is not used by the mature Stephen, but we discover the operation of this concept in Joyce's early work, though the Stephen of *Ulysses* mocks at his earlier belief in it. Even his own name with the mythical association of Daedalus and his son Icarus "seemed to him a prophecy.... Now, at the name of the fabulous artificer [Daedalus], he seemed to hear the noise of dim waves and to see a winged form flying above the waves and slowly climbing the air" (183). The epigraph of *A Portrait* is taken from Ovid's *Metamorphoses* (VIII: 188), denoting the Daedalian theme. Gifford annotates it in the following words: "And he sets his mind to work upon unknown arts". It alludes to "Daedalus's creation of wings for his (and his son Icarus's) escape from the Cretan Labyrinth and from Crete. Daedalus in Greek means 'cunning artificer', and in Greek mythology Daedalus is the archetypical personification of the inventor-sculptor-architect" (130-31). Ovid's story appears to provide the overall structural rhythm of *A Portrait.*

The concluding chapter represents the motif of flight through repetitive references to the flight of birds giving rise to a "soft liquid joy" in his mind (245). He discovers an affinity between the soft long vowels in words and the "wheeling darting birds" and feels "the augury he had sought...had come forth from his heart like a bird from a turret quietly and swiftly" (245). The language of the second section of the closing chapter appears to echo, according to Gifford, the poeticized prose of Pater, referred to earlier in my discussion, and the influence of his aesthetic philosophy.

The diary entries that constitute the closing part of Chapter V usher in a remarkable change in the narrative style which switches from the third person mode to the first person. It seems Joyce implies by this discoursal change that

Stephen's evolving consciousness has reached some sort of consummation in his ability to free himself from the shackles of the pronominal 'he' and the past tense in which his free indirect discourses are couched by an invisible presence. Besides, we can now trace Stephen's progression temporally as he has to record dates conforming to the mode of diary writing. The primary rationale of ending the novel in a deviant way appears to allow Stephen the unfettered freedom, he has been craving for long, to have a private space to give vent to his own thoughts without the imperatives of quoting borrowed ideas and using others' styles and vocabulary that characterize the rest of the narrative.

We construct the character and his style in a new perspective from his private renderings. We discover him assessing his friend Cranly who "attacked me on the score of love for one's mother. Tried to imagine his mother: cannot" (270). The reference to Emma recurs in the diary entries. He even talks to her, though in the narrative he is hardly found speaking to her. He even confirms, to our surprise, "Yes, I liked her today. A little or much? Don't know. I liked her and it seems a new feeling to me". The lucidity of his confession invests his elusive mind with a new realization. Even his mother who has a skeletal appearance in *A Portrait*, compared to her dominant role in *Stephen Hero*, is referred to twice in his diary on 24 March and 26 April. It seems the hostility, as narrated in the earlier part of the novel, arising from his avowal of loss of faith in the Catholic tenets has been resolved as the recordings exude a warmth as we hear "Mother is putting my secondhand clothes in order. She prays now...that I may learn in my own life and away from home and friends what the heart is and what it feels" (275). As in the preceding sections, the mundane details are juxtaposed with philosophical discourses and abstract thoughts: "The past is consumed in the present and the present is living only because it brings forth the future..." (273). Thus formal and informal thoughts are placed in the records with profuse allusive references. He again seems to hear voices, but they come from alien lands claiming them to be his "kinsmen" exhorting him to get ready for his flight. It is followed by his recording of his mother's stitching the secondhand clothes. The realistic reference is enveloped by his exultant assertions: "Welcome, O life! I go to encounter for the millionth time the reality of experience and to forge in the smithy of my soul the uncreated conscience of my race" (275-76). His referring to the Irish as "my race" is a remarkable shift in his stand as he does not support the nationalistic fervour of Maccan in *Stephen Hero* and Davin in *A Portrait.* The narrative comes to a close with an invocation to "Old father, old artificer, stand me now and ever in good stead" (276). Deane perceptively annotates the closing line thus: "Stephen, as ever, is harping on the father—in this case, Daedalus. He is both an Icarus asking for support...and an Icarus asking that Daedalus stands in his place—i.e. that the son will become like the father and survive to create his own labyrinth (*Ulysses*, *Finnegans Wake*)" (329). The narrative of *A Portrait* thus acquires cosmic dimensions by encompassing the biological father's imaginative rendering of a tale and the invocation to the spiritual father to empower him "to give the word to future humanity" (Parrinder, 88). He appears to be liberated from the nets of country, religion and language, but we find Joyce getting more and more entwined with the labyrinth of his language, city and religion as he proceeds in his literary journey after *A Portrait of the Artist as a Young Man.*

WORKS CITED

Attridge, Derek. *The Cambridge Companion to James Joyce.* Cambridge: Cambridge University Press, 1990.

Burgess, Anthony. *Joysprick*. London: Andre Dentch, 1973.

Ellmann, Richard, Ed. *The Letters of James Joyce*. Volume 2. New York: The Viking Press, 1966.

Gifford, Don. *Joyce Annotated.* California: University of California Press, 1982.

Joyce, James. *A Portrait of the Artist as a Young Man*. Ed. Seamus Deane. London: Penguin, 1992.

Kershner, R.B. Joyce. *Bakhtin and Popular Lit Chronicles of Disorder*. Chapel Hill: The University of North Carolina Press, 1989.

Parrinder, Patrick. *A Portrait of the Artist* Ed. Mark A. Wollaeger. Casebook. Oxford: Oxford University Press, 2003.

Peake, C.H. *James Joyce: The Citizen and the Artist*. London: Edward Arnold (Publishers) Ltd., 1977.

Riquelme, John Paul. "*Stephen Hero, Dubliners*, and *A Portrait of the Artist as a Young Man*: Styles of Realism and Fantasy". *The Cambridge Companion to James Joyce*. Ed. Derek Attridge. Cambridge: Cambridge University Press, 1990.

11

Labyrinths of Human Psyche: Text and Sub-Text: Psychoanalytical Study of Manju Kapur's *Difficult Daughters*

Sandhya Saxena

During the past few decades, female question is being empathically and persistently raised by Indian writers writing in English. A host of our Indo-Anglian novelists—especially our women writers have undertaken the task of presenting the thought process, emotions, reflections, actions and reactions of their female characters. With more women writers emerging at the forefront, the women question is much more widely discussed. However, its form is gradually changing. The shift is from feminist approach to 'women studies' through which the lives and character of women are studied in a broader perspective.

The purpose of the present study is not to highlight the shifting paradigms of female question, the focal point; here, is a psychoanalytical study of a character called Virmati in Manju Kapur's *Difficult Daughters*. The novel "is the story of a woman torn between family duty, the desire of education and illicit love. Virmati, a young woman born in Amritsar into an austere and high minded household, falls in love with a neighbour—the Professor—a man who is already married. That the professor eventually marries Virmati, installs her in his home (alongside his furious first wife) and helps her towards further studies in Lahore, is small consolation to her scandalized family or even to Virmati, who finds that the battle for her own independence has created irrevocable lines of partition and pain around her" (Cover page of the novel). This apparent simplicity of the narrative, when studied in the light of psychoanalysis, submits to unmark the layers of human mind providing a deeper inner reality around which a sub-text could be woven. Psychoanalytical criticism can study a text in four different ways, depending on its object of attention. The focal point of the study may be the author; the content; formal constitution and the reader. The present venture is centered on the psychoanalysis of 'content' touching, alongside, the peripheries of the psychoanalysis of the 'reader', weaving thereby a sub-text. The psychoanalysis of 'content' facilitates the reader with a deeper probe into the psychoanalytical significance of objects or events in the text as well as into the unconscious motivations of characters.

Psychoanalytical criticism is grounded into the idea that the repression of the 'pleasure principle' by the 'reality principle' is the fundamental cause of human misery as it thrusts—*id ego* and *super ego* into a state of conflict. Sigmund Freud is to be credited for presenting the first comprehensive theory of personality. For Freud, personality is a three-tier structure founded upon *id ego* and *super ego*. "Id is the contact point between the psychic structure and the instinctual energy emanating from the body. It is the storehouse of psychic-energy"[1] and "a cauldron full of seething excitations."[2] Operated by the 'pleasure principle', Id always instigates the gratification of instinctual urges, entirely disregarding the objective reality that an organism is bound to accept in the external world. Ego, on the contrary, is guided by the 'reality principle'. "By exercising the 'function of reality testing' it regulates the satisfaction of instincts so that the organism is not harmed. The mode of its operation is termed 'secondary process' (thinking in realistic terms) and all higher mental functions are placed at its service";[3] Super ego can be interpreted as "an internalised version of the ideals and moral expectations of society."[4] In Freud's own words super ego is "the representative of every moral restriction, the advocate of striving towards perfection".[5] Super ego is always at war with the demands of id, and hence, it continuously hampers the gratification of instinctual urges. Broadly interpreting, these three tiers of personality—*id ego* and *super ego*—may be "treated as representatives respectively of the body, mind and society in the psychic structure of man".[6]

The consequent possibilities of the ever-going conflict between *id* and *super ego* are: either tension may be reduced through gratification of urges, or the rejection of instinctual urges may cause frustration. In both the conditions, one voice is unheard. In the first state super ego is neglected and in the second one, id's demands are left unnoticed, hence, the tension persists. The function of ego, similar to that of human mind, is to establish a balance between the demands of these two entities.

New dimensions may be explored on studying Virmati's character in the context of this persistent conflict. Virmati's ego is strained to maintain a balance between the claims of her id representing her desire to marry the professor and thus continuing a socially unacceptable relationship and her super ego which restrains her at every step from surrendering to her passion. Virmati's example is an intricate one. Her desire for education—which is a noble virtue, traditionally an appropriate representation of super ego—turns to be another version of id which is otherwise 'a cauldron of seething excitations'. This desire for education brings her in close communion with the Professor, facilitating her with the situation that paves the way for illicit love. Who knows if her desire for education is but an escape from the burdensome domestic duties that she is bound to perform because of numberless pregnancies of her mother? However, her hunt for education prepares a ground for Virmati's war with the society, and the war is not to attain education but to obtain her socially unacceptable love. The sociologically-oriented interpretations which Freud started brooding upon in his later life are equally applicable to Virmati life. "He began to treat cultural, religious and philosophical questions from the psychoanalytical standpoint."[7] Human beings are perpetually in search of pleasure and they long for the absence of misery. This "programme of the pleasure principle"[8] determines the purpose of life. However, the civilization, which is an agency to interpret the regulations of the universe, runs counter to it. Man is compelled to struggle furiously at three levels; against his body, the external world and human relationships. The last of these three throws man into the most difficult situation. The natural reaction to these encounters may be into two directions—either a man may create an alternate delusional world where the ugly and unpleasant features of reality find no place or he may get a qualified satisfaction by surrendering his passion into a voluntary isolation.

> One way in which we cope with desires we cannot fulfill is by 'Sublimating' them, by which Freud means directing them towards a more socially valued end. We might find an unconscious outlet for sexual frustration in building bridges or cathedrals. For Freud, it is by virtue of such sublimation that civilization itself comes about: by switching and harnessing our instincts to these higher goals, cultural history itself is created.[9]

Virmati, too, attempts to sublimate her unfulfilled desire through a higher ideal beyond love—dedicating herself to the goal of uplifting the simple girls of Pratibha Kanya Vidhyalaya at Nahan. By that time, she had undergone diverse experiences under the influence of Shakuntala and Swarnlata at Lahore. However, her appetite for education and yearning to serve the nation "melted into nothingness" as soon as love overpowered her. She wrote to Harish from Nahan: "If he couldn't make up his mind to marry her then she might as well devote herself seriously to her career".[10] It is evident that career is her second choice now—only an effort to 'Sublimate' her passion. In Virmati's life Freud's idea of the reality principle repressing the pleasure principle is turned upside down. Virmati's hunt for education thrusts her into the traps of illicit love but her inner self is in conflict with the external world. The society refuses her to marry the man who is already wedded to someone else.

Human relationships represented by the family also stand against her illegitimate relationship constantly imposing upon her the pressure to sever her ties with the professor. Yet Virmati marries Harish under the sway of emotion without reflecting over the consequences of an illegitimate relationship —repressing reality principle by the pleasure principle—and encounters conflicting state no less tortuous than that which one suffers *vice versa*. Very soon, she finds herself helplessly dislocated and disconnected. The severity of her isolation could be realized when her father died; Virmati felt "Like pariah on the outskirts of her family circle" and "she longed to break down and weep in the midst of the circle that surrounded her mother. She wanted to be in its warm inclusiveness as well."[11]

Virmati could never be assimilated into Harish's family, nor could she herself develop a living relationship with them. It was difficult for her to spend her holidays with Harish's family; "I feel so utterly left out", she sighs, "so utterly cold. Will there be any change in my life I wonder?"[12]

She went home reluctantly and when the time to return to Lahore after summer holidays approached, she felt "secretly relieved".[13] She could never be a part of the family. The hostile gaze of Ganga (Harish's first wife) and Kishori Devi (Harish's mother), silent disapproval of Gudiya (his sister) and Chhotti (his daughter), the pricking murmurs of Giridhar (his son) about this 'gandi (wicked) lady' on the day of their marriage made her feel guilty. She conveyed her feelings to Harish;

> I should never have married you, she said slowly, and it's too late now. I have never seen it so clearly. It's not fair.[14]

Moreover, she suffered the pangs of conscience, cried and sighed and repented over her wrongdoing; "God was speaking. He was punishing her for the first time. May be she could never have children. She had robbed her own womb three years earlier, just as she had robbed another woman of her husband."[15]

These outpourings of Virmati's heart are the expressions of what super ego is meant for. The tortures that Virmati endured in her social life, her isolation in the family of Harish and her dispossession by her own family, despite "all those years of care, concern, sacrifice and responsibility"[16] when she thought of nothing except bearing Kasturi's children, evince that her marriage with Harish could never get a social sanction because she robbed another women of her conjugal rights. Man's psychic structure is such as does not let him escape from suffering. Man suffers when the 'pleasure principle' is overlooked and he equally suffers at the hands of the society and civilization if 'reality principle' is overthrown. Virmati's strife exemplifies the failure of the 'pleasure principle' when 'reality principle' is neglected. Her ego struggles perpetually to establish a balance between both. Jaques Lancan's theory, reinterpreting Freudianism in terms of language, a pre-eminent social activity, explores the relations between the unconscious and human society. He establishes that unconscious is not something tumultuous within us, it's rather an effect of our relations in the society. "The unconscious is, so to speak, 'outside' rather than 'within' us—or rather it exists 'between' us as our relationships do. It is elusive not so much because it is buried deep within our minds, but because it is a kind of vast, tangled network which surrounds us and weaves itself through us, and which can therefore never be pinned down."[17] Language is the best image for such a vast network. When one enters the symbolic order of human psyche, he enters the language itself yet this 'language' for Lancan, as well as for the structuralists, is an entity beyond individual's control. An individual can, by no means, entirely dominate or subdue language, as one shall never be able to reject the dominant role that our parents perform in our constitution. Language, the unconscious, the parents, the symbolic order are, in Lancanian theory, intimately allied, though not synonymous. Sometimes Lancan speaks of them as 'Other'. For Lancan our unconscious desire is directed towards this 'Other' in the form of some ultimately gratifying reality to attain which is almost impossible, on the other hand our desires are, in the same way, received from the 'Other' too.

The desire is the result of our being, caught into linguistic, sexual and social relation. The psychoanalytic criticism studies the desire in terms of language and thereby constructs a 'subtext' for the work. Interpreting Lancan, we can hold that "a novel does not exactly say what it means or mean what it exactly says."[18] All the literary works contain one or more subtexts. "The work's insights, as with all writing, are deeply related to its blindnesses; what it does not say and how it does not say it, may be as important as what it articulates; what seems absent, marginal or ambivalent about it may provide a central clue to its meanings."[19]

The narrative, in *Difficult Daughters,* yields to the subtext, when studied with probing analytical approach. What could have been the picture of Virmati's life had her adolescent yearnings not been thwarted by the yoke of responsibilities and domestic duties which she had to bear because of her mother's numberless pregnancies? The question can be studied in the light of the conversation that took place between Virmati and Kasturi during their short stay in the mountain regions where Kasturi was taken for recovery:

> What is all this nonsense? In Amritsar you were bad-tempered because you were busy and tired, here you are bad-tempered because you are idle, retorted Kasturi. 'May be I should go back to Amritsar, Pitaji can take me the next time he comes'. The language of feeling had never (lowed between them, and this threat was meant to express all her thwarted yearnings.
>
> 'May be you should' said Kasturi crossly. Why was her daughter so restless all the time? In a girl, that spelt disaster.[20]

The conflict between mother and daughter is the result of the repression of pleasure principle which manifests itself here, in the form of Virmati's 'thwarted adolescent yearnings' which, later, led to another 'disaster' that Kasturi had already smelt. The 'disaster' that appeared in the life of Virmati in the form of her illicit love for Harish may also be interpreted in terms of Harish's estrangement from his first wife Ganga. Harish's infatuation for Virmati is not exclusively responsible for his withdrawal from Ganga. In one of his letters he reveals to Virmati the causes of his retreat from his wife:

> Then, Vir, consider, what is it that takes me away from the woman I live with?... She is a good woman, runs the house to perfection.... Despite all this, I am lonely, lonely, lonely. We have nothing in common.... Who is responsible for this state of affairs? Society, which deems that their sons should be educated but not their daughters, society that decides that children-babies really should be married at the age of two and three as we were. As a result both of us needlessly suffer for no fault of ours.[21]

The simple narrative gives bent to some relevant questions which, if probed through the layers of secondary revision, would expose something of the sub-text which, like an unconscious wish, the work both conceals and reveals. Virmati's resentment and Harish's alienation from his marital life are the 'signifiers' that provide a sub-text. Had Ganga been an educated woman Harish's life would have been different. Unfortunately, Ganga is not a suitable companion for him and consequently, havoc is caused in the lives of Harish, Ganga and Virmati. Had Virmati lived a normal childhood and adolescence she would not have sought shelter into the sort of love that society does not approve of. It is because of her insatiate soul that she was infatuated with the scholarly professor, and finally, fell into the pit of illicit love. Hence, the secondary revision of the text opens the hidden possibilities.

As "the structure of literature is in some sense the structure of mind",[22] literature and psychoanalysis may be viewed as two very intimately related intellectual disciplines, Freud, himself, acknowledged, "poets and philosophers discovered the unconscious long before he did".[23] It is true about the novelists also as the function of a novelist is to provide a very subtle study of the intricate human emotions and passions. A profound probe into the character of Virmati reveals a fresh perspective. Her defiance against the family and society can be studied in terms of the 'repression of the pleasure principle' and also in terms of 'structural unconscious' composed of signifiers.

NOTES

1. Rajeshwer, M., *Indian Women Novelists and Psychoanalysis*, Atlantic Publishers & Distributers, New Delhi, 1998, p. 2.
2. Freud, Sigmund, *New Introductory Lectures on Psychoanalysis*, trans. James Strachey, Harmondsworth, Penguin, 1973, p. 106.
3. Rajeshwer, M., *Indian Women Novelists and Psychoanalysis*, p. 2.
4. *Ibid.*
5. Freud, Sigmund, *New Introductory Lectures on Psychoanalysis*, trans. James Strachey, p. 98.
6. Rajeshwer, M., *Indian Women Novelists and Psychoanalysis*, p. 2.
7. *Ibid.*, p. 3.
8. Freud, Sigmund, *Civilization and its Discontents*, Harmondsworth, Penguin, 1964, p. 163.
9. Eaglelon, Terry, *Literary Theory and Introduction*; Blackwell, Cambridge University, 1996, p. 152.
10. Kapur, Manju, *Difficult Daughters*; Penguin Books India (P) Ltd., 1998, p. 173.
11. *Ibid.*, p. 220.
12. *Ibid.*, p. 230.
13. *Ibid.*, p. 231.
14. *Ibid.*, p. 195.
15. *Ibid.*, p. 227.
16. *Ibid.*, p. 205.
17. Eaglelon, Terry, *Literary Theory and Introduction*, p. 173.
18. *Ibid.*, p. 177.
19. *Ibid.*, p. 178.
20. *Difficult Daughters*, p. 11.
21. *Ibid.*, pp. 94-95.
22. Brooks, Peter, "The Idea of a Psychoanalytic Literary Criticism", *Critical Inquiry*, 13.2, Winter, 1987, pp. 336-37.
23. Rajeshwer, M., *Indian Women Novelists and Psychoanalysis*, p. 101.

12

The Namesake and *Unaccustomed Earth*: A Study in Otherness and Transnational Identities

Ketaki Datta

'Otherness' is a feeling that springs from the lack of a sense of belonging. The feeling may also have its roots in the clash of culture and identity. Generally speaking, 'Otherness' is deeply embedded into the history of colonization. Tzvetan Todorov argues in his *The Conquest of America* that the conquest, colonization and destruction of the indigenous culture of the Americas set the pattern for much of the history of Western colonization thereafter. This was tied up with the creation of the 'Other', that is to say the creation of the social group, who are not 'I' or 'We' in the writings and discourses about the 'other' people in 'that' [therefore also other] place. As Todorov says 'Others' are also 'I's:

> Subjects just as I am, whom only my point of view—according to which all of them are out there and I alone am in here—separates and authentically distinguishes from myself I can conceive of these 'Others' as an abstraction, as an instance of my psychic configuration as the Other—other in relation to myself, to me: or else as a specific social group to which we do not belong. This group in turn can be interior to society, women for men, the rich for the poor, the mad for the normal or it can be exterior to society, i.e. another society which will

> be near or far away, depending on the case: beings whom everything links to me on the cultural, moral, historical plane or the outsiders whose language and customs I do not understand, so foreign that in extreme instances I am reluctant to admit that they belong to the same species as my own. (3)

Remarkably enough, we hardly come across such feeling of 'Otherness' in the short stories of Jhumpa Lahiri, which won her Pulitzer Prize in 2000. The alter ego I [a male] of the author in the story *The Third and The Final Continent* might have been a victim of this feeling but Mrs. Croft left no lacuna for him to get entangled in that. So, we fail to get a 'misfit' in the alien culture like the narrator of J.M. Coetzee's *Youth* or a bewildered Arun in Mrs. Pattern's household having interaction with a queer, foreign culture as in Anita Desai's *Fasting, Feasting*.

Jhumpa Lahiri's *The Namesake* (2004) has the fetishism of such 'otherness' throughout the novel. Ashoke Ganguli, a doctoral candidate in Electrical Engineering at M.I.T., marries Ashima of North Calcutta. Ashima is flown abroad to lead a different life, to give birth to a small baby boy whose christening awaits a name to be sent by her grandmother. But it never arrives as she is taken ill back in India and breathes her last consequently. He is named Gogol as Ashoke got a new lease of life after a hair-breadth escape from a devastating accident on his way to Jamshedpur, where his grandparents lived, with crinkled pages of Nikolai Gogol's *The Overcoat* in his clutch. Hence, the christening was instantaneous and emotion-ridden. Though Ashoke and Ashima build a shack together with the small baby boy at Pemberton Road, Boston, they look forward to the perennial warmth of their Bengali friends there. An extended Bengali family, as it were, to remain cocooned, to turn to for moral and emotional support, to be precise and fair. It was of course thrilling to "have enough old issues of the Globe stacked in the corners of the apartment to wrap all their plates and glasses and the whole year's of *Time* magazine to toss out" (51). Only because it was as if a dream come true to an Indian expatriate. Ashima and Ashoke have a full realization of the diasporic existence. Jhumpa writes without reservation, with her heart dangling on her sleeves blatantly, "For being a foreigner, Ashima is beginning to realize, is a sort of lifelong pregnancy, a perpetual wait, a constant burden, a continuous feeling out of sorts. It is an ongoing personality, a parenthesis, in what had once been ordinary life, only to discover that that previous life has vanished, replaced by something more complicated and demanding. Like pregnancy, being a foreigner, Ashima believes is something that elicits the same curiosity from strangers, the same combination of pity and respect" (50).

Ashima gives birth to a baby girl, Sonia. Both Gogol and Sonia grow up quite comfortably in the American ambience, surrounded by their hundred-and-one American pals. They talk in American accent, feel at home with frequent weekend parties, so-called American ways of life. Gogol had been taken on a school field-trip to a site of historical interest. It was when Gogol was in the sixth grade, only a boy of eleven years, they set off in their school bus to reach a cemetery. They were told not to draw the gravestones but to rub their surfaces. Here, for once, Gogol was struck with the feeling of being an 'outsider, an alien': "The children began to scamper between rows of the dead over leathery leaves, looking for their own names, a handful triumphant when are able to claim a grave they are related to, 'Smith' they holler, 'Collins', 'Wood'! Gogol is old enough to know that he himself will be burned, not buried, that his body will occupy no plot of earth that no stone in this country will bear his name beyond life" (68). On his return home, as he sits to narrate the day's experience to his mother, she muses to herself, "Only in America [a phrase she has begun to resort to often these days] are children taken to cemeteries in the name of art. What next, she demands to know, a trip to the morgue? In Calcutta, the burning ghats are the most forbidden of places, she tells Gogol" (70). A conflict of cultures comes to the fore as well as construing life with its sundry intricacies. According to Ashima, "Death is not a pastime, not a place to make paintings" (70).

America-born Gogol and Sonia become so attuned to the culture of the alien land that they are no less the Americans, shedding off their commitment to their own culture, the Indian culture. When they come to Calcutta to spend eight months on their father's sabbatical, they feel flaked out within a few days, cheesed off, to be frank and fair. Their parents, Ashoke and Ashima cry their hearts out to wave hands to their kith and kin in the aerodrome, while Gogol and Sonia feel relieved to get rid of this out-of-the-way, boring ambience. They heave sighs of relief to be back to their familiar surroundings, daily banters, usual norms, deportments and the brands of American commodities they are frantically accustomed to! Jhumpa in the sincerest manner etches, "After a single trip to supermarket, the refrigerator, the cupboards fill with familiar labels: Skippy, Hood, Bumble Bee, Land-o-Lakes. Gogol and Sonia sleep as long as they want, watch television, make themselves peanut-butter and jelly sandwiches, at any time of day. Once again they are free to quarrel, to tease each other, to shout and holler and say shut up. They call up their American friends who are happy enough to see them but ask them nothing about where they have been. And so the eight months are put behind them, quickly shed, quickly forgotten, like clothes worn for a special occasion or for a season that has passed, suddenly cumbersome, irrelevant to their lives" (80).

Gogol and Sonia grow up to be the citizens of America. Once when on his mother's insistence he goes to attend a panel discussion on Indian Novels written in English, actually to meet a distant cousin, Amit, he suddenly comes across a term, ABCD meaning "America-born confused Deshi." He learns that C could also stand for "conflicted." He knows that Deshi, generic word means countrymen, i.e. the Indians. He knows that his parents and all their friends always refer to India simply as Desh. But Gogol never thinks of it, as Americans do, as India. Why so? Is it because he is afraid of being stamped as an Other? Or simply because being born of Indian parents he feels marginalized among the flock of his American friends? Of course, he never feels like the Spivakian 'subaltern', because he can speak, that too with thunderous assertion.

Gayatri Spivak in her famous essay, "The New Historicism: Political Commitment and the Postmodern Critic" declares, "If the subaltern can speak, then thank God, the subaltern is not a subaltern anymore." Though Gogol's parents suffer from a 'Other' syndrome he and Sonia hate to think in that vein. But it assails Gogol sometimes, though not always. For Gogol, any nook of America becomes 'home', in an instant. As Gogol shifts to a hostel at New Haven for his studies, he mistakably mentions it as 'home' to his parents. "His father asked him to bring the Yale decal so to paste it on the rear window of their car. He replied, 'Sorry, I left it at home.' His mother blew her top and outrageously observed, 'Only three months and listen to you,' she says, telling him that after twenty years in America, she still can't bring herself to refer to Pemberton Road as home" (108).

Gogol gradually grows up into a man, holding a job, having covert relationships, even overt ones, with sundry women unabashedly. He was reared up in America, he took up the lifestyle of the Americans and naturally, free hobnobbing with women is no taboo for him. His first American girlfriend, Ruth, with whom he enjoys being young and in love bestows on him a sense of fulfillment, so far unknown to him. Writes Jhumpa, "His relationship with her is one accomplishment in his life about which they are not in the least bit proud or pleased. Ruth tells him she does not mind his parents' disapproval, that she finds it romantic. But Gogol knows it isn't right. He wishes his parents would simply accept her, as her family accepts him, without pressure of any kind" (113). But, in reality, both his parents disapprove his relationship with an American blonde, marriage with whom is the last thing they can think of. The 'Other' syndrome springs up to make them point at examples of Bengali men they know who have married Americans, marriage that has ended in divorce. Presumably Gogol's relationship with Ruth also sours. The author observes, "But within days of being together again in New Haven, in an apartment he had rented on Howe Street with friends, they'd begun fighting, both admitting in the end that something had changed" (120).

Immediately after, he falls head over heels in love with Maxine, who stays with her parents and who goes a step ahead to share the bed with him upstairs almost on all evenings since their acquaintance. Her parents, Gerald and Lydia, form a picture of perfect togetherness, which is something new to Gogol. He knows 'togetherness' in somewhat Indian way, but this, no doubt, is of a different kind. Gogol in his mind compares their togetherness with his parents', Their lives bear no resemblance to that of Gerald and Lydia, expensive pieces of jewelry presented on Lydia's birthday, flowers brought home for no reason at all the two of them kissing openly, going for walks through the city or to dinner, just as Gogol and Maxine do. Seeing the two of them curled up on the sofa in the evenings, Gerald's head resting on Lydia's shoulder, Gogol is reminded that in all his life he has never witnessed a single moment of physical affection between his parents. Whatever love exists between them is an utterly private, uncelebrated thing. When inquired by Maxine whether his parents want him to marry an Indian girl, he feels vexed to answer, "I guess so. It doesn't matter what they want" (139). Gogol thinks himself more an American than an expatriate Indian, with roots sunk deep in some distant soil! He even felt enraged at the thought of being a part of a staunch Indian matrix to which hardly he belongs. While keeping Maxine's company at her parents, Gogol even feels "no nostalgia for the vacations he's spent with his family and he realizes now that they were never really true vacations at all. Instead they were overwhelming, disorienting expeditions, either going to Calcutta or sight-seeing in places they did not belong to and intended never to see again" (105). Again Gogol keeps on comparing his parents with that of Maxine's and sees them standing against each other as Cultural Other: "He can't picture his family occupying a house like this, playing board games on rainy afternoons, watching shooting stars at night, all their relatives gathered neatly on a small strip of sand. It is an impulse, his parents have never felt.... They would have felt lonely in this setting, remarking that they were the only Indians.... His mother would not put on a bathing suit or swim" (155). Frantz Fanon in his "On National Culture" in the frankest possible term opines, "The Real Other for the

White man is and will continue to be the Black man. And conversely. But going a step further we can easily add that it is not just colonial racism that is at work, but it is the cultural difference."

Gogol, however, gets a jolt to his feelings, when Maxine asks him to reconsider his plans of going to his parents on his birthday. They could go to New Hampshire to see Maxine's parents instead where they were holidaying. Gogol cannot pooh-pooh his Mother's avid call and nor can ignore Maxine who keeps pulling strings to make the plan go awry. Gogol decides at last to drop in at his parents' for a couple of hours on his way to New Hampshire with Maxine. He does so; Maxine tries hard to be polite and sweet with his parents while addressing them as Ashima and Ashoke respectively which they seem not to take in so easily. That is for the last time he sees his father, however. His father has to go to Cleveland on a lecture-tour for nine months, leaving his mother behind. There he dies of a stomach-ailment, followed by a severe heart-failure quite unexpectedly. All these transpire abruptly in quick succession. Maxine drives up from New York to Gogol's Pemberton residence to share his grief, to condole the sudden demise of his father. Now, Gogol cannot put up with the pretentious demeanours of Maxine. He can see that she feels out of place in the house "full of Bengalis". She even presses him to leave his mother alone in that bereaved state! "I am so sorry", he hears her say to his mother, knowing full well that his father's death does not affect Maxine in the least. Gogol readily spurns her offer of paying a-visit to New Hampshire which might do him good, "getting away from all this!" He replies sternly instead, "I do not want to get away."

Gogol feels shattered within when his relationship with Maxine terminates. His mother suggests to see Moushumi Mazumdar, the daughter of their long-time friend Dr. Mazumdar, the renowned chemist. During his childhood he had seen her quite a few times at different parties, poring over a book all the time, a glass perched on her nose. When he meets her, goes out dating, falls in love and marries, his mother's cresting joy makes him happy too. Moushumi too has a gash of frustrated engagement in her heart. Graham was the American, with whom she fell madly in love and even took to Calcutta to get him acquainted with her relatives there. But she was crestfallen rather flabbergasted to hear him talk to their friends in a party, a few weeks before their wedding in an objectionable manner, she heard Graham talking about their time in Calcutta. To her surprise; he was complaining about it, commenting that he found it taxing, found the culture repressed. All they did was visit her relatives, he said,

> ...it was one thing for her to reject her background, to be critical of her Family's heritage another to hear from him. She realized that he had fooled everyone including her. (217)

Moushumi was really devastated after Graham walked out on her snapping all ties. Gogol's overture to see her at this point seemed like a welcome gush of fresh air. They keep ruminating their childhood memories. Moushumi becomes truly sad to learn about Gogol's father's sudden demise. Moushumi falls in love with Gogol, Gogol reciprocates and they marry. Sonia is going to marry Ben, an American, he learns. Their roots are now ramifying in the American soil, he senses. To her utter dismay, Moushumi too proves unfaithful by dating with her once-upon-a-time fiance, Dimitri, in Paris, as she chances upon a resume he submits at her faculty. In the meanwhile Ashima decides to divide her time between the States and India as Gogol's father is no more and the house is too big to remind her of her overbearing loneliness all day long.

Could not Gogol dissuade Moushumi from carrying on with her clandestine bond with Dimitri? He was not again a stranger to this sort of flings. Then why did he react so violently on learning it? Why did the Other syndrome get the better of him? Of course, here he himself is the Other and Dimitri being a white individual is the Native. Here, Gogol dons on the Other image inherited from his parents, unawares. He shares the identity with his namesake, Nikolai Gogol, who remained a bachelor till death.

We, however, never expected Gogol to behave as an Other, moving tangentially off the Zeitgeist. A mind-boggling conundrum teases us out of thought. Is an expatriate *Indian an Other, everywhere, in all possible nuances of the term*?! [italics mine] Desperately the Other, we mean. Perhaps, from the sense of insecurity engenders the feeling of Otherness. Says Ortega Y. Gasset, in his essay "The Self and The Other" as incorporated in L. Brander's *Window on the World*, "This thing we call 'civilization'—all these physical and moral comforts, all these conveniences, all these shelters, all these virtues and disciplines which have become habit now, on which we count and which in effect constitute a repertory of securities which man made for himself like a raft in the initial shipwreck which living always is all these securities are insecure securities which in the twinkling of an eye, at the least carelessness, escape from man's hands and vanish like phantoms. History tells us of innumerable retrogressions, of decadences and degenerations. But nothing tells us that there is no possibility of much more basic retrogressions than any so far known, including the most basic of them all; the total disappearance of man as man and his silent return to the animal scale to complete and definitive absorption in the Other. The fate of culture, the destiny of man depends our maintaining that dramatic consciousness ever alive in our inmost being and upon our feeling, like a murmuring counterpart in our entrails that we are only sure of security" (100).

Another noted thinker Albert Schweitzer in his famous essay "Civilization and World View" as appears in L. Brander's *Window on the World*, says, "How little reflection is present in the Western impulse to action becomes evident when this tries to square its ideas with those of the Far East. For thought in the Far East has been constantly occupied in its search for the meaning of life and forces us to consider the problem of the meaning of our own restlessness, the problem which we Westerners shirk so persistently. We are utterly at a loss when we contemplate the ideas which are presented to us in Indian thought..." (82). Does not it sound much like "East is East and the West is West and the twain shall never meet again?" One is surely the Other to either of the two.

Jhumpa Lahiri in both her previous works have pointed out the fact that the 'other' syndrome is applicable to all authors of the diaspora. Even in their works the characters are shown to be caught in such unsavory question of the 'other' that they ultimately suffer from either the sense of alienation or absolute aping of the alien culture to fit into the foreign ambience, quite successfully. The question of acceptance is a big and problematic one, no doubt!

In almost all the stories of the recent collection, *Unaccustomed Earth*, the *transnational* identity of the individuals irrespective of sexes, get jumbled up with their national identities. It appears as though a glocal [*global+local*] identity is taking birth gradually. Ruben Silie in his article "Transnationality—A New Phase of Migration", is cogent in remarking, "Transnational Communities function as a form of integration of sectors which for essentially economic reasons have decided to migrate and once in the destination country, have developed mechanisms to secure their ties with the country of origin and even to improve their social standing there, while at the same time planting their roots in the receiving country. This ability of migrants to conquer their spaces in both the receiving country and the country of origin enables that transnational community to play a decisive part in defining their lifestyle."

Ruma, the heroine of the first story of the collection, *Unaccustomed Earth*, is married to Adam, an American youth and is the daughter of a transnational individual, caught between two cultures [Indian and American] and again Akash grows more attached to his grandfather as and when he comes to stay with them while his father is away on a business tour. Ruma is keen on keeping her lonely father in her own family as her mother is no more. But, just like other transnational individuals, Ruma's father is co-operative, diligent, agile and accommodative. He chips in to take part in domestic chores spontaneously. He spins yarns to little Akash when he goes to sleep at night, which even makes Ruma envious of her own child. Surprisingly enough, though Akash is a product of two cultures because of his parents' belonging to diversifying cultures, he comes under the spell of his transnational grandfather, despite his strong individualistic and insular mindset right at this early age,

> She took him downstairs, where she had prepared the guest room. The space was divided into two sections by an accordion door.... She opened the door to the bathroom and pointed to the wicker basket where he was to put his laundry. "You can close this off if you like," she said, pulling at the accordion door to demonstrate....
>
> "All the way, Mommy," Akash said.... "close it all the way."
>
> "No, Akash."
>
> "This is my room when I get bigger," Akash announced....
>
> "Hey, don't walk on my bed with your shoes on/her father said suddenly to Akash, who had gotten onto the bed and was walking with large, deliberate steps around the bedcover....
>
> For a moment Akash continued exactly as he was doing, ignoring them. Then he stopped, looking suspiciously at his grandfather. 'Why?'
>
> Akash dropped his head. Quickly, to Ruma's surprise, he slithered onto the floor, briefly crawling as if he were a baby again...." (15)

The transnational identity of an individual brings out a cooperative self, an adjusting one to prove his success in straddling two different cultures. But, no man can live without emotional bondage and hence Mrs. Bagchi steps in the life of Ruma's widower father. The twist in the tale is really interesting as the daughter, after her father's departure, finds the note written to his paramour and decides to post it to her address. Ruma feels that her father's loneliness after her mother's death is excruciating and hence the friendship, which maybe a love affair, should not be denigrated.

In the next story of Part One, *Hell-Heaven*, the transnational identity of the individual cannot get the better of his innate instincts. Pranab Kaku [Uncle] though marries Deborah, a devoted woman of alien culture, cannot remain devoted to her love and allegiance till the last. This flippant mentality is not due to clash of cultures but a reflection of an individual mindset. Again, a transnational identity exposes the individual to multicultural choices but faithlessness is not the result of any healthy culture but individual taste and inclinations. Again, psychologists say that in building relationships after relationships often the factor of *sense of insecurity* works unobtrusively. Maybe an alien culture have choices galore shoving one to the verge of promiscuity, yet, the transnational individual must have his ethical sense intact to choose the right path. The narrator's mother had fallen head over heels in love with Pranab Kaku to such an extent that she was about to immolate herself immediately after his wedding!! However, the narrator at one point harps upon the issue of *transnational identity* once again, when she says, "Their hearts had been broken by the same man, only my mother's had long ago mended, and in an odd way, as my parents approached their old age, she and my father had grown fond of each other, out of habit if nothing else.... My mother and I had also made peace; she had accepted the fact that I was not only her daughter but a child of America as well. Slowly, she accepted that I dated one American man, and then another, and then yet another, that I slept with them, and even that I lived with one though we were not married..." (81).

In another story *Nobody's Business*, Farouk's promiscuity reminds us of Pranab Kaku of *Hell-Heaven* once again. However, though, Sang was deeply enamored of Farouk, she finally came to know the truth that he was no more than an ordinary philanderer. Paul, her housemate warned her of Farouk's intimacy with another girl named Deirdre, who kept calling Paul, quite often, just to make him aware of the fact that she was the only love of Freddy and she was told by him that Sang was his cousin!! Anyway, Sang after hearing a telephone talk between Paul and Deirdre [Paul arranged for it] moved away to her native place and got engaged to Charles, who came later to that rented apartment to collect her belongings. In fact, Sang or Sangita Biswas, belongs to a transnational culture which lies latent at some corner of her heart, which disallowed her to be a party to any promiscuous relationship. Farouk, however, carried on with his meaningless flings till the end of the story! Sang settled with Charles at some corner of the world and Sang began to discover a new meaning out of her life! Paul ends up being just a friend of Sang who remains as a witness of all the happenings in her life!!

In the postmodern era, regionalism can be extended to transnationality, in which the immigrant is exposed to certain states of mind which is irrespective of his own land or beyond! For example, in *Only Goodness*, Rahul leads a dissipated life not because he is an expatriate Indian boy, but, just like any other individual he is frustrated for some reason or other, mostly related to existential complexities. Rahul even has no complaint against his parents' shift to an alien country, where adjusting to an alien culture may be a pressing problem:

> While Sudha regarded her parents' separation from India as an ailment that ebbed and flowed like a cancer, Rahul was impermeable to that aspect of their life as well 'No one dragged the here,' he would say. 'Baba left India to get rich, and Ma married him because she had nothing else to do?' That was Rahul.... (138)

A conflict of cultures is felt throughout the story *Only Goodness*. In fact, a specification of certain things is made in an abrupt manner, which is neither regionalism nor transnationalism. It is better to call it *culture-clash*. The following conversation is a pointer to a daring yet common problem of all cultures being made nation or culture-specific,

> 'I think Rahul might have a drinking problem.'
>
> 'Sudha, please,' her mother said. 'I gather everyone at American colleges drinks.' She spoke as if drinking were an undergraduate hobby, a phase one outgrew.
>
> 'Not like that.'

> 'Didn't you drink in college?'
>
> 'Not like that,' Sudha repeated. Not enough to get arrested, she was tempted to say.
>
> 'That's the problem with this country,' her mother said. 'Too many freedoms, too much having fun. When we were young, life wasn't always about fun.'
>
> Sudha pitied her mother, pitied her refusal to accommodate such an unpleasant and alien fact, her need to blame America and its laws instead of her son....
>
> What could there possibly be to be unhappy about? her parents would have thought. 'Depression' was a foreign word to them, an American thing. In their opinion their children were immune from the hardships and injustices they had left behind in India, as if inoculations the pediatrician had given Sudha and Rahul when they were babies guaranteed them an existence free of suffering. (143-44)

A positive aspect of the above statements of Rahul's mother is that she does not gloss over the flaws of his own national culture and only romanticize with it. That is the beauty of the inner construing of a transnational individual. Though he/she is caught between two contending cultures, he/she knows how to be critical as well as appreciative of both the cultures in a considerable and justified manner.

In a story of this collection, *A Choice of Accommodations*, there is already a wedding of cultures when Amit an India-born *transnational* individual marries an American bride, Megan. But, as he goes to attend an old friend, Pam Borden's wedding, an unusually nostalgic fling gets the better of Amit. However, he also suspects of Megan falling in love in an instant with Ted Schultz and even at one point he keeps thinking, "Could it be that Megan was flirting with Ted? Instead of being jealous Amit felt oddly liberated, relieved of his responsibility to Megan, to show her a good time" (109). A traditional twist of his own culture makes him a bit envious of Megan's proximity to Ted. At one point, Amit is so stung by his love of his own nationality that he seemingly rues the fact that, "His daughters looked nothing like him, nothing like his family, and in spite of the distance Amit felt from his parents, this fact bothered him, that his mother and father had passed down nothing, physically, to his children. Both Maya and Monika had inherited Megan's coloring, without a trace of Amit's deeply tan skin and black eyes, so that apart from their vaguely Indian names they appeared fully American. 'Are they yours?' people sometimes asked when he was alone with them, in stores, or at the playground in the park" (94).

In the Part One of the collection *Unaccustomed Earth*, there are stories in which we find the *transnationalism* of the expatriate Indians who can hardly do away with their own national culture and again become part of the *other* culture. But, in Part Two, the writer delves into the cultural identity as well as the nooks of individual psyche. For example, when the Choudhuri family shifts from Bombay to the United States to stay with Hema's family, there is an innuendo at the forceful adaptation of Choudhuri family, especially Mrs. Choudhuri, to the alien culture. In *Once in a Lifetime*, Hema keeps narrating, "My parents, who had never set foot in a liquor store, wondered whether they should buy another bottle—at the rate your parents were going, that bottle would be drained by tomorrow, my mother said. She remarked that your mother had become 'stylish', a pejorative term in her vocabulary, implying a self-indulgence that she shunned" (236).

The family which came to stay with that of Hema was going to face a sad happening in near future, which they concealed from Hema's parents. Kaushik's mother was suffering from breast cancer and her days stood numbered. However, Kaushik's parents buy a new house and shift there within a few months. And, sadly enough, Kaushik's mother dies within months. But, whether she wants it or not, Hema cherishes the memory of Kaushik staying in their house, long back, for some months.

In *Year's End*, Kaushik takes up the role of the narrator and here he is no transnational individual caught between two cultures, but, a motherless youth, who feels down and out but never lets anyone know it, not even his father, let alone,

Chitra, who comes to replace her mother, in the lonely world of his father. Kaushik's instant reaction to see her mother's photographs being scattered on the 'gray carpet' and watched by the two daughters of Chitra—Rupa and Piu. Kaushik scolds the sisters, blow his top by hurting their feelings and thus exposing his unhealed wound after his father's re-marriage rather abruptly, "Well, you've seen it for yourselves, how beautiful my mother was. How much prettier and more sophisticated than yours. Your mother is nothing in comparison. Just a servant to wash my father's clothes and cook his meals. That's the only reason she's here, the only reason both of you are here" (186-87). Irrespective of all cultures, here the individual's psychological plight plays a vital role, no doubt. In a famous essay, "Freud: Within and Beyond Culture", Lionel Trilling [cf. *Beyond Culture*] says,

> It was he [Freud] who made it apparent to us how entirely implicated in culture we all are. By what he said or suggested of the depth and subtlety of the influence of the family upon the individual, he made plain how the culture suffuses the remotest parts of the individual mind, being taken in almost literally with the mother's milk. His psychology involves culture in its very essence —it tells us that the surrogates of culture are established in the mind itself, that the development of the individual mind recapitulates the development of culture. (105)

But, it is really heartening to see in *Going Ashore* that as Hema and Kaushik come in proximity to each other abruptly, Hema is lately jilted by Julian and awaiting a wedlock with Navin who is to join her from India, non-Bengali Indian. Kaushik is alone, yet to form any lasting relationship with anyone. It seems, as if, Kaushik was waiting all these days of agony and loneliness for Hema only! Is there any diasporic tension or tension regarding cultural identity which debarred Kaushik from getting a bride from the other culture or Hema from entering into wedlock with an American boy. It is crystal-clear from Hema's statement that her wedding was just a sort of panacea of all the problems she was passing through:

"But you don't wear an engagement ring."

> "I don't have one."
>
> He studied the bangle, turning it slowly around. "What kind of man proposes without a ring?"
>
> She explained that there had not been a proposal, that she hardly knew Navin. She was looking away, at a dried-out plant on the terrace, but she felt his eyes on her, intrigued, unafraid.
>
> "Then why are you marrying him?"
>
> She told him the truth, a truth she had not told anybody. "I thought it might fix things."
>
> He did not question her further. *Unlike her friends back in America, who either thought she was doing something outrageously stupid or thrillingly bold Kaushik neither judged nor commended her.* (313) [italics mine]

A cultural tension shared by each other, no doubt.

What is the basis of such need for cultural identity when an individual with transnational standing is welcome in the alien society to share its culture? Perhaps, Stuart Hall, in Padmini Mongia's *Contemporary Postcolonial Theory: A Reader*, has some veritable observation to proffer,

> There is, however, a second, related but different view of cultural identity. This second position recognizes that as well as the many points of similarity, there are also critical points of deep and significant *difference* which constitute 'what we really are'; or rather—since history has intervened—'what we have become'...Cultural identity, in this second sense, is a matter of 'becoming' as well as of 'being'. It belongs to the future as much as to the past. It is not something which already exists, transcending place, time, history and culture. Cultural identities come from somewhere, have histories. But, like everything which is historical, they undergo constant transformation. Far from being eternally fixed in some essentialised past, they are subject to the continuous 'play' of history, culture and power. Far from being grounded in a mere 'recovery' of the past, which is waiting to be found, and which, when found, will secure

our sense of ourselves into eternity, identities are the names we give to the different ways we are positioned by, and position ourselves within the narratives of the past. (112)

It is really crystal clear in the conclusion, that, Hema was shaken by shock to learn that the victim of Tsunami on the Thailand coast was Kaushik, a frustrated, deprived soul who craved for a haven of love and expressed it so candidly to Hema! Jhumpa sounds suggestive, "Those cold, dark days I spent in bed, unable to speak, burning with new life but mourning your death.... It might have been your child but this was not the case. We had been careful and you had left nothing behind" (333). Typical manifestation of inner emotions of a *glocal*, transnational human being of the diaspora, who fights off all cultural tensions, to take pride in calling one's own as one's own, being responsive to the call of asserting one's own cultural identity!

WORKS CITED

Brander, L. (ed.). *Window on the World*. OUP: London, 1972.

Fanon, Frantz. 'On National Culture', *The Wretched of the Earth*. Penguin: London, 1969.

Lahiri, Jhumpa. *The Namesake*. Harper Collins: India, 2004.

——. *Interpreter of Maladies*. Harper Collins: India, 1999.

——. *Unaccustomed Earth*. Random House: India, 2008.

Mongia, Padmini (ed). *Contemporary Postcolonial Theory: A Reader*. OUP, 2000.

Silie, Ruben. 'Transnationality: A New Phase of Migration', *The Greater Carribbean this Week*. <http://www.acs-aec.org/column/greatCarib05042006_en.htm>

Spivak, Chakravarty Gayatri. *The Postcolonial Critics: Interviews, Strategies*. Dialogues. Routledge: London, 1990.

Tilling, Lionel. *Beyond Culture: Essays on Literature and Learning*. Viking: New York, 1965.

Todorov, Tzvetan. 'The Conquest of America', *The Question of the Other*. Harper Perennial: London, 1992.

Walder, Dennis. *Postcolonial Literatures in English*. Blackwell: London, 1998.

13

The White Tiger: A Prophecy or a Warning?

Shirish Chindhade

Writers of social realism usually feel the compulsion to state in clear terms what they want to communicate in a work of art because they value the content more than the craft, the message more than the manner of telling the story. In *The White Tiger* Adiga renders this service very clearly to his readers right in the salutation section of the letter which his protagonist Balram, a halwai-turned-entrepreneur, has written to the Chinese Premier Mr. Wen Jiabao. Balram says, "I'm a man of action and change" (5). This is rounded off for reinforcement in the leave-taking section of the epistle where Balram tells the Premier, "You see, I'm always a man who sees 'tomorrow' when others see 'today'" (319). The entire narrative spells out this process of change of Balram's status from a half-literate boy born and brought up in the Darkness called Laxmangarh to Mr. Ashok Sharma, a flourishing entrepreneur settled in Bangalore. He continuously hones two tools useful in this upward mobility, namely, insatiable greed and vaulting ambition. The stages in this journey are only a few but well-marked and speedy. Although mortally afraid of lizards, Balram is marked out earlier on as a "white tiger" by a perceptive school inspector. "You, young man, are an intelligent, honest, vivacious fellow in this crowd of thugs and idiots." The inspector knows that this rough diamond needs to be cut for facets in "...a real school—somewhere far away... you need a different uniform and real education" (35).

The "real education" in Balram's case is done not within the four walls of any formal school but in the wide, wild and weird world of India. The range of his teachers is mind-boggling, from hotel hands, drivers, domestic menials, pimps and prostitutes, to police personnel, government servants, ministers, politicians and entrepreneurs. These are teachers who would easily put to shame Dickens' Fagin, the celebrated "professor" of crimes in *Oliver Twist*! The lessons that Balram learns under such eminent army of tutelage are so effectively bold and bald that he soon outdoes all his teachers and is "...corrupted from a sweet innocent village fool into a citified fellow full of debauchery, depravity and wickedness" (197). Now, whatever the colour of the tiger, white or black or brown, yellow, striped or spotted, as a rule, once it tastes human blood it grows into a man-eater and kills when and where it pleases. Balram the village chicken, jostling in a rooster coop, breaks the cage and emerges as a dinosaur, a cold-blooded murderer of his master and then as a serial killer exterminating even his own entire family, and still manages to float with ease in the elite world of modern India Incorporate.

Even this brief outline of the story declares *The White Tiger* to be a disturbing and exciting book as it raises certain interesting questions about its structure and certain other fundamental ones about its content. The questions relating to the structure can be addressed first as they are obvious and facile. However, it is to be admitted that in a good work of art the form and the content merge together and create a unified impact.

First of all, is *The White Tiger* a latter-day picaresque novel? The prototypical picaroon belongs to a high but initially unidentified or anonymous parentage; he is proverbially innocent, incorruptible and eminently impervious to temptations of all varieties. Finally, after having been tried and tested in the furnace of life, the picaroon is eventually reinstated in honour and legitimized in lineage. As for *The White Tiger,* it tells a tale of progressive and incremental corruption of the protagonist. He is an easy prey to every kind of canker, physical, mental and moral. Appropriately enough, the writer's choice of the letter form as a mode of narration is a subtle hint. As a genre of expression the letter is a highly personalized communication. Its first person narrative mode is said to be highly conducive to the confessional vent of a consciously or subconsciously guilt-ridden mind. Balram's letter operates almost on the level of an interior monologue of a rank and seasoned criminal without a trace of contrition.

The second question is: can *The White Tiger* be considered as a *bildungsroman*? It is a genre that deals with the education/ development of the young. Balram certainly learns his bizarre lessons in the school of life with classrooms filled with weird class-mates such as lizards, mosquitoes, and cockroaches and located in dingy rooms, call centres, hotels, markets, malls, roads, pavements, and night clubs often supplying yellow learning materials. They all suggest a welter of manners and morals. Naturally, all that Balram learns is suspect and obviously pejorative. In the process he has corrupted himself inside out and finally "woken up" (315) in a world of the *nouveau riche* following a new mercenary morality in "A new Bangalore for new India" (318) where both God and Gandhi are irrelevant and not allowed to "corrupt" anyone's heads! (319) As a result, Balram emerges as a man with an entirely darkened (as against enlightened) soul, admitting like Lady Macbeth, "All the skin-whitening creams sold in the markets of India won't clean my hands again" (318). This, however, is not said in penitence because Balram's soul is thoroughly benumbed to such sentiments now, and he has committed all crimes in full awareness that "...it was all worthwhile..." (321). He has now struck a lucrative bargain in life and sold his soul to Satan. We are aware that the protagonist of a *bildungsroman* matures from an ordinary, diffident, fumbling and faltering youth into a mature man of merit who can make informed and healthy choices in life. His suffering/mistake becomes a furnace that purifies the dross of his mettle, rendering him into a man of elevated conscience and heightened sensibility touched by a transcendental knowledge.

In other words, a *bildungsroman* traces the process of culture acquisition involving a status shift which is gradual, positive, ethically evolved and socially acceptable, much above Balram's upward mobility from a driver to a business tycoon. An interesting example is seen in Rama Mehta's Geeta of *Inside the Haveli* or an endearing and impressive example is available in R.K. Narayan's Raju Guide (*The Guide*) rising from a railway tourist guide to a spiritual visionary. How does Balram answer this test? Let us now turn to the third question: Is *The White Tiger* an allegory? We understand that an allegory is a well-worked out, extended metaphor in which the object of the allegory and the message simultaneously run parallel and eventually separate in the reader's mind. The exercise often becomes a symbolic representation of reality. As for the present novel Balram is neither a metaphor nor a symbol. He is not a non-descript cardboard figure of Everyman of the old morality plays. He is tangible in flesh and blood, a man caught in a situation from which there is no turning back. The tunnel here opens into a world of inner and infernal darkness. There are no redemptive diversions on the road; the movement has to be linear as the felonies are incremental. The predictable end can come in the inevitable eventuality of Balram's death in a shoot-out on the roads or on the gallows as a process of the law of the land (if the hands of law can ever reach him!).

A circle is complete: he comes from one Darkness and reaches another, and is permanently damned. Since he is not Everyman, he is not allegorical also.

The crucial question that now remains to be addressed is: What is Balram's story about? What does the writer want to suggest? As noted above, Balram is a man of action and change and set to seek a great tomorrow. However, action without worthy goals leads astray and is vulnerable to corruption. If the goal of life is success, then its nature and the ways to attain it have to be analysed patiently and understood perspicaciously. This is the way to avert tragedy. One needs to answer several questions to do so.

For example,

1. Is success a fulfillment of one's dreams, desires and aspirations at any cost, irrespective of its qualitative fall out?
2. Is success an assertion that man's destiny is a product of his inexorable action which has purely amoral implications?
3. Is success another name for worldly glory and prosperity, pure and simple?
4. Is success only a result of a price or is it an addition of value to one's life?
5. Is success a frank declaration that the old dictum of "pie in the sky" is a silly hoax in a world groomed to respect money, material mirth and mandate?
6. Is Balram's story a reminder that the road to crime has no escape route and that once a sinner is always a sinner?
7. Is the emerging new world (of India) going to be a place where God and Gandhi are totally out of synch, where only Mammon and Machiavelli will rule the roost?

Perhaps, one may also ask if Adiga is trying to hint at a new kind of education that the world in general and India in particular need in times of suffering from a speedy decline of morals. In simple words, is Adiga taking on the primordial conflict of ends and means with a specific reference to India? Is he asking us to close our Charwak and open our Gandhi, by trying to attempt an unsparing and ruthless critique of the sea change coming over the globalized India, sweeping away all time-honoured values and morals that once characterized and sustained the quality of the culture? Modern India is a fast urbanizing society in which avarice and quick success seem to overrule values. The city corrupts fast and corrupts thoroughly, as the case of Ashok and Balram testifies. Do their catastrophes declare the old doctrine that the end does not justify the means, and that the society that defies the sanctity of the means to achieve its ends speedily degenerates into decay and self-destruction? Since ample universal proof can be cited to support this truth, how should one read *The White Tiger*—as a prophecy or as a warning?—Or as both?

REFERENCE

Adiga, Arvind. *The White Tiger*. NOIDA, India. Harper Collins Publishers, 2008. (All the page numbers parenthetically mentioned in the essay are keyed to this edition.)

14

"Novel"ising the Autobiography: Tehmina Durrani's *My Feudal Lord*

Shabina Nishat Omar

'An autobiography', wrote James Olney in his seminal work *Metaphors of the Self,* 'is a monument of the self as it is becoming a metaphor of the self at the summary moment of its composition.'[1] Its objective is 'to build a metaphoric bridge from subjective self consciousness to objective reality.'[2] Olney argues that if all selves are unique and if they are constantly evolving and transforming then it would be difficult to define such a self and even more difficult to give a sense of it to anyone else. The only way to communicate such a self to others is to do so by discovering or creating some similitude for the experience to evoke the same experience in others. The psychological basis of the metaphorizing process, according to him, is to grasp the unknown through the known or to 'let the known stand for the unknown and thereby fit that into an organized patterned body of experimental knowledge.'[3] In the same book Olney discusses several male-authored self narratives to illustrate how each of them invents a unique, exclusive and fresh metaphor to express the self. Jung, Montaigne, Mill, Newman, Darwin or Gandhi—each of these men invents a special objective correlative to reach his as reader. Olney's theorizing from this point onwards becomes patronizing, imperative and patriarchal. In an extremely declamatory fashion he prescribes pre-conditioned for the metaphorizing process and perspective stating that such a view and practice 'must be' unitary, especially human and personally unique.[4] This specifically excludes the minorities and the marginalized entities from the metaphorizing process. Georges Gusdorf had earlier advocated the 'individualizing paradigm of the centrally located isolate autobiographical self'[5] and thus excluded the marginalized entities, blacks and women from the purview of autobiographical writings and studies. Similarly Olney overlooks the marginal identity here, thus confirming his affinity with the school of critical thinking which regarded minorities as either unfit to be autobiographical subjects because of their lack of 'isolate individual self' or maintained silence over their attempts at autobiography writing and thus excluded them from the canonical discourse.

These patriarchal theorists missed a very important point. As Susan Stanford Freidman writes in *Private Self* the 'self creation and self-consciousness are profoundly different for women, minorities and non-westerners.'[6] She further argues that Gusdorfs theory does not take into consideration the importance of the culturally imposed group identity for the minorities including women. If 'separate selfhood is the very motive of creation [autobiography]' and if autobiography is 'a mirror in which the individual reflects his own image', then this mirror does not reflect back a unique image to women, 'it projects an image of WOMAN, a category that is supposed to define the living woman's identity', writes Shari Benstock.[7] As a result 'an awareness of the meaning of the cultural category "woman" [dictates] the patterns of woman's individual destiny',[8] writes Freidman. The feminist theories of the nineties and onwards like those of Estelle Jelinek, Shari Benstock, Sheila Rowbotham, Nancy Chodorow, Susan Freidman and Maison, et al. expose the inapplicability of Gusdorfian theory to the autobiographies by the minorities and assert the need for a separate poetics for such self-referential writing which will take into account the socio-cultural attributes of their personality.

Olney's theory of the autobiography as a metaphor of the self is indeed patriarchal and exclusionist. The three preconditions of the self that he establishes for the metaphorizing self are luxuries of the privileged classes which cannot be enjoyed by or even availed by minority groups. Logically metaphorizing of the minorities, the deprived, the exploited and the marginalized would be extremely different from that of the elite, the hegemonic and the privileged. These metaphors, like their personalities, would be collective instead of individual and repetitive instead of unique and fresh. Although James Olney's theory is acceptable upto the point of every autobiography being a metaphor of the self, one must also assert beside it a special space for women and minorities in the theory of metaphorizing and a respectful acknowledgement of such an act by the canon. Instead of dismissing female authored autobiographies on the basis of gender [which are both male constructs] and incompatibility [again a male view]; it is the responsibility of the serious scholars of the genre to explore the specificities of women's self-writing from a gynocentric view.

Autobiography as a literary genre has always been a contested category in India as well as in the West. It was valued for an interpretation of life in its totality but not as a literary text. With the loosening of the formalists New Criticisms hold on literary scholarship, several critics began reading autobiography as a literary text rather than documented history. Within women's studies autobiographies acquired a special position as women's arrival on the language scene if not on the literary scene. It was on the one hand a step into the public sphere and on the other an expression of the private self. Though fiction and autobiography are supposed to be two poles, autobiography does have the narration of a structured "I". Within women's tradition where women were assigned identities and role models by the patriarchy, autobiography meant arriving at a site of one's own choice. The autobiography creates a self in the very act of seeking it. An autobiography projects a single radical and radial energy originating in the subject centre, an aggressive, creative expression of the self, a defence of individual integrity in the face of an otherwise multiple, confusing, swarming and inimical universe. Psychoanalytic critics of autobiography often focus their analyses on the way in which self-creation in the text negotiates the writer's past inter-relations with his/her parents. According to psychoanalytic theory the psychological development moves from identification to separation. Feminist critics lay emphasis on the sense of identification, interdependence and community. The double consciousness of women and minorities can be understood better in the light of these considerations. For instance, Nancy Chodorow uses the phrase, 'a more complex relation constellation than man's'[9] for the relational world of women. Her analysis of self in female autobiography uses the concept of interdependent existence which is useful while addressing concerns of family in autobiography. The family is the most important part of the female experience as it is the primary cultural space available to a woman. The male members of the family as well as the women breadwinners who go 'out in the world' bring public life—or part of it into their homes. A woman is conditioned to perceive family as her protective shell, she is also tutored into being the protector of the family, upholder of its traditions, etc. Anyone outside the immediate family circle or outside the extended family is relegated to the position of the other or outsider. Women's autobiographies derive their value from their subjectivity and subjectivity, as Raymond Williams asserts, 'The notion of experience as subjective witness is offered not only as truth but as the most authentic kind of truth as the ground for all reasoning and analysis.'[10]

Postcolonial feminist writing is extensive and variable. Its analyses range across representations of women in formerly colonized countries and in Western locations. Criticism and analyses have focused on the constructions of gender differences during the colonial period with the representations of women in postcolonial discourses and with special reference to the work of women writers. At the level of theory, postcolonial feminist critics have raised a number of conceptual, methodological and political problems involved in the study of the representations of gender. It is as challenging to define feminism as to define post-colonialism. The variable range of work that can be called 'feminist' makes it difficult to summarize feminism. One can begin with a reading of the introduction to *The Feminist Reader: Essays in Gender and the Politics of Literary Criticism* (ed. Belsely and Moore, Macmillan, 1989). Catherine Belsely and Jane Moore argue that 'a feminist reader is enlisted in the process of changing the gender relations which prevail in our society and she regards the practice of reading as one of the sites in the struggle for change.'[11] They suggest that a feminist reader might ask of a text questions about gender relations such as 'how it defines sexual difference'.[12] In referring to the 'struggle for change' we can understand that feminist reading practices are involved in the contestation of patriarchal authority. The term 'patriarchy' refers to those systems political, material, social, cultural and imaginative which invest power in men and marginalize women. Like colonialism, patriarchy asserts certain representational systems which create an order of the world presented to the individuals as normal or true. Also like colonialism, patriarchy exists in the midst of resistances to its authority. There are various forms and levels of patriarchy. This is a particularly important point in the postcolonial feminist criticism. So feminism and post-colonialism share the mutual goal of challenging forms of oppression. Third world feminist writers cover a range of issues that share a concern with gender and how their female protagonist's self and sexuality are constructed and controlled by indigenous patriarchies and British colonial practices. Further they show how patriarchy and colonialism collude to worsen a woman's predicament. Although women writers do not romanticize a pre-colonial past, they are well aware of how indigenous and colonial patriarchies collude as represented in Zimbabwean Tsitsi Dangaremba's complex first novel *Nervous Conditions*. Even as patriarchy is critiqued Third World theorists reveal the historical and cultural specificities of patriarchy.

We live 'in a world with powerful histories of resistance and revolution in daily life', notes Chandra Talpade Mohanty in her introduction to *Third World Women and the Politics of Feminism.*[13] She asserts that 'these challenges suggest new questions for feminist historiography and epistemology as well as point toward necessary re-conceptualizations of ideas of resistance, community and agency in daily life.' Mohanty does not posit any homogeneous configuration of third world women who form communities because they share a "gender" or a "race" or a "nation".[14] Her essay "Under Western Eyes" demonstrates the problems in associating third world women with images of underdevelopment, oppressive traditions, high illiteracy, rural and urban poverty, religious fanaticism and other stereotypical concepts. Mohanty suggests a useful direction in stating that 'any definitions, descriptions and interpretations of third world women's engagement with feminism must necessarily be simultaneously historically specific and dynamic, not frozen in time in the form of a spectacle'.

Just as there is no single homogeneous category of 'western women', similarly there is no 'automatic unitary group' of 'third world women.... It is Third World women's oppositional political relation to sexist, racist and imperialist structures that constitutes our potential commonality.'[15]

Postcolonial literature consists of a body of writing emanating from Europe's former colonies. It addresses the concerns of history, identity, ethnicity, gender and language. The term "postcolonial literature" is to date one of the most convenient and flexible ways of embracing the gamut of literary responses to the challenges presented by decolonization and the transition to independence and post independence in a variety of political and cultural contexts. An important consequence of post-colonialism has been the acknowledgement and reappearance of women's experience after its remaining concealed from the histories of colonial societies. Many of the fixed representations of non-Western women have been powerfully rejected in a plethora of contemporary writings; most of them in their different ways refute western imaginings about them. Writers like Jean Rhys, Anita Desai, Buchi Emecheta, Olive Senior, Nadine Gordimer,

Grace Nichols and Arundhati Roy, observes Nabaneeta Dev Sen, have placed women at the centre of history as makers and agents of history, not mute witnesses to it. Writing is an extremely difficult task and has been regarded primarily as male territory. Now of course women have stormed this bastion but have usually been regarded as trespassers. The woman who writes has stepped out of her own perceived area of the senses and appropriated a male gesture. When a woman writes she is not just describing life as we witness it, but is rather transcribing experience into words. Critical dogmas, a patriarchal experience, often distract her from the concrete to the abstract and create academic distance between her and reality. All across the world, especially in the Indian subcontinent, the act of writing is for a woman essentially an act of breaking her silence because her repressive patriarchal/racial society has taught her to be culturally silent. The feminine is essentially the marginalized consciousness that operates on the periphery of patriarchal discourse. As Virginia Woolf wrote: 'A woman's writing is always feminine; it cannot help being feminine; at its best, it is most feminine; the only difficulty lies in what we mean by feminine.'[16]

Such an insight into the marginalized feminine self is provided by Tehmina Durrani's *My Feudal Lord*. Tehmina Durrani, a Pakistani English author, in her autobiography *My Feudal Lord* describes her traumatic marital life with Gulam Mustafa Khar, an important politician in the Zulfiqar Ali Bhutto government, who later became the Chief Minister of Punjab. Professionally a charismatic champion of democracy, on the personal front he was an inveterate wife abuser. This autobiographical novel won the Italian Marrissa Bellasario prize and was later translated into several languages. An Afghan Pathan by birth, and born into an educated and affluent family, Tehmina was just seventeen years old when she married Anees Khan, and had a daughter, Tania. She divorced him in 1976 and then married Khar. Subsequently she had to give up claim of her daughter's custody. It was Tehmina's second marriage and Khar's the sixth marriage. After thirteen years of conjugal life and having four children, the couple divorced. After her divorce, Tehmina wrote her autobiography called *My Feudal Lord* in 1991, describing her marriage with Khar. The book hit the international bestseller list, but created controversy in Pakistan for its graphic description of her marriage, the mental and physical abuse inflicted on her by her husband, a powerful and prominent political figure, and the book was thus initially banned in Pakistan. The book elaborated how Khar beat Tehmina, kidnapped their children, flaunted his extra-marital affair with her youngest sister, and even forced Tehmina to strip naked, when she disobeyed his orders. She argued in the book that the real power of feudal landlords like Khar is derived from the distorted version of Islam that is supported by the mullahs and maulvis. Khar later went on to marry Tehmina's younger sister.

My Feudal Lord is divided into three parts respectively aptly entitled Lion of Punjab, Law of Jungle, and Lioness. Throughout these sections one can map the progress of Tehmina from an ordinary elitist housewife to an emancipated human being contesting for equal rights and women's empowerment. In Pakistani society, where the Muslim patriarchs dominate, the entity of women is that of inferior beings, both intellectually and socially. Her main *raison d'etre* seems to be an instrument for the satisfaction of the man's sexual desires and perpetuation of the species. Tehmina herself was no exception to this rule and fashioned herself mechanically to cater to her husband's preferences, be it in appearance, attire or makeup. Moreover she reveled in the conventional social expectations of the behaviour expected of a married woman. Tehmina writes:

> The women in our circle did not seem to look beyond their raised noses. They chattered endlessly about disobedient servants, clothes, jewellery and interior decorations.... Many a day in the lives of these women was completely devoted to the topic of what to wear that evening.[17]

Tehmina herself is no exception as she revels in the same and after her marriage to Mustafa she fashions herself mechanically to satisfy his whims and fancies. She writes, "I was flattered when Mustafa noticed me and upset when he did not." This is a norm of her society and being born and bred in such a culture Tehmina herself has been brainwashed into accepting male supremacy and female inferiority. In the first part of *My Feudal Lord*, Mustafa is portrayed as a man who revels in the total subjugation, repression and oppression of his female counterpart. Tehmina's conventional upbringing, conditioned by her patriarchal social environment in which she lived, made her accept her husband Mustafa's physical assaults and sexual brutality as a part of her destiny. That was the social ethos which inculcated itself into her being. Her mother's comment aptly illustrates this:

> If a husband behaves in a strange or unreasonable manner, you should treat him like a sick human being, like someone who needs medical care and treatment. Deal with him like a psychiatrist.[18]

Yet Mustafa is neither sick nor unreasonable. He is simply insanely and irrationally possessive in a manner reminiscent of the Duke of Ferrara in Robert Browning's *My Last Duchess*. For, according to Mustafa, a woman, like land, is "power, prestige and a property"—a commodity meant for utilization and consumption in whichever way the owner/master deems fit. Surprisingly, when Tehmina becomes pregnant as a result of Mustafa's violent rapist tortures, he takes a lot of personal care of her. However, a close reading of the novel makes the reader realize that it is not out of love for her but in the hope of a male heir that Mustafa is attending to Tehmina. The following lines amply illustrate her repulsion and hatred:

> By the time I was eight months pregnant, Mustafa's rich force-fed diet has caused me to balloon from my normal eight stone to almost eleven stone. I looked and felt like a bloated cow.[19]

Her endurance of Mustafa's tortures is the result of an archaic patriarchal value which inculcates a sense of slavery into the essence of womanhood. This extends to sexual domination of the wife by the husband. Patriarchal discourse does not regard sex as a means of mutual physical enjoyment but rather as a tool of dominion. This is why Tehmina tries to perpetuate her marriage bond with Mustafa, realizing fully well that in her society a divorced woman is the most despicable of the human species. Her heart-rending description of her loveless marriage is revealed as:

> There was not a day that Mustafa did not hit me.... For some reason, the food was late, his...clothes were creased. I just tried my best not to provoke him.... He continued to use my first marriage as a stick to beat me with, my divorce and remarriage had proved to him that I was capable of adultery. I was afraid that my slightest response to his advances would reinforce his image of me as a common slut. This was a feudal hang-up: his class believed that a woman was an instrument of a man's carnal pleasure. If the woman ever indicated that she felt pleasure, she was a potential adulteress, not to be trusted. Mustafa did not even realize that he had crushed my sensuality. I was on automatic pilot...responding as much as was important for him but never feeling anything myself. If he was satisfied there was a chance that he would be in better humour. It was at these times that I realized that prostitution must be a most difficult profession.[20]

Part Two of the novel is set in a politically turbulent atmosphere of General Zia's coup, overthrowing the Government of Prime Minister Zulfiqar Ali Bhutto and establishing a military regime. Mustafa, a Bhutto loyalist now falls from grace in the new regime since his loyalties are suspect and along with Tehmina, goes to London via Mecca. Before leaving his country, Mustafa promises the Government of General Zia that he will bring back some important documents from London and these will help in the total liquidation of the Bhutto Government and will thus prove Mustafa's loyalty to the present military regime of Pakistan. Yet once Mustafa reaches London, his dilemma is resolved and he decides to remain loyal to the Bhutto Government and so he starts contacting all possible exiles there. In London Mustafa and Tehmina start a fashionable life as exiles. At this point both Tehmina and her family have accepted Mustafa with all his perversions and atrocities and they are living in an apartment owned by Tehmina's parents who want their daughter and son-in-law to live happily together. They also urge the two not to file for divorce. Her father tells her:

> You can only leave his home in a coffin.[21]

Emboldened by his father-in-law's approval and attitude, Mustafa starts behaving as before and to make matters worse, he seduces Tehmina's younger sister Adila, while physically assaulting Tehmina regularly. Overcome by his physical assaults, Tehmina finally raises her voice telling him:

> This is my father's house and I do not think that you should dare to lift a hand on me here.[22]

However her protests become feeble once she realizes that her family will not support her at all and she can hardly hope to receive support from anyone else. Left with no material and mental support and with the hope of a bleak future before her, Tehmina reconciles yet again with her brute of a husband. Her only consolation is in the power of the Almighty to whom she prays constantly to alleviate her sufferings and to make her husband realize his shortcomings. The last straw comes after Tehmina becomes pregnant again and unforeseen circumstances compel her to visit a male doctor. This hurts Mustafa's enormous ego and he sees Tehmina's visit to a male doctor as an unforgivable transgression whereby she has insulted his manhood and his right over her as her husband. He beats the pregnant Tehmina brutally. This is an insight into the sexual ego of the feudal master who treats his wife as a possession. For the first time in her life she considers divorce but realizes that she might have to forgo her right over her daughter. So she once again reconciles with her destiny:

> A prisoner ultimately settles into a monotonous routine. Anger recedes; senses dull. The spirit is crushed.[23]

It is not as if Tehmina is immune to all the insults and violence heaped on her. She lacks the courage to protest as she has been taught that women are meant to be soft, forgiving, enduring, having infinite patience and capacity for stoicism. The fact that despite all tortures a woman must have unquestioned loyalty to her husband or patriarchal master is an embedded concept in her psyche. She thus understands that she lacks the conviction to stand up for her self-respect and is aware of the reality of being a single divorcee in a male-dominated patriarchal society. She tries to perpetuate her marriage with Mustafa by reconciling herself with her socio-cultural environment. In the course of time, Mustafa develops an incestuous relationship with Adila, his sister-in-law, which is subsequently discovered by Tehmina. Yet Tehmina blames not her husband but her sister and complains about the affair to her mother that her sister has been seducing Mustafa. The reason for Tehmina's one-sided complaint is that she may protect her husband's honour in her parent's house. But the results of these are drastic as Mustafa batters her with the butt of his double-barrelled shotgun and strips her nude, taking away from her even the last vestige of security. This episode has an oppressive effect on her soul and she describes:

> This episode would cripple my spirit—perhaps beyond salvation. From this movement forward, it would be nearly impossible for me to function as an individual. There was not one iota of self-esteem left. The shame had burned it down to ashes.[24]

Politics in Pakistan begins changing with the execution of Bhutto in 1979. The Soviet invasion of Afghanistan helps Zia consolidate his position in the domestic politics of Pakistan with the support of the American Government. Bhutto's sons mobilize the support and sympathy of a large number of Pakistani people in exile. And this exiled community dreams of dislodging Zia forcibly. Mustafa senses the futility of this attempt and feels that this revolutionary group aiming at overthrowing the Zia Government will strengthen Zia and give him an excuse to eliminate all the supporters of Bhutto who were still in Pakistan. So Mustafa changes his potential strategy. He starts traveling the entire continent, mobilizing support from those in exile, tirelessly delivering lectures at public meetings for a sensible change in the Government of Pakistan. At this stage of his life and career, he appears to be a champion of democracy in public life, although he is still an inveterate wife-abuser in his private life. His words enthuse Tehmina and she starts believing that soon her country shall be free from the clutches of martial law imposed by the military government.

The basic teaching imparted to every woman in a patriarchal society is to remain a silent spectator, even as a victim to any injustice meted out by the man and to be very careful of not going public with any personal crisis which may harm the "honour" of her man. However even social constraints have their limits and one day Tehmina cannot take it anymore. So Tehmina retorts in fury when he next tries to hit her. She warns him not to raise his hand on her again for she can also react by taking a knife and killing him.

After the warning, Tehmina remains with her husband and visits India with a diplomatic mission. After the meeting, she visits the Holy Shrine of Ajmer and her prayer reveals her deep devoutness and reverence for her religion:

> My two shadows were at my side as I entered the shrine. Their Hindu presence disturbed my Islamic prayers.... I asked God to curb Mustafa's bouts of violence and insanity. 'I want a normal home with peace and harmony', I prayed. I asked that God would give Mustafa respect and end his exile.[25]

After their return from India, Mustafa and Tehmina file for separation under the court of law in England. This is granted, and after the legal separation, Tehmina decides to cut her hair thereby sending a message to Mustafa that she will never return to him, as he had been besotted with her beautiful hair and the act of cutting it is symbolic of her cutting him out her existence. She writes:

> He knew that I had finally decided not to return to him, ever again. Otherwise I would not have done away with what he loved most about me. Without my hair, he was a weak Samson.[26]

However now that she has forsaken him, Mustafa's male ego is affronted and he begins wooing her back with a vengeance. Eventually he succeeds in winning her over by enthusing her with his noble mission of returning home to rescue his country from the clutches of its martial government. A kind of ideological affinity makes the two of them return together to Pakistan upon which Mustafa is immediately arrested at the airport. Tehmina, being his wife, receives much public attention and is for the first time accepted as a leader of the people. Being a dutiful wife, legal separation notwithstanding, Tehmina visits the jailed Mustafa regularly and tries to mobilize public support for him. He has no alternative except her and so he controls his temper. Eventually however his perversions dominate him and his lust for her resurfaces making him rape her in jail on his birthday. Tehmina is physically ravaged by the wounds he inflicts as she is still recovering from surgery. This ends her optimistic endurance and she applies for the Islamic *Khula* or divorce granted to a woman as long as she relinquishes all her claims to property. Mustafa tries desperately to prevent the termination of their marriage because she is the sole means of his release from jail. So successfully does he brainwash her into dreaming of an ideal society and envisioning him as the champion of democracy that she relentlessly and successfully campaigns for his release. When Mustafa emerges from jail his real self is revealed—he is not the champion of the downtrodden masses, but the same selfish, jealous, egoistic and possessive man. Amazed at the public image and support built by Tehmina around herself, he raves with jealousy and does not acknowledge all her efforts in his release from jail and, on the domestic front, resumes his illicit relationship with his sister-in-law Adila. Tehmina, however, is no longer docile, compromising, submissive and tolerant. As she tells him in the presence of all:

> Your marriage, according to the Koran, was over years ago when you slept with my sister. I have been living with you in sin. The contract stood null and void long ago.[27]

She now decides to complete the divorce proceedings and also begins to write an autobiography. She believes that ethical compulsions demand this act of courage and she owes it to her closed and repressive society to reveal the deepest personal secrets of her life. The new emancipated Tehmina has a courage born out of enduring oppression, and believes that:

> Silence condones injustice, breeds subservience and fosters a malignant hypocrisy. Mustafa Khar and other feudal lords thrive and multiply on silence. Muslim women must learn to raise their voice against injustice.[28]

The inter-related tropology of gender, space and ethnicity in Tehminia Durrani's *My Feudal Lord* gestures towards a possible resolution of the expressive dilemma articulated by Virginia Woolf in her comment on women's writing.[29] For Tehmina Durrani, the feminine is the marginalized consciousness that operates on the periphery of patriarchal discourse. However the marginalized or peripheral consciousness can centre itself through a radical act of subversion by turning the master discourse inside out as it were—by reconfiguring the periphery as the frontier or point of entry into an alternate realm of possibility. The new Janus-faced identity is capable of negotiating multiple realities as it looks back towards the periphery and forwards to the frontier and can hence be re-conceptualized as being empowered instead of marginalized. The duality of this vision underscores the potentialities rather than the problematics of the marginalized self-marginalized both in terms of identity and gender. The socially passive and culturally silenced female voice is suddenly focalized and vocalized as being assertive and empowered through the very act of self-expression. Space is a crucial ingredient of this tropology. Space functions in discourse as a mimetic concept since spaces, literal as well as metaphorical, are very often culturally constructed imperialist and/or patriarchal 'mapping' of experience. Destabilizing space and the markers that define it in the dominant discourse is one way of claiming agency. Through negotiating gender, space and identity Tehmina Durrani interrogates the very basis of the relationship posited between gender, spatial and cultural location and identity. Tehmina Durrani becomes not one of Homi Bhabha's shadowy and derivative neo-colonial 'mimic men' (the products of mimesis) whose identities are subsumed within the externally imposed metaphor but the activator of fresh analogies and the producer of new metaphors. Patriarchal discourse limits and transcribes the image and identity of Tehmina but she inverts the social and familial constraints to emerge as a new woman. She strives against all odds to escape from all forms of essential categorizing that render the subaltern or minority woman both the victim and unwilling perpetrators of damning stereotypical metaphors both by Eurocentric imperialism and the patriarchal tenets of her Islamic society, the power politics in Pakistani Government and the social ethos of Pakistani marital life. Tehmina is urging her readers and other socio-culturally repressed sisters to rediscover their marginal self and thereby gain emancipation and empowerment. Pakistan's famous author says fearless expression of thoughts on social evils and wrong alone can save the country from chaos. "One of the things that I became one hundred per cent sure was that one must not be afraid to raise one's voice against what one feels is wrong and finds painful. If one does not break the silence one can't correct disorder. There is a disorder, because we are so silent.... We do not want to become inconvenient by putting ourselves in roles which will not be immediately accepted. That silence of ours is a very major reason for social and political malaise. I see lethargy everywhere, in everybody,"[30] says Durrani in an honest outburst about Pakistan's society.

NOTES

1. Olney, James, *Metaphors of Self: The Meaning of Autobiography* (Princeton University Press, November 1981), p. 12.
2. *Ibid.*, p. 13.
3. *Ibid.*, p. 14.
4. *Ibid.*, p. 15.
5. Gusdorf, Georges; "Conditions and Limits of Autobiography," trans. James Olney, *Autobiography: Essays Theoretical and Critical* (Princeton: Princeton University Press, 1980), p. 8.
6. Freidman, Susan Stanford, *Mappings—Feminism and the Cultural Geographies of Encounter* (Princeton University Press, 1998).

7. Benstock, Shari, *The Private Self: Theory and Practice in Women's Autobiographical Writing* (Routledge, 1998), p. 12.
8. Freidman, Susan Stanford, "Women's Autobiographical Selves: Theory and Practice" in Benstock, Shari, *The Private Self: Theory and Practice in Women's Autobiographical Writing* (Routledge, 1998), p. 36.
9. Chodorow, Nancy, *Feminism and Psychoanalytic Theory.*
10. Williams, Raymond, *Culture and Society* (Columbia University Press, 1958), p. 33.
11. Belsely, Catherine and Moore, Jane, eds., *The Feminist Reader: Essays in Gender and the Politics of Literary Criticism* (Macmillan, 1989), p. 1.
12. *Ibid.*, p. 1.
13. Mohanty, Chandra T., *Third World Women and the Politics of Feminism* (Indiana University Press, 1991), p. 4.
14. *Ibid.*, p. 5.
15. Mohanty, Chandra T., "Under Western Eyes: Feminist Scholarship and Colonial Discourses" in *Colonial Discourse and Post-colonial Theory*, ed. Williams and Chrisman, pp. 196-220.
16. Woolf, Virginia, *A Room of One's Own,* quoted by Elaine Showalter in Showalter, ed. *The New Feminist Criticism: Essays on Women, Literature and Theory* (London: Virago, 1986, rpt. 1993), p. 247.
17. Durrani, Tehmina, *My Feudal Lord* (Corgi, 1996), p. 65.
18. *Ibid.*, p. 130.
19. *Ibid.*, p. 109.
20. *Ibid.*, p. 127.
21. *Ibid.*, p. 126.
22. *Ibid.*, p. 134.
23. *Ibid.*, p. 143.
24. *Ibid.*, p. 165.
25. *Ibid.*, pp. 233-34.
26. *Ibid.*, p. 236.
27. *Ibid.*, p. 362.
28. *Ibid.*, p. 375.

29. Woolf, Virginia, *A Room of One's Own,* quoted by Elaine Showalter in Showalter, ed. *The New Feminist Criticism: Essays on Women, Literature and Theory* (London: Virago, 1986, rpt. 1993), p. 247.
30. Tehmina Durrani in her interview to Muhammad Najeeb in *Mid Day*, October 26, 1998.

15

An Intertextual Reading of Barbara Kingsolver's *The Poisonwood Bible* and Joseph Conrad's *Heart of Darkness*

Shymasree Basu

Graham Allen in his monograph *Intertextuality* has remarked on the multiple meanings of the word which serve to establish its problematic nature. However, he adds that the act of reading a text, in the postmodern age, is all about establishing the relations between that text and others. Meaning becomes indeterminate and something which exists between a text and all the other texts to which it refers and relates (Allen, 1). Allen Kristeva coined the term/intertextuality while discoursing on Bakhtin's theory of dialogic (in her essay "Word, Dialogue, Novel") to describe it as a permutations of texts (Allen, 15). Edward Quinn in the *Collins Dictionary of Literary Terms* describes two types of intertexuality: citation and presupposition. Citation includes not only direct quotation and allusion, but also literary conventions, imitation and unconscious sources (Quinn, 173). Presupposition involves assumption regarding the reader, the situation being referred to and its context (Quinn, 173). In this paper I shall consider Barbara Kingsolver's novel *The Poisonwood Bible* as a text which responds to both kinds of intertextuality. Kingsolver uses motifs, images and tropes used by Conrad in *Heart of Darkness* to document the Price family's experiences in the Congo. Exploring the relations between the two texts, we shall see whether Kingsolver is successful in creating a writerly text which stimulates exercises in intertextuality.

One of the earliest examples of intertextuality is the instant when Leah, one of the narrators of Kingsolver's novel, recaptures the momentous occasion of Patrice Lumumba coming to power in the Congo and roughly translates his victory speech:

> My brothers...we have suffered colonial oppression in body and heart and we say to you all of that is finished. Together we are going to make a place for justice and peace, prosperity and grandeur. We are going to show the world what the *homme noir* can do when he works for freedom. We are going to make the Congo, for all Africa the *heart of light*. [italics mine] (*The Poisonwood Bible*, 184)

Lumumba describes his nation, the Congo as the 'heart of light'. Marlow in his narration in *Heart of Darkness* often refers to his journey towards the Inner Station as a journey into the heart of darkness. Lumumba asserts his patriotism by deliberately subverting associations or images of darkness with that of Africa. In his description of the African nation as the heart of light, we see the ability of the post-colonial nation to define its own nationhood, sometimes by discarding Eurocentric images associated with the nation's identity; in this case Africa's association with darkness. As in the case of Marlow who comes to the Congo with preconceived notions of the virtues of European colonialism, especially in its avowed aim to civilize the savages, Nathan Price, a Baptist comes to Congo to spread the word of Jesus and dies believing that the natives were beyond salvation.

Kingsolver situates her epic narrative in the 1960s and the political turmoil of the Congo is compared to the turmoil that the Price family faces while adjusting to the country and trying to overcome their American selves. As in Conrad's depiction of Marlow's journey, Kingsolver also emphasizes on the curious ways in which the African continent claims the outsiders and forces them to re-examine themselves, until they question the Western civilization which they represent. The preacher's wife Orleanna like Marlow critiques the Western civilization which had used Congo for its economic gains. She is critical of Dr. David Livingstone for starting the trend of opening missions in Africa for the betterment of the savages. She remarks at the beginning of the novel:

> Why, Dr Livingstone, I presume, wasn't he the rascal! He and all the profiteers who've since walked out on Africa as a husband quits a wife, leaving her with her naked body. (*TPB*, 9)

Orleanna Price's disgust at Western attempts to civilize Africa has the same tone of disgust as that of Marlow when he sees the chained African labourers and talks about 'this objectless blasting' (*Heart of Darkness,* 25) and his scathing comment on the colonial enterprise as that of a 'flabby, pretending, weak-eyed devil of a rapacious and pitiless folly' (*Heart of Darkness,* 25). Very early in *Heart of Darkness*, Marlow comments on the colonizer as immigrant and his arrival in an alien land that is a wilderness. He delineates the process in the following manner:

> There's no initiation either into such mysteries. He has to live in the midst of the incomprehensible, which is also detestable. And it has a fascination, too, that goes to work upon him. The fascination of the abomination.... The longing to escape, the powerless disgust, the surrender, the hate (*HD*, 8).

Orleanna Price and her daughters go through the same motions. In her summation of the African experience there is the same sense of being initiated into some kind of 'mystery'. She remarks on her African experience:

> I trod on Africa without a thought, straight from our family's divinely inspired beginning to our terrible end. In between, in the midst of all those steaming nights and days darkly colored, smelling of earth, I believe there lay some marrow of honest instruction. Sometimes I can nearly say what it was. If I could, I would fling it at

> others, I'm afraid, at risk to their ease. I'd slide this awful story off my shoulders.... But Africa shifts under my hands...refusing to be any place at all, or anything but itself. (*TPB*, 9)

Orleanna Price's awareness that there was some 'marrow of honest instruction' in her African experience recalls Marlow's comments immediately after his hearing Kurtz's last words 'The horror! The horror!' (*HD*, 118) Marlow calls this cry an 'appalling face of a glimpsed truth' (*THD*, 119). He believes that Kurtz's cry was an honest one since he believed himself to have transgressed and Marlow, because he had been tempted feels that those words condensed the feelings one had when poised just above the precipice ready to fall into the abyss of nothingness. Orleanna Price, however, does not feel that she has transgressed and unlike Marlow she does not feel that her experiences have to be guarded carefully. She wants to enlighten herself as well as others but is aware how Africa and its way of life elude her. She is unable to give it any concrete meaning although apprehending that there is some important significance in those events. Thus like Marlow, the Congo experience remains an inconclusive and a liminal one for Orleanna.

Kingsolver layers her narrative by adding the narrations of Leah, Adah, Ruth and Rachel to contrast whether any amongst their could arrive at a more conclusive evaluation of the African experience as they doubt, defy and gradually shed off their American selves. Nathan Price, their father, an overzealous preacher is the only one who is unable to reconcile to the African experience although his family realises how ineffective his sermons were in the Congo. During the famine his wife and daughters realize that they could survive only if the villagers helped them by giving them food and supplies. Nathan Price's religion becomes a failure as there is no one to support his claim that Christ will eventually help them through this crisis if only they repose their faith in Him. It is another missionary who tells Nathan Price about the need to reorder conservative Christianity to accommodate it with the Pagan religion of the Congo. He tells Nathan Price that it is his belief in Creation, more than Jesus Christ's word that has helped him to sustain his faith. He cites the example of the *Book of Romans*, chapter ten where it is said that if 'the root of a tree is consecrated, so are the branches' (*TPB*, 251). He uses this metaphor and remarks:

> Brother Price, don't you sometimes think about this, as you share the food of your Congolese brethren and gladden your heart with their songs? Do you get the notion we are the branch that's grafted on here, sharing in the richness of these African roots? (*TPB*, 252)

Brother Fowles advocates the superiority of the African way of life by calling it the 'root' and themselves as the 'grafted branches'. Thus he is also critiquing the ways in which African culture has always been relegated into a secondary position whereas the European/Western culture is automatically given supremacy by its position of enlightenment. This is an instance of intertextuality that is also presupposition since Kingsolver deliberately alludes to the post-colonial theory of acknowledging the other in the self. Marlow in *Heart of Darkness* hints at Kurtz's participation in pagan rites and alleges that such a transgression occurs because the latter lacked restraint. Conrad unconsciously betrays a sense of racial superiority, but Kingsolver through Brother Fowles, and later on through the daughters of Orleanna Price is able to establish how easily the other can be accommodated in the self.

After their retreat from the Congo, the Price family try to evaluate their African experience and uniformly affirm how the continent has become a part of them. For Leah Price, this affirmation comes with guilt since she acknowledges the reality of the American intervention into the politics of Congo, especially in the assassination of Patrice Lumumba. Leah marries a freedom fighter Anatole and experiences the difficulties of living the life of a fugitive and her faith is severely tested when he is imprisoned for his political activities. She learns the value of African culture and there is a deeper understanding, an urgency to know the other. As she tells her sister: 'You just can't assume that what's right or wrong for us is the same as what was right or wrong for them.' (*TPB*, 490)

Leah feels rewarded as the Americans are gradually driven off from Angola and like Brother Fowles she develops a faith in Creation and technically forsakes her Christian religion which according to her forced her to believe in a 'tyrannical, exacting God'. She feels defined by her existence in Africa and at the end of her narration she remarks:

> I wake up in love, and work my skin to darkness under the equatorial sun. I look at my four boys, who are the colors of silt, loam, dust and clay, an infinite palette for children of their own, and I understand that time erases whiteness altogether. (*TPB*, 526)

Adah the twin sister of Leah returns to America and becomes a successful doctor. However, her pioneering work is done in the field of African parasites. Studying their variety and their myriad manners of invasion, she develops a scepticism about the effectiveness of total medical solution that western medical research proposes. She sees the ways in which western vaccines have failed to affect permanent cures in Africa. Africa, as Adah sees it, survives by a balancing act and their belief in voodoo is conditional by their equal respect for death and life. Thus she believes:

> God is everything, then god is a virus. Believe that when you get a cold. God is an ant. Believe that too, for driver ants are possessed, collectively, of the size and influence of a Biblical plague. (*TPB*, 528)

Adah along with her sister Leah appreciates this dialectical nature of African existence. In fact she feels a kinship with this culture precisely because of this duality. As she studies the indeterminate nature of the Congolese words, she understands the fallacy of Western religion. Her father had proclaimed from the pulpit—'Tata Jesus is bangala' (*TPB*, 70). Literally translated it meant 'The word of Christ is beloved' (*TPB*, 70). She later realizes bangala also meant—Poisonwood—the poisonous plant which grows on African soil. Adah ironically observes that her father was actually setting down the tenets of the poisonwood Bible by preaching what he believed was the Gospels. She remarks:

> We are the balance of our damage and own transgressions. He was my father. I own half his genes, and all his history. Believe this the mistakes are part of the story. I am born of a man who believed he could tell nothing but the truth, while he set down for all time the poisonwood Bible. (*TPB*, 533)

Thus not only do the words elude absolute signification, Adah with her penchant for anagrams discovers that one is never able to arrive at a fixed meaning as the meanings keep shifting. Very consciously she treats the word of God (something the western civilization has valued as absolute) as indeterminate. Unlike Marlow, Adah and Leah talk about the inconclusiveness of their experience and are comforted by the fact that they are inconclusive since human existence consists of dualities which are indefinable. Adah's remark is also significant because intertextuality as a theoretical concept is based on this indeterminacy of the text and the shifting signification of words. Kingsolver invites the readers to undertake a comparative/intertextual reading between her text as well as Conrad's *Heart of Darkness*. Conrad had one of the narrators describe Marlow's yarn as something which has an elusive quality. He says:

> But Marlow was not typical (if his prosperity to spin yarns be excepted) and to him the meaning of an episode was not inside like a kernel, but outside, enveloping the late which brought it out only as a glow brings out a haze, in the likeness of one of these misty halos that sometimes are made visible by the spectral illumination of moonshine. (*HD*, 7)

As Adah and Leah clarify their experience, they become more and more sceptical about the word of God. Living in close proximity to the Congolese, they begin to appreciate the fractures within the language which made faithful translation of the Bible not only absurd but also catastrophic. Graham Allen in his study *Intertextuality* has remarked about the indeterminacy in the Bible and in the word of God. He also cites Barthes' 'Death of an Author' (Allen, 61-94) to emphasize his contribution to the theory of Intertextuality especially his propounding the concept of text as existing in language and therefore liable to evolve its own meanings. Adah's observation of Nathan Price's ministry as evolving into a separate text—a Poisonwood Bible—is significant because more than Marlow in Conrad's novel, Kingsolver deliberately appropriates the concept of a writerly text, as all the members of the family try to make their own meaning of the Congo experience. Kingsolver implements presupposition in her text because the popularity of post-structuralist discourse has given currency to intertextuality and it is one of the essential aspects as arising out of the phenomenon of the writerly text.

Kingsolver writing the novel in 1998 does not camouflage the meaning of the Congo experience as Conrad made Marlow do in his interview with Kurtz's Intended. She reveals the multiplicity of meanings that Congo assumes in the lives of the women in the Price family. In recounting their experience in the Congo they review their beliefs, their faith and finally their identity. For each of the Prices Congo teaches them the value of life and like the Barthesque notion of the "text", it keeps changing forever.

WORKS CITED

Allen, Graham. *Intertextuality*. New York: Routledge, 2007.

Conrad, Joseph. *Heart of Darkness*. New Delhi: Oxford University Press, 1999.

Kingsolver, Barbara. *The Poisonwood Bible*. New York: Harper Collins, 1998.

Quinn, Edward. *Collins Dictionary of Literary Terms*. Glasgow: Harper Collins, 2004.

16

Theorizing Fiction, Some Concepts of the Traditionalists: A Comparative Study

Piyali Das

When we read a novel we find a close imitation of men and manners and along with it we see the very web and texture of society as it really exists and as we meet it when we face the real world. So a novel is basically an art of imitation and it depends on the individual novelist how successfully he carries out his task of imitating the society of which he himself is a part. Like any other artist the novelist is a maker, as he is essentially making an imitation of life and creating a fictional world removed to some extent from the real world. He is making, it might be said, a working model of life as he sees and feels it; his conclusions about it being expressed in the characters he invents, the situations in which he places them and in the very words he selects accordingly for those purposes.

This article aims to discuss the views of Henry James, Somerset Maugham and E.M. Forster related to fiction. Many of their views are similar in nature and point out the basic structure and characteristics of a novel. As already stated, a novel is in its broadest definition a personal impression of the contemporary society of the novelist and its value is greater or less according to the intensity of the impression of life, felt and reflected in this work of imitation. So the aspect of value judgment is necessarily linked with this work of art, but there shall be no intensity at all and therefore no value, unless there is the freedom to feel and say. The execution belongs essentially to the creator; it is what is most personal to him and we measure him and also his creation by those standards. The advantage, the luxury as well as the torment and responsibility of the novelist is that there is no limit to what he may attempt as an executor—and thereby no limit to his possible experiments, efforts, discoveries and successes.

So far we pointed out that the novelist recreates the world of reality in his work and that is what Henry James in his *The Art of Fiction* points out: "The novelist must write from his experience and characters must be real and such as might be met within actual life" (p. 14). Therefore the stress is given on the fact that the imitation must be as perfect and as real as possible and that is the vital task to be fulfilled by the novelist. James further states: "The air of reality (solidity of specification) seems to me to be the supreme virtue of a novel—the merit on which all its other merits (including that conscious moral purpose of which Mr. Besant speaks) helplessly and submissively depend" (*The Art of Fiction*, p. 16). Thus the key to a novel is 'the air of reality', as pointed out by James, that it creates in producing an illusion of life, a finite blend of reality and imagination. Art for James is to be selective in terms of the aspect of reality/human experience he wishes to write about, but part of this selectivity is to be definitely inclusive. This suggests that the novel must deal with aspects of reality that many may not consider to be morally good. To be moral in writing is to be complete and faithful to human experience.

Maugham differs to some extent from the view of James that reality is the basic principle behind the creation of a novel. Maugham has definite views on the relationship between art and the novel, which is of course a form of art and life. He is of the opinion that the world of art is different from the actual world. Art cannot possibly copy life which is chaotic, complex and indefinable. A work of Art, however outstanding, cannot be the literal transcript of life.

Naturally a novel does not present life as it is, but is only an arrangement of some of its aspects in consonance with the novelist's individual attitudes and ideas. According to Maugham, the novelist as an artist does not simply copy life but he makes an arrangement out of it to suit his own purposes. Life itself furnishes the novelist with material for artistic creation. But he selects, alters and arranges it in his own way so as to create a world of his own. The novelist, for Maugham, is akin to the painter or the sculptor, who sacrifices truth for the sake of achieving his effect.

When we come to Forster, what he stresses most in the novel is its human quality. He affirms that the novel is basically sogged with humanity, and if it is alienated from it, it will come to nothing. A novel can make a definite progress only when it is sensitive to the life around it and deals with it as thoroughly as possible. Since it is inseparable from human nature, its development implies the development of humanity.

To quote Maugham "The aim of the writer of fiction, is not to instruct but to please" (*The Art of Fiction*, p. 9). Maugham's idea that fiction is primarily a source of entertainment and that it should be necessarily readable is in essence the ideal of the Victorian novelists. He asserts that a novelist should tell a tale of absorbing interest, that he should obviously create characters marked by individuality and complexity and replete with vitality and that he should be both an entertainer and philosopher. Once again to quote Maugham: "I think it an abuse to use the novel as a pulpit or platform and I believe readers are misguided when they suppose they can thus easily acquire knowledge. It is a great nuisance that knowledge can only be acquired by hard work. It would be fine if we could swallow the powder of profitable information made palatable by the jam of fiction. But the truth is that, so made palatable, we can't be sure that the powder will be profitable, for the knowledge the novelist imparts is biased and thus unreliable and it is better not to know a thing at all than to know it in a distorted fashion" (*The Art of Fiction*, p. 8). Thus Maugham stresses on the fact that the novel should be entertaining and it is the essential quality of the novel, without which as he says no other quality avails. Maugham is of the view that even if the novelist's theme is not based on universal facts, it must be widely interesting. To him, the novel is a story first and foremost. Further he states: "A sensible person does not read a novel as a task. He reads it as a diversion. He is prepared to interest himself in the characters and is concerned to see how they act in given circumstances, and what happens to them" (*The Art of Fiction*, p. 2).

Similarly, James considers, a good novel to be good because it is interesting. The point of interest lies in the way it represents life and has the odour of reality. The odour of reality in turn has its major source in the experience of the author. James' major contribution to the modern novel deals with the point of view or the relationship of the narrator to the material he selects for himself to write. Actions he notes are of limited interest unless they deal with or are reflected in an engaged consciousness. Characters are interesting he believes only in terms of their ability to feel their respective situations in which they are placed in the novel.

This view of James leads us to the next basic aspect of the novel—the art of story-telling. Maugham pinned his faith in the age-old art of story-telling. Naturally he thus keeps up the great tradition of the English novel, the tradition of novelists like Fielding and Scott. Despite Forster's attempt to relegate the story to the low position, Maugham continues to regard it as the most fundamental element of the novel. His dictum that the novel is a story first and foremost is a matter of faith with him. He firmly believes that the function of the novelist is mainly to tell a story, to device a plot and to invent characters. The greatness of a novelist, according to Maugham, lies in the power of narration—the ease, grace, freshness and the spontaneity with which he tells a tale. That is how the interest of the readers is sustained in the novel. In the chapter on the 'story' in *Aspects of the Novel*, Forster begins with the assertion that the novel, in its most basic definition, tells a story. He goes on to say that a story must be built around suspense keeping in view the question of what happens next. The only skill of a storyteller as Forster believes is his ability to wield the weapon of suspense making the audience eager to discover the next event in the sequence. The basis of a novel is necessarily considered to be story—the narration of events in the order they happened—but story telling alone can never produce a great novel. A novelist can only begin to explore the value of human experiences by developing the characters of the story.

The Art of Fiction expresses in clear terms how serious James was about the craft of story-telling. He desired to achieve in art completeness about any given situation; he also aimed at an ultimate artistic perfection which should reveal the reality of the imagined situation. Never did he underestimate the difficulty of achieving such completeness. This perpetual concern with completeness explains his fastidious care in writing his novels and his search for the exact phrase to convey his meaning. He was the first novelist in English language to believe that how a thing said was equally important as what was said.

Along with the element of the story, the plot is also essential. A plot according to Forster demands intelligence and memory on the part of the reader who remembers incidents and creates connecting threads between them. This allows the novelist to delay explanations and introduce human mystery to the narrative. The novel has to have integral structure. Part of the reader's evaluative judgment is based on its ability to hang together for us. A novel has individual character, it has its own tensions, physiognomy and atmosphere. Maugham does not draw a clear line of demarcation between the story and the plot, and thus he greatly differs from Forster. Maugham holds that human nature is made of discordant elements and that men are not all of a piece. Since Maugham was greatly influenced by the French novelists and their sense of form, therefore in his theory of fiction he attaches considerable significance to form and structure. This accounts for his conviction that the novelist's story must necessarily be well-constructed with a definite beginning, a middle and an end. He affirms that a story cannot have a form unless it is brought to a conclusion.

James speaking about the structure of a novel states: "a novel is a living thing, all one and continuous, like any other organism, and in proportion as it lives will it be found, I think, that in each of the parts there is something of each of the other parts" (*The Art of Fiction,* p. 16). So he focuses on the close-knit structure of the novel and it being considered a living one, takes on a life of its own. Once again according to Maugham a novel cannot be made of mere facts alone. Their use is to develop an idea or illustrate a theme, and the novelist does not have only the right to change them to suit his purpose, to stress them or leave them in shadow, but is under the necessity of doing so. So as a matter of fact, the artist is naturally obsessed with his theme and it is with a view to exploring and conveying it that he creates a work of art. He is primarily concerned with it and the techniques he uses are only a means to present it effectively.

The next important aspect which characterizes a novel is the character. Character and characterization play an important part in imparting life to the novel. For Forster the speciality of the novel is that the novelist can talk to us about his people, can talk through them and can enable us to hear what his people talk to themselves. Besides he can know and portray his and his people's subconscious self fairly well. In chapter three, titled 'People', Forster states: "a character in a book is real when the novelist knows everything about it" (*Aspects of the Novel,* p. 70). Forster emphasizes that characters are not real people, rather they are like real people. People in a novel can be understood completely by the reader if the novelist wishes; their inner as well as their outer life can be readily exposed. It is this completeness that allows characters to take on the air of being real; and this reality as already quoted depends on the novelist's complete knowledge of it. Central to the *Aspects of the Novel* is Forster's notion that there are in the novel mainly two forces: human beings and a bundle of various things, not human beings, and it is the novelist's business to adjust these two forces and conciliate their claims. Forster believes in the primacy of people over form, of life over art, in the novel. According to Maugham, characters in the novel should posses individuality and vitality. The novelist as Maugham believes, has a multiple personality as he has to project himself into different characters. He also points out that James could not fully succeed in making his English characters life-like and credible because he, being an American, could not become one with them, and also because he unfortunately lacked the quality of empathy. James speaking about the character argues that the distinction is of no importance as character in any sense in which we can get at is action and action is plot. Any plot which hangs together, even if it pretends to interest the readers, plays upon emotion, suspense, by means of personal references. We care what happens to people in proportion as we know what people are. James further states that a novel always undergoes transmutation in the writer's consciousness under the pressure and heat of imagination. James thinks that a character in a novel should not be contrasted with an incident or situation. He demands that a novel deals with what he called the dramatization of consciousness.

To sum up, it can be said that the novel cannot be a literal transcript of life but nevertheless is an impression of life and the novelist only arranges the facts, of his observation and experiences of life according to his own personality. The worth of a novel depends directly on the amount of felt life concerned in producing it, and thus, ultimately on the kind and the degree of the artist's prime sensibility which is the soil out of which his subject springs. The novelist does not recreate life as it is and does not tell a story for its own sake. He expresses his vision of life through his story and the portrait of life he presents. Thus a novel is a personal and direct impression of life and along with it the novel must be interesting. It should be enjoyed as it deserves and should be explored to its utmost extent. The readers should reveal it and rejoice in it. The duty of the novelist is to be complete as far as possible and to make a perfect a work.

WORKS CITED

Allen, Walter. *The Novel Today*. Longmans Green & Co., 1960.

Forster, E.M. *Aspects of the Novel*. Penguin Books Limited, 1927.

James, Henry. "The Art of Fiction". In *Essentials of the Theory of Fiction*, eds. Michael J. Hoffman and Patrick D. Murphy, Durham & London: Duke University Press, 2005.

Maugham, W. Somerset. *Ten Novels and Their Authors. Vintage*, 2001.

Van Ghent, Dorothy. *The English Novel: Form and Function*, London: Harper Touchbooks, Harper and Row Publishers, 1953.

Watt, Ian. *The Rise of the Novel*. London: University of California Press Limited, 1971.

17

Raja Rao's *The Cat and Shakespeare*

Suresh Chandra Pande

Raja Rao who webs a trio with R.K. Narayan and M.R. Anand as a novelist and short story writer was brought to full-length assessment by the maiden efforts of Prof. C.D. Narasimhaiah[1] and Prof. M.K. Naik.[2] Soon after winning Padma Bhushan and Sahitya Academy awards, Raja Rao once more as first illustrious Asian was seen at a glittering ceremony held in Oklahoma University receiving the most prestigious £ 25000 Newstadt International prize for literature. In an age of hectic global literary upsurge as is evident through Media announcements, Raja Rao is taking his place among the well-known scientists of the world whom he not only greeted by his mellifluous voice but also kept dumb-founded in World Science Congress—Bangalore (India) recently. One can trace propensities of his scientific bent of mind as early as *The Serpent and the Rope* (1960)[3] and later further strengthened and enriched by the trilogy *The Chess Master and His Moves* —(1988)[4] in which the central character Srinivasa Sastri is a mathematician.

I feel it genuinely difficult to write a tribute commemorating the sad demise of 'a half sensuous saint'[5] of non-duality—*Advaita*, who had an aura around him and who spat much of metaphysics. Jawaharlal Nehru was indeed surprised to see Raja Rao spitting much of metaphysics when he introduced Nehru with Andre Malraux in Paris (not to undermine the contribution Raja Rao levied on a tribute—book to Nehru) even before the publication of *Kanthapura* (1938). Nehru loved and admired Raja Rao but could never get an access to his metaphysics. Metaphysics, of course, was not Nehru's cup of tea. Similarly, E.M. Forster who came to India in 1945 asked jovially to a friend—Where is Raja Rao? Where is he hiding now? Hiding—yes, Raja Rao once shut up himself in a room at Benaras (India) nearly for forty days engrossed in meditation. Actually, 'he was worldly in a very unworldly manner'.[6] Alas! With his passing on Saturday, July 8, 2006 in his home town Austin (Texas) at 96, India has lost a soul whom *Calvinists* would have called 'Pre-destined' and eschatalogical studies of the East on metempsychosis would like to call a pilgrimage to the mythological abode—*Vaikuntha*. I feel highly thankful to K. Natwar Singh—a contemporary friend of Raja Rao, who at least took pains to contribute, an empathetic tribute[7] bidding a good bye and a farewell to dear Raja Rao.

First written in Trivendrum and published in U.S.A. by MacMillan Company in 1965 with two more subtitles *A Tale of Modern India* and *A Metaphysical Comedy*. Raja Rao's *The Cat and Shakespeare* stands as a rare piece of art ever written. The sheer popularity of the novelette can be gauged by the book reviews which appeared in and across the U.S.A. in 1965. Ray Lewis White, a Professor of English, Illinois State University, then prepared a diligent collection later presented it to JIWE.[8]

Initiated into writing by Sri Atmanand Guru, Raja Rao's *Kanthapura*, *The Serpent and the Rope (*1960) and *The Cat and Shakespeare* (1965) respectively comprise the themes of selfless action or *Karma yoga*, self-knowledge or *Jnana yoga* and self-surrender or *Bhakti yoga* as a way of deliverance from birth-death cycle called *Jiva* or life meticulously elaborated in *The Bhagwad Gita*.

Much debatable title which has intrigued critics as well as interviewers of *The Cat and Shakespeare* is indeed profound by symbolic. The Cat as mother symbolises primordial cosmic creator—the Almighty mother worshipped as feminine principle: *Paraskti* or *Jaganmata*, while Shakespearean part unfolds a puzzle as it encompasses an entire world of day-to-day trivialities, joys and sorrows of mundane existence.

As the novel was written in Trivendrum, the tale centres round pre-independence Kerala. In Raja Rao's own words the novel 'as an allegory, a poem or a fable'[9] explores three dimensional meaning of Trivendrum. The foremost dimension represents geographical/historical reality, the second allegorical and the last represents absolute reality which like sky covers everything.

As such the novelist succeeds in capturing vivid reverberations of the sights and sounds of social and naturally deep-seated life lived during World War II. Although social life is ingrained in superstitious, traditions, casteism and corruption, yet it seems instantly intermixed in the multiplicity of effervescent hues and a vivacity surviving along the undercurrents of *Visistadvaita*. Meanwhile corruption is put forward by matter of fact portrayal of a ration office. The ration office is a den of corruption. Seventeen sacks of rice were lost and office files were supposed to be allegedly eaten by the rats. Fake cards were issued to those able to grease the palm of the authorities. Against this backdrop is a picturesque, live presentation of a historical procession of the Maharaja with elephants and horses soaked in the erstwhile princely state of Travancore. A deft realism of the sound of the sea, whispering wind rustling coconut trees, smell of cardamom and tamarind further evoke an enchanting sea-landscape at once reminding us of Anita Desai.[10]

Before analyzing these two symbols separately, I would, as I have mentioned earlier, like to asseverate the ideal of *Bhakti Yoga* presented by Raja Rao with an overlay of humour. This beautiful book of less than 120 pages like a cat marks an unequivocal shift in the ontology of Raja Rao's philosophy. Really a stiff-legged leap from *Jnana* into *Bhakti*, from the *Advaita* of Acharya Shankara into the *Visistadvaita* of Ramanujacharya. The doctrine of *Prapatti* or total self-surrender to God as a way of salvation or emancipation partly owes to Ramanuja and partly to the Tenkalai school of thought—an offshoot of exuberant Bhakti movement of the South. Truly, the comic dynamics of Raja Rao's modified non-dualism erects a playful edifice around the novelette which at once causes difficulties to Western readers unable to comprehend Eastern philosophies as the tenuous tale turns its back and stalks unconcernedly away, but rooted as it is in the long enduring culture of India's antiquity it seems amicably delightful to the Orientalist. Actually, this handy book is a lovey-dovey bundle of scientific West and mythological East.

The Cat as visible mother, as an invisible protector and we as kittens held safely in Her mouth carried to respective destinations is a traditional philosophical analogy malleable both in Northern as well as Southern parts of India. Devotion to this primordial origin of creation has been the sole concern of man from time immemorial. However, it involves a dual response—total surrender of the kitten on one side and love, care, grace and protection of the Cat on the other. If the devotion (*Bhakti*) of the devotee (*Bhakta*) is one-sided, i.e. mere surrender, it fails in invoking the grace of the deity Esta. So, faith, total reliance in and realization of benign cosmic mother is absolutely necessary. Known as *Marjara-Shishu-Nyaya*, it illustrates the life and its movements as enacted by the kitten in its blind surrender to divine cause of care.

Govindan Nair who belongs to middle class Brahmin family and works as a clerk in the ration office is projected by the novelist not only an ardent exponent of Cat-Kitten ideal but also as an already initiated person—a dispassionate soul caring for nothing. A true Indian paradox. In an enigmatic and riddling way the novelette grows along velvety thoughts contemplated and then stated by Govindan Nair. The secret of his emancipated state of mind is that he talks only of what he sees. It means either he talks little or he does not talk at all. In fact nowhere in literature or in real life we come across a clerk like Govindan Nair. This 'otherness' of Govindan Nair from an American, German or French clerk is indeed remarkable. In spite of being aware of his low status as a clerk in the ration office he looks jovial, carefree and serene. The conviction of truth he has imbibed and is initiated into imparts him bliss—

Ananda of a rare sort—'Ah, the kitten when its neck is held by its mother, does it know anything else but the joy of being held by its mother...'.[11] Not only this but also he likes to fondle feline ways—The Kitten is being carried by the cat. We would all be kittens carried by the cat. Some, who are lucky (like your hunter) will one day know it, other live hearing 'Meow-Meow'.... I like being the kitten.[12] Really, it is not an intensity of joy or feeling of ecstasy the writer wants to pinpoint for the annihilation of botherings and ramblings of wavering minds but a sense of overpowering bliss—*Ananda* which is experienced in itself by surrendering blindly to the mother cat—'The mind that is not when the cat carries kitten is happiness'.[13] Although he looks apparently unconcerned yet his concern is with all and sundry. Once asked by an agricultural expert he spoke on manure as if he was professor. Also he glides smoothly from the monotony of mundane newspapers to highly sophisticated Sanskrit text—*Astavakra Samhita*. John one of his office colleagues is supersaturated by the saving grace of Govindan Nair's Mother cat—'Learn the way of the Kitten then you are saved. Allow the mother cat, sir, to carry you.'[14] Besides, truth he used to say, as he once told to a Judge during trial in court, can be realized by being it. Be truth, if you want to know it, is Govindan Nair's *mot juste*.

This ideal of cat-kitten theory is further upheld by protagonist-narrator Ramkrishna Pai. A Brahmin and a clerk in the Revenue Board, initially uninitiated, unlike Govindan Nair, Ramkrishna Pai's search for ultimate reality assumes manifold roles as he seems to stumble due to strange and bewildering ideas of varying ideologies—Indian as well as antipodean. Being Govindan Nair's disciple, he tells in an arrogant tone that he has no bond or ties with this world. It is because he proceeds or appears to be proceeding periodically towards emancipation. So, his story is a heroic tale—a gradual growth of consciousness from mundane to the grace and illumination. In early stages of life, as depicted by the novelist, the sole concern of Ramkrishna Pai is to amass wealth like John Doe. His dream of three storeyed building and of Kartikura House provides enough evidence for his material pursuits. Also he seems at par with the confessional heroes of Dostoevsky, Andre Gide, Albert Camu and Jean Paul Satre. Like St. Augustine he not only speculates on problems of existence but also ponders over the why and how of things—an eschatological probe into existence. His musings on causations are just and interesting—philosophical dialogues with Upanishadic overtones. Although he looks afflicted, unbalanced and disillusioned with his wife Saroj, daughter Usha and son Vithal, yet its compensation and fulfilment is gained through Santha's extramarital love. One day while following the cat he all of a sudden sees ultimate—Reality—the vision of life as harmony reconciling diversities and opposites and divine principle as perfection incarnate.

The world of Shakespeare into myriad forms leaves through the world of illusive (*maya*)—the imperfections of the world called *Samsara*. As such the novelette is ego's game of trying to be on the side of this life to suffer the miseries of *Samsara* like the narrator rather than go beyond it and live a full life. The transgression of the phenomenal reality is to go beyond the veil of *maya*. And it was revealed to Raja Rao as he always felt that Shakespeare was a sage. The sage is a being who has no ego and the cat represents an impersonal principle. Thus the cat reaches back to Shakespeare and Shakespeare absorbs the cat as it were—yet the two are one: *Ekam Advayam*.

NOTES

1. C.D. Narsimhaiah, *Raja Rao* (New Delhi: Arnold Heinemann).
2. M.K. Naik, *Raja Rao* (New York: Twayne Publishers Inc.).
3. Raja Rao, *The Serpent and the Rope* (New Delhi: Orient Paperbacks, 1968).
4. Raja Rao, *The Chessmaster and His Moves* (New Delhi: Vision Books Pvt. Ltd., 1988).
5. K. Natwar Singh, "Remembering Raja Rao", *The Hindu* (New Delhi, Monday, July 10, 2006).
6. *Ibid.*
7. *Ibid.*

8. White Ray Lewis, "Raja Rao's *The Cat and Shakespeare* in the U.S.A." (*JIWE*, Vol. 7, No. 1, July 1979, pp. 24-29).
9. Ayyappa Paniker, "A Conversation with Raja Rao on *The Cat and Shakespeare*" (*Chandrabhaga*—N.D., pp. 14-18).
10. Anita Desai, *Where Shall We Go This Summer* (New Delhi: Orient Paperbacks, 1982).
11. Raja Rao, *The Cat and Shakespeare* (New Delhi: Orient Paperbacks, 1971, p. 11).
12. *Ibid.*, p. 10.
13. *Ibid.*, p. 11.
14. *Ibid.*, p. 74.
15. Nar Singh Srivastava, *The Mind and Art of Raja Rao* (Bareilly: Prakash Book Depot).

   (As there is ample room for further study and a wider scope for detailed discussion on Raja Rao as an innovator of fictional techniques, I feel elated in summing up the book for it seems to make a pleasant reading, but simultaneously afraid of the reviewer—a desperado—who in Baltimore Sun, February 14, 1965 taunts that *The Cat and Shakespeare* of Raja Rao is nothing more than a stringing of abstruse Hindu thought and pseudo-profundities and a verbal necklace genuinely Indian but strictly brass. As a matter of fact, all that is gold does not glitter—one has to remove the soot in order to know the substratum of light.)

18

A Study of Cross-Cultural Conflict in Jhumpa Lahiri's *The Namesake*

Nilofar Akhtar

Immigration as a global phenomena has, of late, become a social trait as well as a literary genre. The growing trait of immigration has given place to dislocation, dispossession, disintegration and rootlessness of the one who migrates. He stands confused as the experience of expatriation uproots him from his homeland making him straddle between the two worlds—the one which he leaves behind and the other, he chooses to make his home.

Jhumpa Lahiri, in her first novel—*The Namesake* has raised the question of identity of those who are displaced not only geographically and physically but culturally as well. Jhumpa Lahiri belongs to the second generation of expatriate writers who have totally assimilated themselves into foreign culture. She was born and bred in America. She is an American Indian writer who began with a hyphen but later on merged herself completely from any title. Like her own self, her characters often straddle simultaneously in two cultures, the reality which they face day to day while living in America and the memory of Indian tradition.

Having won the 2000 Pulitzer Prize in fiction for her debut story collection *The Interpreter of Maladies: Getty Images*, she has repeatedly made nationality, tradition and belongingness her fictional themes. She belongs to the category of second generation of diasporic writers who have a heightened degree of assimilation and involvement with their adopted homeland. However, this urge to assimilate themselves in the mainstream culture leaves them dually alienated as the acceptance, there, is minimal. Thus, they stand polarized between nationality and exile. An immigrant's cultural affinity with his native land makes him an alien in his adopted home where he repeatedly tries to transmute and transform his self.

The themes of dislocation and cross-cultural conflict in Jhumpa Lahiri's fiction spring from the fact that she herself faced such complexities of expatriation and struggled for four decades to feel like an American, on an emotional plane. She avers:

> For me, there is a sort of a half-way feeling (of being American).[1]

The Namesake captures the agony and the ecstasy of an immigrant Bengali Indian family who faces a cross-cultural conflict during their stay in America. Ashima and Ashoke are steeped in Bengali culture and find themselves isolated in the mainstream American culture. They speak English but are betrayed by their heavy accents. They dress up in a traditional way and are identified within no time as non-Americans, wherever they go. Ashima and Ashoke belong to the first generation of immigrants who consciously try and hold on to their Indian tradition. There is a virtual line of demarcation of culture, which they dare not cross, a barrier which they would never overcome. This alienation or unwillingness to belong remains not only on the part of the immigrant but also on the part of their country, which they choose to make their abode. Thus, they seem to be tied to the two different parts of the world. This state of dislocation and then, relocation makes their sustainability a difficult phenomenon. This experience of inhabiting two cultures yields to subtle tension of alienation and disintegration. However, the second generation migrants like Ashima and Ashoke's children (Gogol and Sonia) develop a survival strategy against the cultural shock, which their parents had. They construct a multiple identity and develop a hybrid vision, which helps them in the ongoing process of survival through adaptation.

Lahiri, an American writer of Bengali-Indian descent chooses characters who are often Indian immigrants to America and navigate between the cultural values of their birthplace and their chosen abode. She draws her fictional characters on her own life-relations and experiences and delineates through them an immigrant's psychology and behaviour. Thus, *The Namesake* becomes her own story, where the parents try and keep their children close to themselves and their culture. They want them to inherit their culture and to retain Indianness. But, it happens otherwise. The descendants of such immigrants assimilate themselves into the Western culture, where they are born and brought up. Their perception of culture is large and permissive. Lahiri, through the character of Gogol, has depicted this hybridity of the second generation immigrants who are looking forward to their adopted homeland for acceptance and belongingness. Gogol wants to depart from all national, cultural and physical constraints. He also wants to depart from the original ethos and wants to discard "The Cultural Baggage", which he inherited from his parents. The life of Gogol, who is confused at his hybrid upbringing with oriental parents and western peer groups reminds one of the author herself. A confused college student, she did her major in English from Boston University. It was only after her attaining Ph.D. in Renaissance Studies, that she grew disenchanted with the academic world and began working for a non-profit organization for a short while. Writing, which was for her, only a hobby became her career and an act of liberating herself and being in sync with her identity as an expatriate. She reflects on her Indianness thus:

> Writing for me, is a form of meditation, writing is selfish. Most creativity is. I felt that the Indian part of me was unacknowledged, therefore somehow negated by my American environment, leading two separate lives.[2]

The Namesake captures the similar experiences with parents making an attempt to adjust to life in a new culture and their children struggle to assimilate themselves into the same. Thus, *The Namesake* is a fictional mouthpiece of the complex and conflict ridden world of Indian immigrants in the US. Gogol is one such character who tries to build strategies of culture identification through assimilation (which is a milder way of submission). Cultural assimilation and cultural alienation are the two extreme strategies which an expatriate tries to use in a foreign environment. Gogol uses the former, whereby 'Excessively belonging' will nullify his concept of nationality. He is discomfortable with his name, which he feels is 'shapeless and weightless'. When he steps into the outside world, he discards his old name in favour of the new and contemporary Nikhil. He wants to lead his life as any other American. He wants to look, behave, speak and feel like an American. He involves himself with girls who are steeped in Western culture and starts measuring his parents against these girls. He puts a self-willed exile on himself. He desires to live unnoticed.

> For some reason, it is dependence, not adulthood, he feels. He feels free of expectation, responsibility, in willing exile from his life.[3]

However, this self-willed exile ends with the death of Ashoke, his father who had wanted him to inherit his values and cultural affinity with India. In an attempt to overcome the guilt of overlooking his father, he marries an Indian girl but this marriage falls apart shortly due to the oddity of their upbringing. He tries to deracinate himself and loses what he actually is. As a child he struggles to cast off his unique name, as a student to make a mark in an alien society and as an adult to settle his family. Like his author, he struggles in trying to respect his roots while simultaneously adapting to American society. It is only after Ashima decides to shift base that he visits his old home and learns that the solution to the problem lies not in abandoning it or deracinating himself and thus diminishing either culture but in blending the two into one. He is not in sync with himself, his name and his origin until he realizes that he is a hybrid of both the cultures. The Overcoat, which had saved his father's life, also saves him from falling apart. His father had given him the book long back but he had not read it. The book thus not only supplies him answers to all his confusions, it also yields him a new lease of life. He now understands that he does not need to be an American or an Indian. To him, the world seems to be an open platform where different interpretations are possible of one experience. The second generation of migrants have made an attempt to disrupt long established epistemological notions on nationalism and culture. An immigrant is no more an alien, he has become "a global trotter". As a diasporic writer, Jhumpa Lahiri has given authentic literary representations of the diasporic sensibility of an immigrant. As she admits:

> When I first started writing, I was not conscious that my subject was the Indian American experience. What drew me to my craft was the desire to force the two worlds I occupied to mingle on the page as I was not brave enough, or mature enough, to allow in life.[4]

Unlike, their first generation cousins, the writers of second generation diaspora are more in sync with the reality principle, which forms the relationship between a societal core or centre and the periphery or margins. In the end of the novel, Gogol is made to realize that the 'centre' and 'marginality' have become blurred and blended together. He favours 'decentering' much like his author and is in favour of new cultural configurations which will surely have a balancing act upon the attempts of assimilation and understanding of different cultures and societies.

NOTES

1. http://www.reviewsofbooks.com/namesake/
2. *Ibid.*
3. Jhumpa Lahiri. *The Namesake* (New Delhi: Harper Collins, 2004), p. 142.
4. http://www.bookreporter.com/reviews/

19

Structuralizing and Institutionalizing Transformations in Salman Rushdie's *Midnight's Children:* An Orientalistic Approach

Jaba Kusum Singh

Edward Wadie Said in the introductory chapter of his book *Culture and Imperialism* (1993) responds to his critic and recognizes that he had left out of *Orientalism* (1978) those activist and intellectuals responsible in part for decolonization and among those intellectuals he mentions the name of Salman Rushdie too. But the present writing shall see how Salman Rushdie in his celebrated novel *Midnight's Children* manifests *Orientalism* in 'the various stated views about Oriental society, language, literatures, history, sociology and so forth' (Said, 206). As we all know that Said's study is a work of "colonial discourse analysis", making sense of the concealed Orientalism by close reading of individual Orientalist utterances or text; Rushdie too, in his monumental fiction bares forth the untold history of the just independent India as a country and Saleem Sinai, the protagonist expresses all those Indian subjects and their subjugations, that was a common feature of the common man of the post colonial Indian mass. Rushdie through Sinai makes an oriental statement, although garbed in fantasy but it is a statement of Truth, as also stated by Said.

Although as a writer Salman Rushdie opposes Said's view of gendered and racialized power-knowledge but as we go on reading his novel we cannot simply deny that Rushdie's Sinai represents all those subjugated class that is the Orients who 'has helped to define Europe (or the west) as its contrasting image, idea, personality, experience' (*Ibid.*, 1-2).

In the galaxy of Indian English novelist, Salman Rushdie is the only figure, who has almost become a myth by provoking universal controversy and being the object of a death sentence by a leader of the Islamic World. Salman Rushdie belongs to that generation of Indian English novelists, who shot into fame in the last quarter of the 20th century. It is known fact that the factors that influence these novelists pertain to the political, economic and socio-culture milieu of the post independence India. These multi-layered and complex milieus have evoked varied creative responses from Indian English novelists.

Rushdie is one of those sensitive and humanistic writers, who stand for liberty, love of freedom, democracy and anything brushing aside these virtues of modern civilization has extreme aversion for him and thus making him close to the Oriental theory of Said. He upholds this idea of democratic freedom throughout his career. As we know that Salman Rushdie belongs to three countries; India, Pakistan and Britain and thus a critic has accused him of facing the problem of "dislocation" but, quite on the contrary, this has helped him in developing as a sensitive human being and a prolific writer and thus instead of creating problems, it has proved to be quite rewarding. The cultural transplantation of the novelist is reflected in the transformation from the regional to the international in his fictions.

Rushdie comments upon the cultural predicament of the novelist like him, "...sometimes, we feel that we straddle two cultures, at other times, that we fall between two stools...but however ambiguous and shifting this ground may be, it is not an infertile territory for a writer to occupy. If literature is in part the business of finding new angles, at which to enter reality, then once again our distances, our long geographical perspectives, may provide us with such angles: Or it may be that is simply that we must think in order to do our work" (*The Indian Writer*, 79).

Rushdie learnt the art of condensed writing during his career as a journalist, and then switched over to writing novels. Rushdie's idea about the function of literature is revolutionary. Writing a book, according to him, involves daring: for he believes that "...a book is not justified by its author's worthiness to write it, but by the quality of what has been done..." (*The Indian Writer*, 79). So is true about his novel *Midnight's Children* too. While talking about this work of fiction he once said: "Forty years ago, the independent nation of India and I were born within eight weeks of one another. I came first. This gave rise to a family joke—that the departure of British was occasioned by my arrival on the scene—and the joke, in turn, became the germ of the novel, *Midnight's Children*, in which not just one child, but one thousand and one hundred children born in the midnight hour of freedom, the first hour of 15 August 1947, were comically and tragically connected to the birth of a nation" (*Imaginary*, 26).

We can see that Rushdie is clearly stating that the novel is the story of those who are marginals—the narrator is the member of the minority class of India. Not only so Rushdie also portrays the protagonist, Saleem Sinai as one unified whole, a mixture of many diversities, the symbol of India, the country. Thus he celebrates India's diversity and states: one of the most absurd aspects of this quest for national authenticity is that—as far as India is concerned, anyway—it is completely fallacious to suppose that there is such a thing as a pure, unalloyed tradition from which to draw. The only people, who seriously believe this, are religious extremists. The rest of us understand, that the very essence of Indian culture is that we possess a mixed tradition *me lange* of elements as disparate as ancient Mughal and contemporary Coca-Cola American... Eclectism, the ability to take from the world, what seems fitting and to leave the rest, has always been a hallmark of the Indian tradition...like Said, Rushdie too believes that the Orientals must re-write their history focusing their "hybridity". We find this eclectic hybridity in *Midnight's Children*, together with a reflection of the impossibility of linear and homogeneous forms of literature capturing the plurality of the subcontinent.

Midnight's Children has been regarded as *sui generic* for this volumnious novel seems to many critic a "...sprawling, rollicking, aggressive book, mixing fiction and fantasy with an exuberance of language, never seen in Indo-Anglian writing before [and has] invented a new idiom and metaphor, to interpret the multi-textured reality of the sub-continent" (Storm, 26).

Midnight's Children written in four hundred fifty pages and containing more than two hundred fifty thousand words is a novel, that is not only dealing with the birth and achievement of its protagonist but it is mainly talking about contemporary India and the meaning of Indian independence. The harmonious collision and fusion of the national and domestic history throws into focus many related themes of the narrative, such as secularism, national growth and development, the focus is on realizing India as a nation, in its historical and political perspective as pointed out by T.N. Dhar. The novel is in three parts: Book one deals with events from 1915 till the hero Saleem Sinai's birth; Book two deals with the hero's childhood and ends with his being injured in a bombing raid on the streets of Karachi during the Indo-Pakistani war in 1965, the Book three begins with his being used as a 'man-dog' by the Pakistani army for tracking and ends with his suggested disintegration on August 15, 1978.

Dhar rightly comments, "*Midnight's Children* is a first-person narrative, in which Saleem Sinai writes his private history, which is inextricably connected with the history of his country" ("Micro Macro", 20). The novel surely confirms Said's viewpoint that "no one can escape dealing with, if not the east/ west diversion, then the north/south one, the have/have not one, the imperialist/anti-imperialist one, the white/coloured one" (Said, 327).

We find, that the protagonist Saleem Sinai's birth coincides with India's independence and, "...his destiny got handcuffed to history, the narrative and thematic progression in the novel is characterized throughout by a continuous oscillation from the personal story of Saleem to the story of his country" (Dhar, *Problematizing*, 95).

The novel is a first person narrative in which the protagonist Saleem Sinai while writing his personal story writes about the one thousand common human beings of India, who as Rushdie shows is born at the same hour of India's independence. India is personified in Saleem and thus the diversion, as quoted above, is evident throughout the fiction. The story is not a simple narrative of a man born in Bombay but again a strongly woven discourse of a cosmopolitan city that comprises various men belonging to separate caste, creed and language; it represents India which is not yet free from its past torturous history, a country that smells foul for it carries with it the tyrannies and exploitation of the past regime in a new garb. Rushdie narrates the story of the political development of politically free India and Pakistan, where Saleem grows from an infant to a man, thereby benefiting himself "properly from the general 20th century rise to political and historical awareness of so many of the east's people" (Said, 328).

Rushdie re-writes history, the history of the Orientals, a history that must be read and re-read with the eye of the have-nots, if not so the eye of an anti-imperialist, an eye of a beholder who is free from the inhibitions and hypocrisies of so-called imperialistic power structure and then only one can experience the pathos behind the humorous tone of the writer. It is the grievance of all those who are torn between two cultures, people who have nothing to do with the political happenings of the Indian subcontinent yet were compelled to participate in the heart-squeezing, devastating event of Indian independence that is the partition.

Saleem Sinai, grandson of a Heidelberg returned medical practitioners, Dr. Aziz, whose involvement with Germanic revolutionary anarchist movement gives him a past that corresponds with that of the new born Indian subcontinent where everything is framed under the power structure of Western revolution. But our great Dr. Aziz is entrapped by the perforated sheet and ends up into an imbalanced marriage with Saleem's grandmother Naseen with whom Dr. Aziz falls in love in several parts, an apt representation of Indian political imbalances and socio-cultural imperfections that were balancedly instigated by its foreign rulers.

The objective storytelling method of the narrator reminds us of the Indian storytelling custom that gives the novel an Oriental fervor and solves Rushdie's purpose of showing the historical barbarity. The narrative style befits the story line; for the language and the technique are casual and matter of fact that makes the tortures, human disparities and exploitation a day to day matter. Rushdie's aim is to convey that history has been invariably manipulated by the occidentals; therefore, re-writing of history is necessary and here Rushdie in spite of his philosophical and intellectual differences with Edward Said duplicates his theory of Orientalism.

The narrator as well as the listener is important in the act of storytelling and here Padma whom Saleem narrates his life history is no ordinary woman, she is the preserver of vegetables in the jars in the form of Achar thus knows how to preserve invaluable and so she is chosen as the listener to the re-narration of the political history of India. Padma is one of the members of the exploited and have-nots who are supposed to witness the political and social changes of the country like an indifferent onlooker but here she becomes the most important character who shoulders the responsibility of preserving history with a different flavour and taste. Saleem informs Padma "...the past has dripped into me...so we can't ignore it..." (*MC*, 38) and thus we, as readers, have no other choice but to re-read the history, that is the life story of the marginals.

The pangs of the dearer ones who are compelled to leave their home, their relatives, their parents for nothing, not for any of their fault, is pathetically shown by the departure of Emerald and her husband Major Zulfikar, the youngest daughter of Dr. Aziz, to Pakistan. Rushdie puts before us the horrors of all those families whom partition compelled to break into two distinct units with different national identities whom our historians have neglected and forgotten in the rejoicement of political freedom. Rushdie, humanist by heart, finds it necessary to highlight the invariable forgetfulness of the colonial historians.

The character of Lifafa Das, the peep show man, and his interpretation of communal riots, that was burning the entire Indian subcontinent during the time of partition, tells us how pathetic it was for common men to survive in those days of in humanity and barbarism, when a meaningless but ardent urge of a small girl could flare up communal frenzy. The burning down of Ahmed Sinai's factory which made Saleem and his family to leave Delhi and settle down in Bombay is an apt example of communal inharmony and trauma of the minorities.

Rushdie, throughout this novel voices the cry and revolt of the marginals against the ruling power structure. The novel voices the voice of the apolitical people of the subcontinent, the readers are made to realize the actual situation of the divided country when soothsayer says to Amina Sinai, Saleem's mother: "there will be two heads—but you shall see one—there will be knees and a nose and knees...newspaper praises him, two mothers raise him...soldiers will try him...tyrants will fry him...he will have sons without having sons! He will be old before he is old! And he will die...before he is dead" (*MC*, 99). Rushdie sketches the whole graph of Indian subcontinent, which is divided into two halves and where the strong knees shake and propagate might is right and the nose provokes the men of these two nations to fight irrationally, even at the very smell of danger. Everywhere there is chaos in the two nations for they are dead people, there is no discipline, no law, no ethics and nothing seems to be impossible. It is an age, where, nothing but separatism is at work, everywhere there is an air of fragmentation, which the society and the family both have inherited from their near past. Saleem Sinai, even long before his birth and even before he could realize, inherited a fragmented tradition and culture and thus he confesses: "...the conflict between grandpaternal skepticism and grandmaternal reduality; and above all the ghostly essence of that perforated sheet, which doomed my mother to learn to love a man in segments, and which condemned me to see my own life—its meaning, its structure—in fragments also; so that by the time I understood it, it was too late" (*MC*, 124).

Rushdie has hinted at the tussle between Western and Eastern ideals and principles that have been inbuilt in our youth, a fragmentation of thought and action that howsoever we may try, we cannot help to deny and thus follow it blindly and helplessly. Just as Saleem is not the son of his parents, democratic and sovereign India is also not what it is projected as. Both needs reformation and again we see reformation comes in the life of baby Saleem as nurse Mary exchanges the babies of Amina and Vanita, in doing so the mid wife does "her own private revolutionary act" giving a poor baby, a life of privilege. Saleem like India has nothing original; nor his name, neither his parents and thus resembles India which according to Rushdie is a country "which would never exist accept by the effort of a phenomenal collective will—except in a dream, we all agreed to dream...India, the new myth—a collective fiction in which anything was possible, a fable rivaled only by two other mighty fantasies: money and God" (*MC*, 130). And so Rushdie, accepting the challenge chooses to tell tale of the have-nots; they act as the decision-maker of his fiction and thus nurse Mary is the powerful one who has the capability to decide the fate of the protagonist Saleem and Shiva, the actual son of Amina and Ahmed Sinai. Rushdie's aim is quite evident to write an untold history of the common majority class of India who finds no place in the money and power world.

Rushdie makes it clear that Indian independence is not a matter of celebration but on the contrary it is something which brought mass massacre, devastation, trauma and umpteenths pains. L.N. Campbell suggests that it is this pain that is reflected in the self contempt of Saleem Sinai for he is conscious that he is a product of an hour that has created a divide, a perforation mental and geographical. Perhaps Rushdie aims at healing up this perforation by re-telling the trauma and creating a cathartic effect. Saleem's detailed description of his ugly features corresponds with the turbulent partitions and the disintegrated and disfigured political ventures. His unblinking eyes evidence a generally passive nature. At the same time he grows up "with legs that were irretrievably bowed because, [he] had got to [his] feet too early" (*MC*, 54) indicating at the unnecessary hurry in getting political freedom. Saleem represents the whole of India with its ups and downs, dreams and aspiration, its misery and exploitation and its deformities. He represents every man and thus he is bound to witness discontentment and fallacy. His infatuation for the American girl, Evelyn corresponds with common Indian attraction of *goraas*—an infatuation that has dragged Indians to unending slavery if not physical but mental surely. It is this wrong writing of history that Rushdie wanted to rectify, to let people realize that Orientals cannot be befooled anymore. Saleem's pain for not getting his lady, a despair of the subjugated ones for not achieving what aimed for, is aptly corresponded with the language riot of Bombay for both are illogical and irrational. Rushdie highlights that the illogical and irrational partition is followed by further re-division and chaos.

Rushdie is of the view that the new generation of India "represent many things...they can be seen as the last throw of everything antiquated and retrogressive in our myth ridden nation, whose defeat was entirely desirable in the context of a modernizing, 20th century economy; or as the true hope of freedom, which is now forever extinguished; but what they must become is the bizarre creation of a rambling, diseased mind" (*Unriddling*, 155). It is a country where the members of the *Midnight's Children* club represent the entire nation and its essence, their superficial power is suggestive of intense energy and vitality of common man and woman that has been neglected by colonials and their native counterparts. It also symbolizes their ardent urge to reach great heights but we find that these powers are either curved or diverted to evil means. This is represented through his altar ego Shiva, representing knees and nose. Both Saleem and Shiva are indispensable for India for Shiva represents India's strong physique while Saleem is India's mind.

Indian socio political condition finds an apt metaphor in Mary's revelation of Saleem's birth that finds him deserted by his parents and thus he reaches his uncle Hanif and Pia's household. It seems as if the country is "forgetting the new myth of freedom and reverted to their old ways, their old regionalist loyalist and prejudices, and the body politic began to crack" (*MC*, 294).

The novel deliberately juxtaposes the national and personal happenings and gradually Saleem Sinai is liberated from his past and he is in a state of amnesia, which occasions a loss, which is more than a loss of a memory. The year is 1965; the War between India and Pakistan bewilders the common people of the subcontinent and thus they find themselves at a loss of identity like Saleem. Memory is the link, the chain which connects the postcolonial subjects to his disrupted history but Saleem is now the Buddha and thus free from all boundations. The character of Parvati brings a new dimension in the novel. She helps Saleem to return to his birth place, she is the agent for restoring Saleem's identity to him. Here again like *Grimus* and *The Satanic Verses* female plays the role of a refuge and the abyss. Parvati represents the exploited class of women who has no role or little role to play in the manifold of the history of colonials but quite contrary to it in this novel Parvati is the savior of our protagonist.

Saleem returned to magician ghetto followed by his marriage to Parvati and birth of Ganesh, the illegally begotten child, who is a true son of his genealogy, gets its name and thus history is corrected and legalized, for Ganesh is Shiva's and Parvati's biological son; Parvati sets in order the historical injustice, Aadam Sinai or Ganesh becomes the true inheritor of his family. We find that the sour grapes eaten by Saleem's forbearers also set the teeth of his son on edge. Rushdie writes "...mysteriously handcuffed to history, his destinies indissolubly chained to those of his country" (*MC*, 501), this is because he is born at the precise instant when the emergency is declared on the night of 25th June 1975. Symbolically enough the baby is given a powerful medicine to induce it to cry under the belief that "he must weep" or he "will die". The first word the baby utters is Abracadabra symbolizing that it has a bare world in front of him and it is upon him to find out meanings and new dimensions from confusion and chaos. The atrocities of authoritarian rule is shown through the suppression of the agitating mob and the crushing of the innocent masses that resulted in eviction of magician slums that killed Parvati and separated Saleem from other magicians and his son Adam.

Saleem now lands in Benares widow's home, a city well chosen by Rushdie to show India's back march towards an age that the writer considers must be rectified. The vasectomy drive describes vividly talks of the impotency of democracy during the days of Emergency. At the end Saleem's body cracks up indicating the multifarious division of India and the conflicting tendencies appearing in the country. Cracking up can also be interpreted as an act of imbibing all as he does and being omnipotent and omniscient in the tale he is telling, he describes himself as "swallower of lives" and a multitudes are jestling and shoving inside him. These multitudes cause him crack up when he attempts to bring them out in his tale; like the independent India it is impossible to unify Saleem with all his diversities for it has several distorted perforations. Rushdie's tale is thus mainly about these multitudes of perforations that the modern India cannot deny. Rushdie in fact satires the so called picture of India's unity in diversity as proclaimed by the occidental historians of the world. Rushdie lays bare the fact that India comprises several cultures, traditions, class, creed so and so and it is very necessary to recognize the diversities of this country as a whole suggesting the invisible and un-pickled future of the protagonist. It also suggests that the truth of life when narrated is pickled and thus arouses strong taste and tears. The empty jar of pickle is the suggestion of the unknown future that waits for the fresh vegetables and spices to be filled in. Rushdie has shown that Saleem represents multitudes of hopes and aspirations and waits for a new and tougher generation for a new beginning. Rushdie maintains that truth of life is variegated and it is wrong to see history from one angle, it has many facets and can be interpreted in many ways.

To conclude as Edward W. Said writes that Rushdie's *Midnight's Children* is an effective and astoundingly resourceful novel for it has daringly re-appropriated the historical experience of colonialism, re-vitalized and transformed it "into a new aesthetic of sharing and often transcendent reformulation" (Said, 353).

REFERENCES

Dhar, T.N. "Micro Macro Symbiosis: The Form of Salman Rushdie's *Midnight's Children*", *The Journal of Indian Writing in English*, Vol. 13, 1 Jan. 1985, pp. 18-22.

——. "Problematizing History with Rushdie in *Midnight's Children*", *Journal of South Asian Literature*, Vol. xxxviii, 1993, pp. 93-111.

Rushdie, Salman. *Midnight's Children.* New York: Avon Books, 1982.

——. "The Indian Writer in England", *The Eye of The Beholder.* Ed. Maggie Butcher. Commonwealth Institute, London, 1983.

——. "The Riddle of Midnight: India, August 1947", *Imaginary Homeland: Essays and Criticism 1981-1991*, Granta Books, London, 1991.

"Satanic Storm", *India Today*, March 15, 1989, p. 26.

Said, Edward W. *Orientalism*, Delhi: Penguin Books, 2001.

Contributors

Santwana Haldar. Reader, Department of English; Fakir Mohan Autonomus College, Balasore.

Arnab Bhattacharya. A critic of wide repute; 22/2, Praulla Chaki Rd. Kol-36.

Basavaraj Naikar. Professor & Chairman, Department of English, Karnatak University, Dharwad.

Anita Myles. Professor Department of English, D.D.U. Gorakhpur University, Gorakhpur.

Debalina Banerjee. Asst. Professor of English, Vidyasagar Evening College, Kolkata.

V.M. Madge. An Academician and Scholar Critic of wide repute; resides in Pune.

Bishnupada Ray. Head, Department of English, North Bengal University, Darjeeling, West Bengal.

Partha Kumar Mukhopadhyay. An Ex. Associate Professor of English and a Fellow (U.W.A.).

Arpa Ghosh. Department of English, Vivekananda Town College for Women, Barisha, Kolkata.

Tapati Talukdar. Teaches at Barasat College and Rabindra Bharati University, Kolkata.

Sandhya Saxena. Sr. Lecturer, Department of English, V.R.A.L. Govt. Girls P.G. College, Bareilly, U.P.

Ketaki Datta. H.O.D., Department of English, Acharya B.N. Seal College Coach Behar, W.B.

Shirish Chindhade. Principal (Retd.) and an accomplished writer, Flat-7, Neelambari, Opposite Mehendale Garage, Erandwane, Pune.

Shabina Nishat Omar. Assistant Professor and Head, Department of English and also acting Principal, Milli-Al-Ameen College (For Girls), Kolkata. Previously associated with St. Xaviers College and Presidency College, Kolkata.

Shymasree Basu. Assistant Lecturer in English, Barasat College, Kolkata.

Piyali Das. Lecturer in English G.M.S.M. Mahavidyalaya, West Bengal.

Suresh Chandra Pande. Lecturer in English, Government College, Phoolchaur, P.O. Anandpur, Nainital, Uttarakhand.

Nilofar Akhtar. Head, Department of English, Govt. P.G. College, Champawat, Uttarakhand.

Jaba Kusum Singh. Asst. Professor & H.O.D., Department of English, Upadhi (P.G.) College Pilibhit, U.P.